Recriminalizing Delinquency provides a detailed account of one state's attempt to control violent juvenile crime by redefining previous acts of delinquency as crimes, and delinquents as juvenile offenders. It begins with the
brutal violence of a 15-year-old chronic delinquent, and the subsequent
passage of waiver legislation, which abruptly lowered the age of criminal
responsibility for juveniles charged with violent offenses. But the reasons
for bringing juveniles into criminal court, Singer argues, go beyond sensational acts of violence and the immediate concerns of elected officials to do
something about violent juvenile crime. Instead, recriminalization is seen
as a product of earlier juvenile justice reforms and modern-day political
and organizational interests in classifying juveniles with a diverse set of
legal categories. Singer shows that waiver legislation has not eliminated the
need for juvenile justice nor has it reduced the incidence of violent juvenile crime.

Recriminalizing Delinquency

Cambridge Criminology Series

Editors:
Alfred Blumstein, *Carnegie Mellon University*
David Farrington, *University of Cambridge*

This new series publishes high-quality research monographs of either theoretical or empirical emphasis in all areas of criminology, including measurement of offending, explanations of offending, police courts, incapacitation, corrections, sentencing, deterrence, rehabilitation, and other related topics. It is intended to be both interdisciplinary and international in scope.

Also in the series:

J. David Hawkins (editor), *Delinquency and Crime: Current Theories*

Recriminalizing Delinquency

VIOLENT JUVENILE CRIME AND JUVENILE JUSTICE REFORM

Simon I. Singer

State University of New York at Buffalo

CAMBRIDGE
UNIVERSITY PRESS

Published by the Press Syndicate of the University of Cambridge
The Pitt Building, Trumpington Street, Cambridge CB2 1RP
40 West 20th Street, New York, NY 10011-4211, USA
10 Stamford Road, Oakleigh, Melbourne 3166, Australia

First published 1996

Printed in the United States of America

Library of Congress Cataloging-in-Publication Data
Singer, Simon I.
Recriminalizing delinquency : violent juvenile crime and juvenile
justice reform / Simon I. Singer.
p.   cm. – (Cambridge criminology series)
Includes bibliographical references and index.
ISBN 0-521-48208-9 (hardback)
1. Juvenile justice, Administration of – New York (State).
2. Criminal justice, Administration of – New York (State).
3. Juvenile delinquents – Legal status, laws, etc. – New York (State).
4. Juvenile delinquency – New York (State) – Prevention.   5. Violent
crimes – New York (State) – Prevention.   6. Law reform – New York
(State).   I. Title.   II. Series: Cambridge criminology series
(New York, N.Y.)
HV9105.N7S56   1996
364.3'6'09747 – dc20   95-19329
                                                                 CIP

A catalog record for this book is available from the British Library.

ISBN 0-521-48208-9 Hardback

In memory of my wife
Adele Bardach Singer
(1950–1995)
for the courage, love, and family
that helped make it all possible

Contents

Figures and Tables

Figures

Tables

Acknowledgments

This book benefited from an enormous amount of assistance from persons inside and outside systems of juvenile and criminal justice. I can only acknowledge a few of the many persons who encouraged me through their advice and friendship.

Murray Levine right from the start has been a guiding light who assisted me in more ways than I can ever acknowledge. Through numerous lunch-time discussions and several drafts of the manuscript, he allowed me to share with him the ideas that shaped its final production.

Several aspects of the research developed from my initial collaboration with Charles Ewing and David McDowall. I thank them for remaining constant sources of support and advice. Various drafts of chapters in the manuscript benefited from the comments of Nachman Ben-Yehuda, Stanley Cohen, Robert Emerson, Martin Guggenheim, Barbara Howe, Frank Munger, Elwin Powell, and Oren Zev. Bruce Jackson carefully read the entire manuscript and in the process made it into a much more readable book.

I can acknowledge the efforts of only a few of the many persons inside juvenile and criminal justice systems who contributed to this book. Richard Ross of the New York State Division of Criminal Justice Services helped to provide me with the state agency data presented in Chapter 5. Sharon Lansing, also of the Division of Criminal Justice Services, gave me an inside perspective on what the numbers really mean and caught numerous errors in my earlier analysis. Gary Almond and Clayton Osborne, current and former employees of the New York State Division for Youth, facilitated the administrative access I needed to gather the data presented in Chapter 7.

That chapter also benefited from the inside view and comments of Michael Quartararo, who is still serving a sentence of 9 years to life as a juvenile offender.

I wish to also acknowledge several past and current graduate students at the University of Buffalo. Xiogang Deng applied his computer skills to the complex task of formatting the raw state agency data. Colleen A. Connolly interviewed several officials quoted in Chapter 7. The dedicated assistance of Suzette Cote and Vanessa Garcia greatly contributed to the manuscript's development.

Thanks are also due to the administrative staff here at the University of Buffalo: Laurie Lanning of the Department of Sociology, and Anne Gaulin and Laura Mangan of the Baldy Center for Law and Social Policy.

I am grateful to David Farrington and Alfred Blumstein for including this book in their "Cambridge Criminology Series" and for their reviewer's extensive comments. For helping to bring this book to press, I wish also to thank the staff of Cambridge University Press, especially Alex Holzman for being an efficient and considerate editor and Eric Newman for his assistance as production editor.

Some pages of this book were adapted from previously published articles that appeared in the journals *Law and Society Review, Law and Policy,* and *Crime and Delinquency.* Parts of the material presented in this book were generated with the support of New York State's Rockefeller Institute of Government, the National Institute of Justice, and the Office of Juvenile Justice and Delinquency Prevention. The University at Buffalo's Baldy Center for Law and Social Policy provided additional research support and a collegial atmosphere for a sociologist to think about the law.

Poor girl! . . . She will come to herself and weep, and then her mother will find out. She will give her a beating, a horrible, shameful beating and then maybe turn her out of doors. Then there will be the hospital directly . . . and then . . . again the hospital . . . drink . . . the taverns . . . and more hospital, in two or three years – a wreck, and her life over at eighteen or nineteen. Have not I seen cases like that? And how have they been brought to it? . . . But what does it matter? That's as it should be, they tell us. A certain percentage, they tell us, must every year go . . . that way . . . to the devil, I suppose, so that the rest may remain chaste, and not be interfered with. A percentage! What splendid words they have; they are so scientific, so consolatory. Once you've said "percentage," there's nothing more to worry about. If we had any other word . . . maybe we might feel more uneasy.

Raskolnikov speaking in Dostoyevsky, Crime and Punishment

Ye shall have one manner of law, as well for the stranger, as for the homeborn; for I am the Lord your God.

Leviticus 24:2

Introduction

THIS IS A CASE STUDY of legislation that redefines previous acts of delinquency as crimes, and delinquents as juvenile offenders. It examines one state's response to violent juvenile crime through waiver legislation that transfers jurisdiction over juveniles from juvenile court to criminal court. Specifically, it focuses on the creation, implementation, and effects of New York's 1978 Juvenile Offender (JO) law, which lowered the eligible age of criminal responsibility to 13 for murder and 14 for other violent offenses.

The JO law is often referred to as *waiver by offense categories* or *legislative waiver*, and it is sometimes called *automatic transfer legislation*. It shifts the initial source of legal decision making on juveniles from juvenile justice officials to criminal justice officials. In contrast to more traditional systems of waiver that initiate with a hearing in juvenile court as mandated by the U.S. Supreme Court's 1966 *Kent* decision, legislative waiver begins with a specific set of offense categories for which juveniles can be considered criminally responsible.[1]

In placing initial decision making in the hands of criminal justice officials, legislative waiver in New York and in other states "recriminalized" delinquency and juvenile justice. Like other newly created criminological words, such as *deinstitutionalization* or *decarceration* (Scull 1977), the word *recriminalization* has not yet entered the dictionary and is in need of a definition. I use it here to refer to the creation and implementation of legal rules that place juveniles in the adult criminal justice system. Recriminalization is an effort to return a part of the juvenile justice system to a period that existed prior to the creation of juvenile courts.

But recriminalization has not eliminated the need for juvenile justice. It

1

exists on top of a shaky foundation of earlier juvenile justice reforms in which juvenile courts still remain as an integral part of the diverse legal avenues for transferring juveniles to criminal courts. Juvenile courts exist not necessarily as first resort legal settings but as another legal avenue in which to classify juveniles as either delinquents or offenders. By re-criminalizing delinquency, modern systems of juvenile and criminal justice are able to provide officials with a larger set of legal avenues in which to identify and track juveniles as either delinquents or offenders.

The need to recriminalize delinquency stems from modern-day political and organizational concerns and interests in maintaining the legitimacy of juvenile justice. That legitimacy is threatened by chronic delinquents who continue to commit serious violent offenses and by brutal acts of juvenile violence. By diverting the most difficult and violent of juveniles away from the juvenile justice system, recriminalization attempts to satisfy public and official demands to see serious delinquents punished in a public, criminal court.

The reasons for recriminalization over the past several decades are dis-cussed in the first two chapters by focusing on the question: Why did New York wait until 1978 to move from a state without any waiver legislation to automatic waiver? The answer is first revealed in Chapter 1 in a brutal set of murders committed by a chronic delinquent on New York City's subway system during a Governor's election-year campaign. I then argue that the type of recriminalization that New York produced went beyond a single juvenile's lethal acts of violence and the immediate political concerns of the governor and other officials. Instead, I see an increasingly complex system of juvenile justice setting into motion the need for recriminalization and waiver legislation. Legislative waiver, I suggest, is not merely triggered by violent juveniles. It is also a product of negotiated orders of justice and loosely coupled systems of juvenile and criminal justice.

In Chapter 2 I extend my argument by taking stock of earlier juvenile justice reforms to explain the unique shape of recriminalization. I see legislative waiver as a product of earlier reforms that I divide into periods of decriminalization and criminalization. That explanation continues in Chapter 3 where I describe recriminalization and the immediate factors leading to the creation of the JO law in New York. My sources of data consist of the historical literature, media stories, commission reports, and legislative debates. I consider the words of officials as important bits of information that help us to understand the political value of waiver re-forms. I further detail the various legal rules related to legislative waiver in New York.

Chapter 4 raises the complex question of implementation. I wish to determine how legislative waiver relates to principles in juvenile justice decision making. Prior research on waiver decisions in states with judicial forms of waiver suggest that juvenile justice officials base their transfer decisions on factors other than the seriousness of the offense. In New York, with its system of legislative waiver, I first show the importance of offense and offender characteristics on the decision to prosecute juveniles as offenders in criminal court with interviews and survey data based on the perceptions of criminal justice officials. I then analyze the effects of nonoffense-related characteristics on one aspect of initial criminal justice decision in the form of a grand jury indictment.

Chapter 5 further examines the implementation of waiver legislation with case processing data on eligible juvenile offenders from their arrest to adjudication and disposition. The data consist of an extremely large number of juveniles arrested as juvenile offenders in various counties of New York. I consider the jurisdictional and temporal context of legal decision making with multivariate statistical techniques of analysis to determine the relative effects of offense and offender characteristics on the arrest, adjudication, and sentencing of juveniles as offenders. Each figure and table presented in Chapter 5 provides a complex statistical picture of the diverse effects of waiver legislation on juveniles in the criminal justice system.

My last set of concerns is directed toward the impact of legislative waiver. In Chapter 6 I take a quantitative approach to address the question: Did the JO law reduce the incidence of violent juvenile crime? The results of an interrupted quasi-experimental time-series design are presented to examine the statistical significance of a model that predicts change in rates of violent juvenile crime because of the JO law. In Chapter 7 I look at the punishment- and treatment-oriented objectives of the JO law as viewed in a maximum security institution that was built as a consequence of the JO law. I relate a familiar story of crisis to the dual institutional dilemma of providing treatment and maintaining control within a maximum security setting. Personal interviews with incarcerated juvenile offenders provide a glimpse of how juveniles perceive their convictions in criminal court and subsequent confinement. I also consider the words of officials in describing how crisis emerged to produce a familiar story of conflict and abuse.

Although this study focuses on one state's political and organizational reasons for assigning criminal responsibility to juveniles, it is important to stress that New York is not alone in its recriminalization of delinquency. Other states have also attempted to maintain the credibility of their systems of juvenile justice by bringing more juveniles into adult criminal courts.

The number of arrested juveniles brought directly to criminal courts increased from 1 percent of all juvenile arrests in 1973 to 5 percent in 1992, according to the FBI's Uniform Crime Reports (UCR) (Department of Justice, 1971: 112, 1992: 282).[2] With more traditional forms of waiver that initiate in juvenile court, the National Juvenile Court Data Archive reveals an increase in transfers from 1.9 percent of all delinquency cases in 1986 to 2.7 percent in 1990 (Butts & Poe 1993: 6).

General support for waiver legislation can be found in opinion polls that show widespread public support for prosecuting juveniles as adults for violent offenses. According to a USA/Gallup survey conducted in 1993, 73 percent of the U.S. adult population favored the transfer of juveniles to criminal courts for violent crime (Prichard 1993, pp. 1 & 6A). Although the poll was not specific in the age of juveniles and types of offenses for which juveniles should be prosecuted in criminal courts, it suggests that the public sees waiver as an effective response to violent juvenile crime. State legislators have responded by revising or creating their waiver statutes. Even federal legislators have recently joined the act of doing something about violent juvenile crime by proposing waiver legislation as an amendment to the 1994 U.S. crime bill.[3]

Thus, now more than ever, it seems waiver policies directed to a population of juveniles below the age of 16 deserve a close examination. By following New York's history of reforms and implementation of the JO law, I hope to show from legislation, arrest, disposition, and incarceration the real reasons for making juveniles younger than 16 criminally responsible for their behavior.

Recriminalizing Violent Juvenile Crime

WHY RECRIMINALIZE DELINQUENCY? Why did New York State wait until 1978 to respond to violent juvenile crime with legislative waiver? To answer these questions, I start with a description of the incident and the juvenile that triggered waiver legislation in New York. I then shift to the reasons for recriminalization that go beyond one juvenile's violent crimes and the immediate politics of election-year campaigns. Some of the reasons for recriminalization I locate in deep-seated political, as well as organizational, concerns and interests in controlling violent juvenile crime. Those concerns and interests I see as rooted in contemporary efforts to classify and to track a segment of delinquents as violent juvenile offenders in complex systems of juvenile and criminal justice.

The Case of Willie Bosket

In March 1978 Willie Bosket murdered two subway passengers and triggered a crisis in New York's system of juvenile justice.[1] Bosket often roamed the city's subways searching for easy targets to rob, such as drunk and sleepy passengers. Soon after his release from a state facility for delinquents, Bosket was back late at night on the subway line near his home, frequently with his older cousin, Herman Spates. One passenger was in the unfortunate position of having awakened to see Bosket searching his pockets when Bosket pulled the trigger of his .22 caliber pistol and shot him in the head. Eight days later on the same subway line, Bosket again shot and killed a subway passenger before emptying the victim's pockets.

Bosket's robbery and killing of subway passengers were not typical of most homicides. Few of the several murders that occur on average each day in New York City are considered of sufficient interest to even warrant media attention. The subway murders differed from "ordinary" acts of homicide because Bosket appeared motivated by the act of theft and was not acquainted with his victims. His victims also resided outside of his impoverished neighborhood in Manhattan. By attacking passengers on the city's subways, Bosket's violent offenses heightened the concern and fears of New Yorkers, particularly those who commuted on public transportation to meet their daily work routines. For many New Yorkers, especially subway passengers who fell asleep between subway stops, Bosket was not a delinquent; he was a modern-day highwayman, a criminal who threatened their personal safety and ability to live without the fear of violence.

Bosket's shooting of subway passengers caused many New Yorkers to shout and scream to their officials to "do something" about violent crime. But officials did not know exactly what to do until the age and legal status of Willie Bosket were announced. Bosket was only 15 years of age at the time and could not be charged in criminal court. He was technically a delinquent and therefore not criminally or legally responsible for the subway murders. Instead, Bosket was placed in New York's juvenile court (technically known as Family Court[2]), where he was still eligible for the treatment-oriented objectives of the state's juvenile justice system. Unlike many other states, New York at the time lacked the legal procedures for transferring a 15-year-old juvenile to criminal court if charged with murder.

Meanwhile Bosket's 17-year-old cousin, Herman Spates, who was at the scene of one of the subway murders and who claimed only to have watched Bosket shoot his victim, was charged and sentenced in criminal court, where he received a maximum of life in prison and a minimum of eight and one-third years as an adult offender. If Spates had not pleaded guilty, he risked a criminal trial by jury and a sentence of 25 years to life. The only variable separating Bosket from the longer sentences of criminal court was his age and New York's legal definition of his status as a delinquent.

The news reports, however, revealed more about Bosket's status as a chronic violent offender than as a delinquent in need of treatment. They quoted Bosket's claim that he had committed over a thousand offenses.[3] And they quoted his apparent lack of remorse for the death of the subway passengers: "I shot people, that's all. I don't feel nothing" (Butterfield, *New York Times*, March 22, 1989). Bosket was also quoted as saying that he did it "for the experience." Bosket's cousin, Herman Spates, told reporters that Willie "got a kick out of blowing them [the victims] away" (*New York Times*, March 2, 1978).

But there is another part to the case of Willie Bosket that caused the public and officials to question his placement once more as a delinquent in New York's juvenile justice system. Bosket was already there. He had already been through numerous juvenile justice agencies and in many juvenile justice facilities. At the age of 9 he was first brought to the juvenile court by his mother, who complained that she was unable to control his behavior. Since then Bosket spent only 18 months outside of his various state agency placements. In his last Division for Youth (DFY) placement just 6 months prior to the subway killings, Bosket was released despite the complaints of several of the institution's staff that stated Bosket was much too dangerous to be returned to New York City. One staff member was reported to have offered to let Bosket reside in his upstate home rather than to see him return.

Deep inside the news reports, it was also suggested that Bosket's need for help was often ignored by officials. He claimed that just one month prior to the subway killings he called DFY officials to request removal from his home and placement in foster care. Later some officials were quick to acknowledge openly that the system simply had lost track of Bosket and could have possibly prevented the subway murders. Even the Governor at the time, Hugh L. Carey, declared that "blame falls squarely on the shoulders of the Division for Youth" (*New York Times*, July 30, 1978: 1).

Responding to Violent Juvenile Crime

It was not long after Bosket's disposition in juvenile court was announced that Governor Carey stated that he wanted legislation to make sure juveniles such as Bosket "never walk the streets again" (*New York Times*, June 30, 1978: 12). There was no time to create another Governor's commission to study again violent juvenile crime and to once more suggest juvenile justice reforms. Such a commission was created several years earlier, and the get-tough reforms were already part of the juvenile justice system. Besides, election day was less than 6 months away, and the governor faced a tight race for reelection in which he was repeatedly accused by his opponent as "soft" on crime (McGarrell 1988). Only 6 months earlier he had vetoed a death penalty bill, and some believed that he wanted to act tough on crime by proposing at the time the most punitive delinquency law in the nation (Smith et al. 1980).[4]

Earlier attempts to pass waiver legislation had been resisted. New York was one of a few states that had set an already low general age of 16 for criminal responsibility. However, in criminal court juveniles between the ages of 16 and 18 could be sentenced as Youthful Offenders (YO) for offenses other than A felony crimes such as homicide.[5] If granted YO status, their records could remain confidential as is the case in juvenile court. Also, as YOs they would receive substantially shorter sentences and probation. In a sense, New York already automatically waived more juveniles to criminal court than states with waiver where general criminal responsibility began at older ages.

But the governor needed to do something about juveniles such as Willie Bosket who could commit acts of murder without ever facing criminal court or criminal punishment until they had reached the age of 16. He also wanted to do something to prevent chronic delinquents such as Willie Bosket from ever having the opportunity to commit subway murders. To do this he needed to propose legislation that would identify violence among juveniles younger than 15 and for offenses that were inclusive of a wide range of violent behaviors. In proposing the JO law, the governor went beyond automatic waiver in other states, such as Pennsylvania (Eigen 1981), which existed exclusively for the offense of murder. By proposing to transfer automatically initial jurisdiction over 13-year-old juveniles charged with murder and 14-year-old juveniles charged with rape, robbery, assault, and violent categories of burglary, the creators of the JO law wanted to do something more than just transfer juveniles such as Willie Bosket to criminal court. They wanted to classify and to track a wider population of violent delinquents as juvenile offenders before they became 15-year-old murderers.

Although Bosket's status as a delinquent triggered a legal reform, it was not the only incident to threaten the political and moral legitimacy of New York's juvenile justice system. Other incidents of serious violent juvenile crime were reported earlier in the media and repeatedly reproduced public and official criticisms of juvenile justice. A familiar story of crisis and reform appeared well before Bosket's acts of murder and long before the governor's decision to seek reelection. In the remaining sections of this chapter, I argue that the reasons for the sudden emergence of waiver legislation go beyond any particular incident of violent crime or momentary political ambition. In other words, Bosket and a governor's reelection campaign triggered crisis and waiver legislation, but they were not the exclusive reasons for doing something about violent crime by recriminalizing delinquency.

Real Reasons for Crisis and Reform

The deeper reasons for the JO law rest in a complex set of political and organizational concerns and interests.[6] Part of those concerns are stimulated by the media and their news reports on juvenile violence and juvenile justice. Reforms are advocated as part of a cyclical effort to do something about juvenile crime and justice. Conservative and liberal critics of juvenile justice provide the ideological ammunition for making reforms sell during certain periods of crisis. In the sections that follow, I divide the sources of crisis into first the political need to do something about violent juvenile crime, and then the deeper organizational concerns and interests that lead to juvenile justice reforms.

Although not everyone in New York would have agreed that there was a crisis, violent juvenile crime and the inability of juvenile justice to control its occurrence became familiar media themes. In the many decisions that editors must make as to what stories will sell newspapers and boost television ratings, the case of Willie Bosket fit well-developed themes and patterns of reporting. But the interests of the media in presenting a story are not necessarily the same as the public's interest in a true presentation of all the facts (Cohen & Young 1981: 17). The media's interest in fitting incidents and persons into preselected newsworthy themes neglects other possible relevant sources of crisis (Ericson et al., 1987; Fishman 1978).

Perhaps in a different period of time, what was considered newsworthy in the case of Willie Bosket would have produced a different portrayal of the factors that led to his violent behavior and a different perception of crisis. Bosket might have been portrayed as a repeated victim of violent abuse. His impoverished home environment might have been highlighted, as well as the culture of violence in his neighborhood and the institutions in which he was repeatedly placed. Recommended reforms might have followed which would have reinforced political and organizational interests in treatment and juvenile justice rather than punishment and criminal justice.

This takes us to reasons for crisis that go beyond the objective characteristics of crime and punishment. Crisis, or what Stanley Cohen refers to as a "moral panic," takes on unique forms to suit particular interests. In his description of a moral panic in a declining English resort town, Cohen tells us that

> societies appear to be subject, every now and then, to periods of moral panic. A condition, episode, person or group of persons emerges to become defined as a threat to societal values and interests; its nature is presented in a stylized and stereotypical fashion by the mass media; the moral barricades are manned by editors, bishops, politicians and other right-thinking people; socially accredited experts pronounce their diagnoses and solutions; ways of coping are evolved or (more often) resorted to; the condition then disappears, submerges or deteriorates and becomes more visible (1980: 9).

In Cohen's analysis new categories of deviance, "mods" and "rockers," were created to help deal with the town's declining social and economic circumstances. The mods and rockers became the new "folk devils" on which editors as well as politicians were able to blame the town's growing troubles (see also Hall et al. 1981: 161).

But what does an English resort town's folk devils have to do with violent juvenile crime in New York City and subsequent juvenile justice reforms? It suggests that at times it became more convenient to blame the deviant for troubles that defy simple solutions. In times of crisis, societies have an occasional need to blame delinquents as offenders, and to develop a legal response that isolates and punishes them for their criminal behavior. Thomas Bernard (1992) in his book *The Cycle of Juvenile Justice* makes this point when he argues that reforms regularly alternate between treatment-oriented and punishment-oriented programs. Officials and the public may start out, as they apparently did before systems of juvenile justice, with the perception that punishment for juveniles is much too harsh and that there are not enough treatment-oriented options. Programs are developed to expand the number of lenient options for officials. After the creation of these treatment-oriented sanctions or programs, calls for reform are repeated when

> justice officials and the general public remain convinced that juvenile crime is at an exceptionally high level. After some time, they begin to blame lenient treatments for the high crime rates. Initially responses to serious juvenile offenders are "toughened up," so that those offenders receive harsh punishments rather than lenient treatments. The responses for average or typical juvenile offenders are also "toughened up" so that they too receive harsh punishments. This process continues until there are many harsh punishments available for responding to juvenile offenders but few lenient treatments (Bernard 1992: 4).

And then the cycle of reforms returns to that which advocates treatment programs.

Yet a simplistic, cyclical view of reforms assumes that there are limited sets of directions in which the system can expand. If the punishments become harsh, treatment programs are eliminated. If treatment programs are advocated, then harsh punishments are no longer considered a viable option. Instead, a more complex vision of reform suggests that when the cycle of reforms produces harsher penalties, treatment programs are not dismantled or eliminated. Similarly, when treatment reforms are advocated, punishment is not eliminated but remains in the background as a last resort, just as it did in more punishment-oriented periods of reform.

Moreover, treatment- and punishment-oriented reforms depend on a political climate in which various ideologies for viewing the nature of deviance can be supported. In more politically conservative times, it is easier to blame offenders for their troubles by producing what Levine and Levine (1992: 8) refer to as the "intrapsychic mode" of dealing with deviance. When deviance is seen as a consequence of "personal weaknesses and failings . . . what must be changed is not the circumstance but the person." The intrapsychic mode contrasts sharply with the situational mode of reacting to deviance which "assumes that people are basically 'good' but have been exposed to poor conditions and therefore have not reached their full potential" (8). The situational model of reacting to deviance is more likely to dominate in less politically conservative times. For example, seeing the offender as the victim of unfortunate circumstances reflected the earlier turn-of-the-century progressive belief that "men were born innocent, not depraved, that the sources of corruption were external, not internal, to the human condition" (Rothman 1971: 69).

In the case of recriminalization, a wider, more complex net is produced in ways that defy a simple cycle of juvenile justice reforms (Austin & Krisberg 1981). There is an intricate web of legal reforms in which waiver legislation can emerge. Waiver legislation has not eliminated the need for juvenile justice and its various treatment-oriented programs. Those programs remain in the background, not necessarily as a first or last resort, but as another legal avenue to track and to classify juveniles into less severe legal categories. Still, resources are limited, and the maximum security institutions that recriminalization requires may force officials to limit the more lenient dispositions that affect the production of treatment programs.

But before the next cycle of reforms can be accepted by officials, officials and the public must be sold on the idea that punishment or treatment is the most appropriate response to juvenile crime (Bernard 1992: 148–52). In the case of waiver legislation, the ideological and academic justification for getting tough on juvenile crime centered on the concept of serious juvenile violence and chronic juvenile offenders. The explicit reasons for reacting to juveniles as adult offenders in criminal court are contained in a chapter titled "What Can Be Done to Curb Crime?" in Ernest van den Haag's (1975) widely circulated book, *Punishing Criminals*. He states simply that the legal boundaries separating violent juveniles from their adult counterparts are no longer needed.

There is little reason left for not holding juveniles responsible under the same laws that apply to adults. The victim of a fifteen-year-old mugger is as much mugged as the victim of a twenty-year-old mugger, the victim of a fourteen-year-old murderer or rapist is as dead or as raped as the victim of an older one. The need for social defense or protection is the same (van den Haag 1975: 174).

In arguing that the victims are the same whether the offenders are juveniles or adults, van den Haag first emphasizes the need to do justice. He asks us to ignore the age of juveniles and instead focus on the harm they inflict upon their victims and society. Second, van den Haag in stating the "need for social defense" shifts direction by suggesting that society should concentrate on punishing *chronic* delinquents.

Van den Haag draws on the frequently cited longitudinal research of Wolfgang et al. (1972). In that study the cohort arrest data for a population of juveniles born in 1945 in the city of Philadelphia showed that 6 percent of arrested juveniles committed five or more offenses before their eighteenth birthday. Chronic delinquents were defined by Wolfgang et al. as juveniles arrested five or more times for violent as well as nonviolent offenses. These chronic delinquents were responsible for slightly over 50 percent of all offenses committed by the cohort population (Wolfgang et al., 1972: 89). The mean severity of arrests (based on a measure of harm committed) for chronic delinquents was substantially greater than for delinquents who committed fewer than five offenses. In fact, chronic delinquents were responsible for most of the violent index offenses that were recorded for the entire cohort period (Wolfgang et al., 1972: 95).

Although there are substantial difficulties in recommending policy based on the Philadelphia cohort studies (see Blumstein & Moitra 1980), the condensed version of Wolfgang's research took on a life of its own in van den Haag's interpretation.[7]

> Wolfgang's data indirectly question legislation that, in most states, provides for young offenders to be treated with leniency and for no public record-keeping of their arrests or convictions. The legislation is based on the belief that young offenders can be reformed more easily than older ones. Wolfgang's data indicate that such optimism is not supported by facts and becomes positively wrong after the third arrest of a juvenile. Legislation should be changed accordingly. After the age of thirteen, juveniles should be treated as adults for indictment, trial and sentencing purposes (248–9).

But in moving from "indirect" support for waiver to recommending that all juveniles over the age of 13 should be convicted as adult offenders, van den Haag takes a giant leap beyond the data to evaluate the effectiveness of juvenile courts. That is, there is nothing in the Wolfgang et al. cohort data, or the rearrest probabilities of juveniles, to suggest the ineffectiveness or effectiveness of Philadelphia's juvenile courts. The mentioned cohort data could just as easily be interpreted to suggest that juvenile courts are very successful in preventing repeated delinquent behavior; after all, only a small proportion of arrested juveniles go on to repeat their offenses five or more times.

There are other pieces of research that van den Haag cites in support of a policy to place juveniles in criminal court. Based on Robert Martinson's (1974) widely cited article that summarizes what works in the treatment of offenders, van den Haag concluded that "given the evidence we now have we should no longer regard rehabilitation as a major purpose to which punishment is suited" (188). If treatment failed to reform the delinquent, then punishment in criminal court appeared as the only logical and acceptable choice.

Yet van den Haag was not the only one to recommend the need to put violent juveniles in the adult criminal justice system. Several years after van den Haag published his book, New York State commissioned several distinguished professors from Harvard University to recommend policy for controlling violent crime. The authors, Mark Moore, James Q. Wilson, and Ralph Gants (1978), prepared a report for the New York Commission on Management & Productivity in the Public Sector in which they stressed the importance of identifying and tracking violent and chronic delinquents. Like van den Haag, they drew on the Wolfgang et al. *Delinquency in a Birth Cohort* study to conclude that

> a relatively small number of offenders account for a large proportion of all serious offenses. The implication is that if we wish to limit serious offenses there may be some advantage to concentrating on chronic offenders. Because chronic offenders account for a large fraction of serious offenses, to some extent this emphasis will occur naturally as a result of concentrating on serious offenses. However, since chronic offenders also occasionally commit lesser offenses, we may want to know something about the criminal records of even minor offenders to assist the judge in choosing a proper disposition. In effect, we want to concentrate on both serious offenses and chronic offenders (Moore et al., 1978: 21).

In suggesting that New York State concentrate on both serious offenses and chronic offenders, Moore et al. also argued that it is important to identify delinquents based on juvenile court records.[8] They also recognized the difficulty that criminal justice officials faced in identifying chronic delinquents because of the confidentiality of those records.

So far I have presented a widely circulated book and a commissioned report as part of the ideological reasons for waiver and recriminalization. Yet ever since the creation of juvenile courts, published and unpublished reports documented the inability of juvenile courts to control delinquents or violent juveniles. The question that remains is: Why did van den Haag and other critics of existing juvenile justice become relevant to policy makers in the seventies and not in earlier decades?

The deeper reasons for reform go beyond cyclical ideological visions of how to control violent juvenile crime. First, I will stress that the purpose of juvenile justice reforms is not simply to control juvenile crime. Reforms provide a convenient legal avenue in which to do something about the intractable problem of crime and justice. Second, I will argue that the political and organizational concerns and interests that lead officials to legal reforms are built on a history of prior reforms that has produced loosely coupled systems of juvenile and criminal justice.

Why not deterrence and incapacitation as the sole purpose for dealing with juvenile offenders? First, contemporary as well as ancient systems of justice were never interested in just preventing crime. They serve other purposes besides that which goes into the prevention and control of crime. Emile Durkheim (1933 [1893]) made this point long ago when he suggested that crime and punishment was a normal and necessary part of every society. Crime and punishment not only remind members of society of what are unacceptable forms of conduct, but they also help to maintain the cohesiveness of society. The public's inability to see Bosket punished for the subway murders added little to its confidence in the legal rules of society.

But Durkheim (1933 [1893]) further suggested that the reaction to crime depends on how society is organized. In contemporary, urban social environments, a complex division of labor leads to the emergence of bureaucratic and civil types of laws to produce more formal relationships. Within the expanding range of civil administrative rules, restitutive forms of justice are more likely to appear. But restitutive forms of justice are more complex and at times less satisfying than the more repressive forms of justice in simpler societies. In contrast to simple societies where a more direct correspondence between the rule of law and public forms of punishment may appear to exist,[9] according to Durkheim, modern societies produce the administrative rules of law that propagate complex systems of juvenile and criminal justice.

The contemporary structural reason for classifying some juveniles as offenders and others as delinquents is for the purpose of doing more than just separating the good from the bad; with delinquent and offender categories there are only levels of badness. There is no simple split between criminals and noncriminals, and much of what is increasingly labeled as criminal or delinquent today is of little interest to the general public. Something more complex is going on. Deciding the appropriate legal response is no longer between the victim and the offender but between the offender and the state and its bureaucratic mechanisms for administering law.

Systems of juvenile and criminal justice join other complex organizational settings in modern societies to create more and more distinct categories for classifying individuals with unique social and legal labels. They reflect a contemporary society that sees the solutions to its problems in terms of its ability to classify and identify deviance. It is a society that likes to classify juveniles into increasingly diverse sets of social and legal categories (see Cohen 1985: 4–9). Within those distinct classes of labels there is something for everyone. In the world of juvenile justice, there is the status offender, the delinquent, the restrictive delinquent, the chronic delinquent, the serious delinquent, the violent delinquent, and, of course, the juvenile offender. Some of the labels refer to the same population of juveniles. At the same time, in the world of education, there are the honor, academic, general, vocational, learning disabled, and mentally retarded tracks. And many of the labels in juvenile justice draw on the world of mental health with its own range of deviant and not-so-deviant labels to attach to delinquents and nondelinquents.

But back in the world of juvenile justice, practical decisions need to be made about the legal status of juveniles. And within the various governmental courtrooms, there is a bottom-line concern with making decisions to best control the delinquent or violent behavior of juveniles. Officials want to identify the serious delinquent and prevent his or her repeated criminal behavior. They want to prevent juveniles such as Willie Bosket from graduating to more serious acts of violence. The dilemma is how to best do so within the limited treatment and punishment options of officials. If treatment is pursued and the delinquent returns for more serious violent offenses, then a crisis may occur and the legitimacy of the system is once more threatened.

George Herbert Mead clearly saw the difficulty that was in store for traditional juvenile courts in their attempt to pursue the "best interests" of juveniles and society.[10] In many ways it is easier, according to Mead, simply to satisfy society's need to punish the offender. This is because it is psychologically impossible "to hate the sin and love the sinner" (1961: 882). Mead

(1961: 882) like Durkheim argued that "without the criminal, the cohesiveness of society would crumble into mutually repellent individual particles." The solidarity that citizens achieve in identifying and punishing the deviant is a way of preventing a different and at times less preferable social response to crime and deviance.

But general societal interests in condemning deviants tell us little about the specific interests in crisis and reform. For example, Nachman Ben-Yehuda explains the European witchcraze during the Middle Ages not only as a consequence of a moral panic but also as a result of the vested interests of the Catholic church, specifically the inquisitors and the Dominicans (1990: 72). In colonial Massachusetts as well, religious heretics were relabeled as witches because the established church hierarchy felt threatened.

Specific interests can be further narrowed in terms of class conflict as the reason for the criminal label (Chambliss & Seidman 1971). According to Chambliss (1974: 37), the creation and implementation of legal reforms is "first and foremost a reflection of the interests and ideologies of the governing class." Anthony Platt similarly presents a class-linked argument to suggest that an elite group of child-saving women created juvenile courts to control the conduct of lower-class youth and to avoid "the potential development of a revolutionary movement" (Platt 1977: xix). Class interests rather than benevolent interests allowed juvenile justice reformers "to create a system that subjected more and more juveniles to arbitrary and degrading punishments" (Platt 1977: xviii).

But the idea that juvenile justice was created exclusively on the grounds of class ignores other internal interests that are more often related to the concerns of those in existing child-care bureaucracies. In an analysis of Toronto's first juvenile justice legislation, Hagan and Leon (1977) suggest that bureaucratic interests rather than just class interests accounted for the creation of juvenile courts. These bureaucratic interests centered around probation and its convenience in reducing rather than increasing the number of institutionalized delinquents (Hagan & Leon 1977: 595). Moreover, they show conflict as well as consensus among officials in demands for the creation of juvenile courts.

Conflicting bureaucratic interests emerge also as part of the negotiated order of justice. The negotiated character of juvenile justice is highlighted in John Sutton's (1988) empirically grounded historical analysis of major U.S. juvenile justice reforms. The reforms rearranged existing juvenile justice practices rather than significantly altering the proportion of juveniles subject to legal controls. Sutton concludes that "the American juvenile justice system is a negotiated order – negotiated to be sure, among unequal participants – not one determined exclusively or even largely by the economic priorities of a single class" (Sutton 1988: 244).

Also there are what Cohen (1985) calls "deposits of power" in all systems of justice. The police, the juvenile courts, and divisions for youth all have their own interest for handling juveniles as delinquents or offenders. They require a negotiated order of justice in which bureaucratic interests emerge to produce systems of justice that are not centered around any singular objective. Instead, the negotiated character of juvenile justice often produces one part of juvenile justice in conflict with another. This is dramatically exemplified in Mark Jacobs' (1990) study of a contemporary juvenile court located in a largely affluent suburb where interagency conflicts make up the world of juvenile justice. For example, Jacobs reports that juvenile court and school officials battled over financial responsibility for the placement of delinquents who were possibly in need of special education. As a consequence, the school system retained "a high-priced legal firm billing hundreds of thousands of dollars each year to represent them." Litigation was the preferred avenue in negotiating juvenile justice rather than settling "issues of casework responsibility and authority solely through the exercise of their good offices" (Jacobs 1990: 75).

At the same time, modern-day bureaucracies are able to perpetuate themselves by maintaining the superiority of their specialized forms of knowledge. Max Weber's sociology of organizations and law suggests that bureaucracies seek "to increase the superiority of the professionally informed by keeping their knowledge and intentions secret" and by hiding their "knowledge and actions from criticism" (Max Weber 1946: 233). The structure of legal obligations and controls arises not only because of how elites distribute power in society but also because of how "power is organized and justified so that it appears to be legitimate" (Sutton 1988: 245). Reform is one important avenue to avoid public criticism by allowing juvenile justice systems to continually reinvent themselves to take on diverse legal avenues and categories.

The system's need to legitimize itself independent of rates of crime is reflected in David Garland's (1985) definition of success:

> The "success" of the penal-welfare strategy – a success which has allowed its persistence for nearly a century – is not, then, the reform of offenders or the prevention of crime. It is its ability to administer and manage criminality in an efficient and extensive manner, while portraying that process in terms which make it acceptable to the public and penal agents alike (260).

The specialized knowledge of officials allows negotiated orders of juvenile justice to achieve success in the wake of repeated examples of failure and a continuous cycle of reforms.

But how does recriminalization work through negotiated orders of justice? Or why would removing a proportion of juveniles from the more insulated and confidential juvenile court to the public criminal court enhance the juvenile justice system's legitimacy and its ability to classify a diverse population of offenders? First, criminal justice is a more public forum only for the small proportion of homicides that attract widespread media attention. Weber's insight into modern-day bureaucracies applies to criminal justice as well as to juvenile justice; the system is hidden and not directly observable for a lot of offenders, especially those charged with less serious offenses.

Second, there is a degree of tension in public and official responses to crime that just never seems to go away. That tension produces conflict and criticism when legal bureaucracies violate certain "ethical principles" (Sutton 1988: 246). For example, the feeling among many New Yorkers that it simply was not right for Willie Bosket to receive a 5-year indeterminate placement for the murder of two subway passengers conflicted with the legal rule that he was a delinquent. Weber (1954 [1925]) saw the difficulty in the more formal rational pursuit of law in contemporary societies when he wrote that

> the democratic ethos, where it pervades the masses in connection with a concrete question, based as it is on the postulate of substantive justice in concrete cases for concrete individuals, inevitably comes into conflict with the formalism and the rule bound, detached objectivity of bureaucratic administration (355).

In other words, modern-day bureaucracies that touch upon the public problem of juvenile crime are influenced by factors that go beyond any stated singular set of objectives. Formal rationality is only an ideal type that inevitably comes into conflict with a broader set of substantive goals. Sutton suggests that we view "formal and substantive rationalization as interactive processes in the analysis of modern societies" (1988: 246–7).

In the world of juvenile justice, the substantive and rational pursuit of justice has produced a diverse set of legal reforms and an uneven story to juvenile justice. Unlike the bureaucratic administration of, say, a licensing bureau, systems of juvenile justice vary considerably in their structure and routine decision making (Stapleton et al., 1982). Those particular routines did not emerge in a vacuum, but they developed from unique local cultures and particular local interests. Various subsystems of juvenile justice were created to produce a diverse set of legal avenues for deciding the status of juveniles.

But these subsystems in textbook descriptions of juvenile justice are too often portrayed as tightly organized around a singular juvenile justice system. Such descriptions mistakenly lead us to assume that juvenile justice decision making centers exclusively on what juvenile court judges do, when in reality other decision makers are just as important. It is not just the juvenile court judge that determines the ultimate legal status of delinquent or juvenile offender, but also school, mental health, the police, probation, division for youth, and criminal justice officials. And each set of officials involved in the legal decision making of juveniles is touched by its own particular agency's organizational concerns and interests in pursuit of the stated best interests of juveniles and justice.

Thus the negotiated order of juvenile justice and its subsystems of juvenile justice like criminal justice may be viewed as producing loosely coupled systems of justice. The "glue" that holds loosely coupled systems of juvenile justice together is "impermanence, dissolvability, and tacitness" (Weick 1976: 3). Applying Weick's (1976) list of the organizational elements to juvenile justice suggests the following: First, minimal regulations and confidentiality act to insulate and buffer loosely coupled systems from their external environment so that juvenile justice is less subject to public criticism. Second, loosely coupled systems in the short run appear cheaper to operate. It takes time and money to coordinate officials and services, particularly in large jurisdictions where there are numerous agencies in the business of treating juveniles with a multitude of organizational concerns and interests.[11]

Meyer and Rowan (1977) characterize loosely coupled educational systems as operating with rules and decisions that are often violated, unimplemented, and with uncertain consequences. Decision making appears vague and involves little coordination. Modern-day educational systems help to perpetuate rationalized myths about the proper techniques of learning to meet their organizational interests. In other words, there is much to be gained not only for students but also for officials in the stated objectives and techniques of modern educational settings.

The objectives and techniques of juvenile justice, however, differ sharply from those of formal education. Bruce Jackson (1984) reminds us that bureaucracies dealing with offenders or deviants are different from other governmental agencies, such as hospitals, schools, and departments of defense. Criminal justice agencies attempt "to get rid of something," while "those other agencies are all deeded to doing something (teaching the kids, curing the sick, making a war)" (Jackson 1984: 299).

Jackson's insight is further reflected in his less than complimentary metaphor:

> The workers in criminal justice are probably closer to the workers in a city's garbage department than anything else: they take off the streets stuff no one else wants or has use for. The portions that are useful are set loose or recycled, and the portions that are considered too contaminated for further use are destroyed or housed in places of extreme isolation – a dump for radioactive or poisonous chemicals for one agency, a dump for long-term convicts on the other (299).

As Jackson observes, legal decision making requires picking out delinquents for either recycling or isolation. It requires what organizational theorists have called "a garbage can model" of decision making in which a considerable amount of time is spent avoiding and delaying decisions, hoping that by recycling or throwing it away the problem will some how also go away (Mohr 1976).

The various organizational goals within and between systems of juvenile and criminal justice can perhaps best be visualized on the playing field of a very large football stadium where there are several teams looking toward a multitude of organizational goals. A few goal posts are facing the direction of treatment, and several others toward just deserts, retribution, and deterrence. Moreover, there are sets of players on each team striving to reach their particular administrative objectives. It is in the interest of the police to go off in one direction, while probation officers pursue another. Unlike a normal football team, players begin to shift their positions based on the prevailing winds of local public and official opinion. Public prosecutors might enter the field as quarterbacks based on the campaign of one district attorney, while being called to sit on the sidelines for another district attorney. Very large football stadiums need only be situated near densely populated urban centers. A different game would of course emerge in a much smaller stadium where fewer politicians, reporters, and citizens are in the stands to tell the players exactly what to do.

The analogy to football is really off-base when we consider the fact that no one in juvenile justice is really keeping score. By not keeping score, officials appear to care less about rates of treatment or punishment and more about maintaining the appearance of a game. This is because success is not measured by the number of delinquents that are rehabilitated after treatment or deterred after punishment. The salaries or promotion of juvenile justice officials are not contingent on rates of recidivism. For legal officials it is how the game is played that counts most in producing success or failure.

Recriminalization, therefore, is just another direction in which juvenile justice systems can enhance and maintain their legitimacy. It creates another legal subsystem for responding to the deviant behavior of juveniles, although such behavior can be extremely serious. In formulating the concept of loose coupling as it applies to a variety of social and biological systems, Glassman (1973: 91) notes that "one method by which a system maintains loose coupling is by having a subsystem which is more tightly coupled." Legislative waiver is such a subsystem; it allows juvenile justice to persist and to maintain itself as a loosely coupled system.

But simply to argue that the recriminalization of delinquency is a product of loosely coupled systems and of the system's need to reinvent itself does not really explain the timing and shape of reforms. It does not explain why there is simultaneously recriminalization of violent juvenile offenses and decriminalization of status offenses. The particular direction which recriminalization takes can best be understood by returning to notions of power and bureaucratic interests. Bureaucratic interests are pursued in avenues that are organizationally convenient. In the cycling and recycling of deviants, a wider net has emerged in which definitions of criminal and noncriminal are constantly revised and consequently blurred.

There are two ends of the legal system's attempt to control deviants that Cohen sees as having expanded in the wake of modern-day criminal justice reforms. First, a wider net in which to identify deviants as offenders has occurred at the "soft end" of the legal process; this involves intake, adjustment, and mediation services. The soft end operates with inclusionary techniques of control. They are inclusionary because they attempt to retain delinquents "as long as possible within conventional social boundaries and institutions, there to be absorbed" (Cohen 1985: 219). They not only give juveniles a second and third chance, but they also provide officials with the threats they need in order to make all those inclusionary programs work.

But for those who resist the repeated warnings of officials in group and individual counseling, or through drug rehabilitation, first offender programs, and even probation, there is the "hard end" of the legal process with its exclusionary techniques of control. This consists of not only last-resort penalties consisting of out-of-home placement but also waiver to criminal court. Recriminalization expands the legal options of officials at the hard end of the system, while at the same time maintaining the soft end of juvenile justice. Inclusionary and exclusionary techniques of control work together to redefine the nature of crime and punishment by creating new legal avenues for identifying juveniles as status offenders, delinquents, or juvenile offenders.

Garland shows that in England a history of delinquency legislation produced a complex system of welfare that created the necessary back-up system that made inclusionary treatment programs work.

> This segregative sector, then, operated as the coercive terminus for the whole penal network, in just the same way that the penal complex as a whole supplied the coercive back-up for the institutions of the social realm. It formed the "deep end" of the complex, which functioned as a sanction of last resort, supporting the others by its threatening presence (Garland 1985: 243).

If exclusion through waiver to criminal court as a last resort for the serious violent delinquent is a necessary, more exclusionary form of control, then why did recriminalization in the shape of the JO law not appear earlier? The answer rests in a dynamic process in which first- and last-resort options are continuously adjusted to maintain the legitimacy of systems of juvenile justice. Officials are in the business of fine-tuning the legal response by expanding their available list of first- and last-resort options.[12] Adjustments are made in line with a diverse set of emerging official and political interests. This is because there are deep pockets of power for both doing good and doing justice.

In doing justice by means of exclusionary forms of control, waiver satisfies political and organizational interests in seeing the offender punished. It satisfies the interest of politicians to show the public that something is being done about violent juvenile crime. It satisfies the elected district attorney's responsibility to fight violent crime. It even satisfies the interests of juvenile justice officials to concentrate their treatment services on the less seriously delinquent juveniles. But, as I will show in later chapters, there are other interests as well that are satisfied through waiver and recriminalization.

Conclusion

So far I have emphasized how functional and conflict approaches contribute to an understanding of juvenile justice reform. I have argued that political and organizational interests produced recriminalization as a way of coping with crisis. In arguing that recriminalization is just one part of a cycle of reforms, I suggested that the reasons for legislative waiver go beyond the actions of one juvenile or election-year politics by a single official. Recriminalization is a part of contemporary society's need to divide juveniles into the good, the bad, and the not-so-bad. It provides officials with another legal avenue to negotiate juvenile justice, and it creates another subsystem within loosely coupled systems of juvenile and criminal justice.[13]

To understand why recriminalization emerged in 1978 and not in prior years requires a review of an earlier history of reforms and the immediate dynamics of reform that led to passage of the JO law. It requires a more extensive review of New York's history than the initially stated reason for waiver in the form of Willie Bosket and a governor's election campaign.

CHAPTER TWO

Taking Stock of
Juvenile Justice Reforms

PART OF THE REASON for recriminalization in New York and in other states is contained in a long history of earlier juvenile justice reforms. A history of reforms takes us beyond Willie Bosket and a governor's election campaign and helps us to understand the specific timing and content of waiver legislation. By moving away from the immediate sources of crisis, we can more accurately see the emergence of the political and organizational concerns and interests that paved the way toward recriminalization. The sources of legal change are in part internal in that each new generation of reforms is directly linked to a set of assumptions inherited from the previous generation of reformers. The assumptions of prior generations were modified and refitted to address the local concerns and interests of each successive generation of reformers (Sutton 1988: 5).

In this chapter I take stock of a history of juvenile justice reforms to see how the assumptions of officials in prior generations set into motion systems of juvenile justice. I seek to understand, not entirely to explain, the social and legal circumstances that produced loosely coupled systems of juvenile justice with diverse sets of legal avenues and legal labels. I highlight crisis, beliefs, and administrative concerns in the system's emerging ability to identify and classify juveniles as delinquents, status offenders, and juvenile offenders.

As I noted early on in my use of the term *recriminalization*, my identification of periods of decriminalization and criminalization is not mutually exclusive and exhaustive. In most states waiver legislation existed alongside legal efforts to decriminalize the status of juveniles. Similarly, during a period of criminalization, there are examples of decriminalization. Within the cycle of juvenile justice reforms, there are minicycles that are not easily placed into one period or the other.

With the above caveats in mind, I identify a period of decriminalization as one marked by the creation of social and legal reforms that worked to treat juveniles as delinquents in institutions that were physically separated first from the penitentiary and then from criminal courts. The creation of reformatories and juvenile courts also redefined a wider range of offenses for which the state could increasingly intervene in the lives of juveniles.

Criminalization marked a shift in first- and last-resort options for legal officials. It is a term that Barry Feld (e.g., 1984 and 1993) noted to describe the emergence of contemporary systems of juvenile justice. During times of criminalization, traditional juvenile courts were no longer viewed as containing the viable organizational settings for dealing with a wide range of delinquencies. Most noticeably, criminalization provided the reforms to make juvenile courts more closely resemble criminal courts by producing legal changes that emphasized procedural due process and diversion for status offenses (e.g., truancy and running away). It also, as I will show, created the organizational concerns and interests that led to the expansion and creation of waiver legislation. In other words, I will argue that distinct periods of juvenile justice reforms were reproduced in periods of decriminalization that led to the criminalization and then recriminalization of juvenile justice.

Decriminalization

A formal treatment-oriented system of juvenile justice did not appear suddenly with the emergence of any particular legal reform. Ancient systems of punishment always incorporated a vision of punishment as treatment, especially when it came to the raising of children. As Francis Allen puts it, punishment was seen "as a kind of cure" (Allen 1981: 4). To understand how punishment can be viewed as treatment, Allen directs us to the particular cultural context in which the techniques of punishment arise. Although penitentiaries today may be viewed as last-resort places for inflicting punishment, they were also initially created as institutions that could treat or rehabilitate offenders. In the early part of the nineteenth century, for example, they were envisioned not just as places to hold the offender but as places to do penitence; the concept of "doing time" was an integral part of the ideal form of treatment.

But techniques of treatment were developed by those working inside the system to serve purposes that went beyond the stated need to rehabilitate offenders. Decisions about what to do with offenders could not be satisfied easily by the whipping post or by prison. Decriminalization allowed the system to expand by developing new legal avenues not only to make the punishment fit the type of offender and offense but also to advance institutions for punishment and treatment to serve emerging bureaucratic concerns and interests. It produced one institution after another so that officials could rely on the orphan asylum and then houses of refuge and then juvenile courts as more appropriate legal settings. But the shift from treating juveniles as ordinary criminal offenders to a class of separate delinquents was not an abrupt one that can be attributed to any one single reform.

Pre–House of Refuge. In eighteenth-century England, Douglas Hay identified the "prerogative of mercy" as the administrative technique for avoiding the severe penalties of law.

> The prerogative of mercy ran throughout the administration of the criminal law, from the lowest to the highest level. At the top sat the high court judges, and their free use of the royal pardon became a crucial argument in the arsenal of conservatives opposing reform. At the lowest jurisdiction, that of the justice of the peace, the same discretion allowed the magistrate to make decisions that sometimes escaped legal categories altogether (Hay 1975: 40).

The "prerogative of mercy" not only worked to spare adults from the stated penalty of death; it also worked to spare juveniles from criminal punishment. The common law defense of infancy was just one legal avenue for justifying the official use of discretion. Although the death penalty in England and the United States covered a wide range of offenses, few juveniles were actually sentenced to death. Pardons and forced transportation or emigration were preferred ways to mitigate the state's response to serious crimes. As is the case today, officials could drop or reduce the charges. For example, between 1801 and 1836, 103 children were sentenced to death in England, but not one was executed (Knell 1965: 199). And in New York State there were no reported executions of juveniles under the age of 16 (Sobie 1987: 17).

The prerogative of mercy or official discretion similarly spared juveniles from the harsh penalties of law. It provided officials with the flexibility they needed to implement eighteenth-century penalties not only for adult offenders but also for juveniles. There was a broad array of penalties that appeared to rely mainly on monetary fines. However, if the offender was unable to pay, officials could resort to physical punishment. According to David Rothman,

> the statutes fixing a penalty of a fine often provided that persons unable to pay the costs were to be whipped. Where one punishment was inappropriate, magistrates had recourse to the other. No clear division by type of offense distinguished those who received a fine from those who received a whipping. The circumstances of the criminal, not just the crime, determined the penalty (Rothman 1971: 49).

It is important to note that it was not just the severity of the offense that determined the kind of punishment an offender received but also his or her characteristics and ability to avoid the harsher penalties contained in early eighteenth-century criminal law.

In the wake of rapid social and cultural shifts in the urban U.S. population, officials needed to adjust their legal options for dealing with offenders. The population in New York City's borough of Manhattan grew from about 33,000 in 1790 to 124,000 in 1820 (Andriot 1993: 461). And with an increase in the general population, there was undoubtedly an increase in the offender population. In response to emerging sources of urban social disorder, officials looked to expand their legal avenues and mechanisms for punishing or treating offenders. Meanwhile, the whip and other corporal forms of punishment appeared less and less attractive as ways of identifying, watching, treating, or punishing a growing population of offenders.

The early eighteenth-century reformers set into motion institutions that were believed to be capable of caring for the vagrant, the deviant, the criminal, and the delinquent. These institutions were seen as less cruel than earlier systems of control and more capable of turning the deviant into a productive member of society. It was no longer as easy to expel the vagrant from the city when the vagrant's labor might be needed and there were no other places to where the vagrant could be expelled. The reformers responded to the increasing chaotic quality of urban life through institutions that were to produce "a highly disciplined and regimented routine which would at once reform the prisoner and inspire the community to emulation" (Rothman 1971: 116).

One way to maintain order in the wake of disorder was to create new institutions to fit newly defined classes of deviants. Institutions were built for the vagrant and the mentally ill as well as for the criminal. Meanwhile, the social extension of childhood increased the age and population of juveniles that were seen in need of institutional care in the absence of parental supervision. The first institution in New York developed exclusively for the care of children, the orphan asylum, was created in 1807 (Sobie 1987: 22). At the time, an increasing proportion of the city's homeless and abandoned juveniles was placed in almshouses so that in one almshouse, 259 of the 622 paupers were children under the age of 9 (Sobie 1987: 20).

Initially, the orphan asylum like the adult asylum was able to distance itself from the problems of almshouses. Children without parents and delinquents were initially placed to receive secular and religious training but later were "bound out to some reputable person or families for such object and in such manner as the [orphanage] board shall approve" (Sobie 1987: 22). But at the same time, the almshouse was able to persist as an institution for children. Support for almshouses continued as reflected in a New York State statute authorizing magistrates to "send" youths to almshouses if they were found begging and their parents were impoverished (Sobie 1987: 20).

Almshouses and orphan asylums expanded despite reports of problems. The dismal conditions of almshouses did not prevent the state from supporting them as institutions for troubled children. The orphan asylum and the practice of boarding out children with reputable families produced their share of complaints. But the families were not always so reputable. There were complaints of abuse against children by persons in these families and instances of children running away, for good reason, from their apprenticeships. Meanwhile, various immigrant ethnic groups accumulated the political clout to generate political concerns over the practice of boarding delinquent children in households with a different religious orientation than that of their natural parents. Catholic and Jewish charities objected to their lack of involvement in the decision-making process leading to commitment.

At the same time, the prison also appeared as a more acceptable legal alternative to physical forms of punishment. For juveniles as well as adults who graduated on to more serious levels of deviance, the Newgate prison, built in 1796 in the Greenwich Village section of Manhattan, appeared as a more viable alternative to corporal forms of punishment. As is the case today, officials in the early nineteenth century were concerned about the potential abuse of juveniles by older inmates in newly created prisons. The Newgate prison was there as a place for punishment, but officials hesitated to use it as a place for punishing and treating juveniles as offenders. Other institutions needed to be created.

Institutions for Delinquents. The House of Refuge appeared at a time when officials needed to do something about the increasing proportion of juvenile offenders for which the prison, fines, or corporal forms of punishment were no longer seen as viable dispositions. There was a level of juvenile offending that could not be satisfied with existing juvenile institutions in the form of almshouses, children's asylums, the state prison at Newgate, or the newly created state penitentiary at Auburn. Reformers wanted to establish an institution that would be more palatable to officials and to the public. An institution devoted to the business of educating abandoned and convicted juveniles could accomplish that task at a time when public school education was seen also as part of the solution to the problem of urban disorder.

The targeted population of juveniles was the urban poor, as partially reflected in the name of the society that submitted the plans for a House of Refuge. The New York Society for the Prevention of Pauperism was composed of distinguished citizens of New York and included the mayor of New York City, Cadwallader D. Colden. In the mayor's report to the Common [City] Council in 1818, he dramatized the need for a House of Refuge when he described the confinement of juveniles in the city's prison.

> There are now there eleven boys under eighteen: several are under fourteen. They are shut up in cells with other convicts. It must be obvious that under such circumstances it would be in vain to expect that their punishment will improve their morals: it can hardly fail to have a contrary effect. It is presumed that some system might be adopted which would separate the aged from the young, and at the same time afford the latter employment and instruction (Young People in the Courts of New York State, 1942: 19–20).

Colden also wrote that the sentencing of juveniles to the city's prison opened the "road to ruin." Juveniles in prisons were educated by "thieves, burglars, counterfeiters, gamblers, perjurers, drunkards, vagrants, and peace breakers (Pickett 1969: 38).

The solution that Colden and other members of the Society proposed was not just to create an alternative institutional setting for those eleven boys that were incarcerated in the city's prison. The House of Refuge was initially envisioned as a place for the treatment of juveniles who could not be fitted into the almshouse, orphan asylum, or city penitentiary. It was an institution restricted to juveniles under the age of 16 so that older juveniles were still subject to the city penitentiary, especially for serious offenses.

Initially, the House of Refuge selected juveniles charged with less serious offenses so that the majority of the juvenile offenders that Mayor Colden referred to would still be sent to the city penitentiary.

The House of Refuge sold to officials as a way of dealing with juvenile crime and delinquents because it provided officials with another legal option. It was an option that was made to fit the prevailing social and cultural climate for treating stubborn and impoverished juveniles. It was based on an eternal belief in universal forms of education. According to Stephen Schlossman (1977: 17)

> the great majority of Americans, judges included, believed that universal education was a social panacea; that children, especially children of the poor, had few legal rights; that impoverished parents lacked moral character and were incapable of providing healthy conditions for child rearing; and that anything which the government could do to instill their children with proper values was for the better.

The initial high hopes of educating delinquents through a reform school were expressed in the praise that the House of Refuge received from many distinguished visitors from around the world (Pickett 1969: 52). For example, the French penologists Alexis de Tocqueville and Gustave de Beaumont, during their tour of American penal institutions in 1831, wrote that

> if it be possible to obtain moral reformation for any human being, it seems that we ought to expect it for those youths, whose misfortune was caused less by crime, than by inexperience, and in whom all the generous passions of youth may be excited. With a criminal, whose corruption is inveterate, and deeply rooted, the feeling of honesty is not awakened, because the sentiment is extinct; with a youth, this feeling exists, though it has not yet been called into action (Beaumont & de Tocqueville 1964: 109).

But the ideology of doing good through a reformatory or refuge is just one part of the reason for its existence. It was not just the desire to treat the juvenile but the administrative convenience of the reformatory that quickly developed early on in systems of juvenile justice. When the House of Refuge opened its doors on New Year's Day in 1825, it received the kind of delinquents that it wanted in order to show success in meeting its reform mission. The orphan asylum was not abolished, nor did the penitentiary cease to house juveniles. Both institutions remained in the background or foreground depending on the nature of the juvenile's future and past offenses.

By keeping admission requirements for the House of Refuge loose, officials selected for placement juveniles who were charged with less serious offenses, such as vagrancy and other minor crimes (Pickett 1969: 58). Robert Mennel suggests that vagueness in the definition of delinquency could be attributed to the initial competition that refuge managers felt "with other institutions founded explicitly to care for deserted, orphaned, or abused children" (1973: 13). This is perhaps the first identifiable source of interagency conflict in New York's emerging systems of juvenile justice.

Identifying appropriate juveniles was only one source of conflict for the House of Refuge. Some delinquents resisted the moral and vocational treatment that the managers of the House of Refuge attempted to instill in its residential population. Their resistance to treatment might have reflected a certain degree of cultural and religious tension between the Protestant beliefs of the managers and the Catholic faith of the Irish, who made up the largest part of the city's offender population (Pickett 1969: 17). Consequently, the initial short periods of time envisioned for juveniles placed in the House of Refuge were gradually extended for more resistant delinquents (Rothman 1971: 224).

Soon the House of Refuge appeared more like an ordinary prison rather than a place for treatment. When it changed from being less of a religious institution to more of a state-supported facility, it was less able to be selective about the kinds of delinquents that it would accept. The state required it to accept a larger population of serious delinquents than might otherwise have been sent to the city prison. As a consequence, the institution's reform message was resisted by its residents, who lived in overcrowded conditions in which the benevolent hand of officials quickly turned into a slap or a whip. Few inmates were spared "the whip, the ball and chain, or solitary confinement" (Rothman 1971: 231).

The House of Refuge's Assistant Superintendent, DeVoe, described how physical punishment became a routine part of maintaining control:

> Corporal punishments are usually inflicted with the Cat or a rattan. The latter instrument is applied in a great variety of places – such as the palm and back of the hands, top and bottom of the feet – and lastly, but not rarely nor sparingly, to the posteriors over the clothes, and also on the naked skin. The rattan is in the hands of the Superintendent and Assistant Superintendent, and Teacher and Assistant Teacher. It is to be found in all parts of the premises, and liable to be used every where and at all times of day (Pickett 1969: 161).

Meanwhile, who got into the House of Refuge continued to be vaguely defined by the state through its parental power (*parens patriae*). Vagueness was seen as a convenient legal mechanism for incarcerating difficult juveniles who, officials felt, did not belong in the orphan asylum or the state penitentiary. Courts supported the ideals of the newly created reformatories despite evidence that they were prisons for juveniles. For instance, in an 1838 decision, the Pennsylvania State Supreme Court denied Mary Ann Crouse's father the right to free his daughter from placement in the House of Refuge. Despite public reports of reformatories acting as prisons, the court stated that it was sold on the idea of reformatories as places to treat delinquents:

> The object of the charity is reformation, by training its inmates to industry; by imbuing their minds with principles of morality and religion; by furnishing them with means to earn a living; and, above all, by separating them from the corrupting influence of improper associates. To this end, may not the natural parents, when unequal to the task of education, or unworthy of it, be superseded by the *parens patriae*, or common guardian of the community? . . . The infant has been snatched from a course which must have ended in confirmed depravity; and, not only is the restraint of her person lawful, but it would be an act of extreme cruelty to release her from it (Mennel 1973: 24).

What the court did not state is that they liked reformatories because they saw no other alternative to these institutional settings for dealing with segments of the delinquent population. As a consequence, reformatories were quickly replicated throughout the United States not because of any proven ability to correct delinquents but because they became organizationally convenient institutions for dealing with delinquents.

But soon more complaints surfaced not just from the parents of incarcerated juveniles, like Mary Ann Crouse's father, but also from prominent officials. The governor of New York, William H. Seward, complained about the fact that juveniles were sent to the House of Refuge for minor offenses. He faced irate but politically connected parents of House of Refuge juveniles who wanted their children released.[1] In an 1839 letter, he expressed his concerns and frustration in having to pardon juveniles placed in the House of Refuge.

> A few days since I granted a pardon to a juvenile convict in the House of Refuge because the judgment was illegal. . . . One of the grounds upon which it was held to be illegal is that persons convicted of petty larceny cannot lawfully be sent to the House of Refuge. I then anticipated that this decision would be followed by other applications for pardon upon the same ground. . . . A petition is now before me for the pardon of Frederick (Pickett 1969: 151).

The letter reflects more than just the inconvenience of having to pardon juveniles placed in the House of Refuge for minor offenses. It expresses confusion as to how these juveniles were committed to the House of Refuge in the first place. The emergence of loosely coupled systems of juvenile justice with the House of Refuge as a newly created subsystem accounts for Governor Seward's confusion in his letter when he stated that juveniles were committed illegally as "convicts."

> I am not clear that it is my duty to pardon . . . convicts in the House of Refuge even when their confinement there is not warranted by law. The responsibility rests with the courts and it may not be improper to leave to them the correction of their own errors (Pickett 1969: 151).

The governor's words illustrate bureaucratic conflict, confusion, and administrative inconvenience. Questions would be raised repeatedly in a slightly different form at each new stage of institutional reform. The public and their officials would ask: How did these particular juveniles receive this particular set of legal sanctions? And is there not a better alternative to the existing legal avenue for treating or punishing juveniles?

Despite the political headaches created by the prior generation of juvenile justice reforms, officials such as Governor Seward did not wish to get rid of the House of Refuge. In fact, he preferred it over the state prison as a place to incarcerate serious delinquents. In contrast, "managers were not always as pleased to receive prison youngsters as the Governor was to send them" (Pickett 1969: 153). At this point to some officials the House of Refuge was a reformatory in the business of helping children deserving of treatment. To other officials it looked liked an ordinary prison. Other institutional settings and subsystems would be needed to fill the apparent gap in the legal dispositions of officials.

An influential and prosperous Quaker businessman, William Pryor Letchworth, devoted himself to philanthropic projects after the Civil War that would further expand the institutional options of legal officials (Mennel 1973: 66–7). In 1876, as president of the New York State Charities Aid Association, Letchworth suggested that the state create separate institutions for four classes of children whom he classified as felons, minor offenders, truants, and the merely homeless. He was advised by Josephine Shaw Lowell: "Keep bad boys in the House of Refuge . . . homeless and truant boys should be sent to entirely other and distinct institutions, when it is necessary to send them to institutions at all" (Mennel 1973: 69). Soon some reformatories appeared stressing more comprehensive vocational education programs. In 1885 the Western House of Refuge was created in Rochester, New York, to house the less serious delinquents. But the larger juvenile justice subsystem that Letchworth would recommend came in the form of probation, which was already established in Massachusetts.

Around the same time significant criticism emerged elsewhere over the limited dispositional options of the criminal court through houses of refuge. This was exemplified by a widely cited Illinois State Supreme Court decision that reflected a significant shift in thinking about the ability of houses of refuge to reform delinquents. In a case that was similar to Crouse, the Illinois Court rejected the criminal court's quick use of reformatories without sufficient due process. In the 1870 case of Daniel O'Connell, the court asked "Why should minors be imprisoned for misfortune?" (Bernard 1992: 70). The court released O'Connell from his indeterminate placement and expressed official frustration with houses of refuge as the only legal avenue for treating delinquent juveniles.

Thus limited institutional and dispositional options for diverse sets of delinquents would stimulate the next major set of reforms in a period of decriminalization. But the assumption of earlier reformers needed to be modified to take into account newly emerging political and organizational concerns as well as interests in classifying and treating juveniles as delinquents.

The Juvenile Court. Juvenile courts emerged as a way of formally implementing Letchworth's earlier recommendation for probation. They institutionalized not only probation but other inclusionary techniques of treating juveniles in their home environments. As the reformers of an earlier era initially envisioned the House of Refuge as a first resort for younger, less serious delinquents, so did the post–Civil War progressives see probation as an effective first response to delinquents. Ryerson (1978) states that

> one of the distinctive features of the juvenile court movement was its primary, if not exclusive, commitment to probation as the most desirable disposition for child offenders. Where other generations had channeled their dissatisfaction with correctional institutions into redesigning such institutions, the progressives concentrated on developing an alternative which could occupy the foreground of juvenile corrections while the last resort (or threat) of institutionalization remained in the background (41).

Organized interest in expanding the range of available dispositions was based on a progressive belief in the ability of governmental institutions to "moralize the lives" of delinquents (Sutton 1988: 130). The reformers known as *progressives* believed that social order could be restored by producing governmental institutions that were more specialized and rational in their administration of services. In New York City, a belief in more governmental institutions evolved from the social disorder that emerged in the wake of another sharp increases in its urban population. In less than 40 years, Manhattan's population grew from 942,292 in 1870 to 2,331,542 in 1910 (Andriot 1993). The motivation for reform was also stimulated by social change in a post–Civil War period marked by rapid industrial growth. The sources of deviance for juveniles appeared more situational to a new wave of reformers; deviance was seen as less a product of innate criminality and more a consequence of impoverished families and communities.

Separate juvenile courts appeared in the large urban centers of New York State to extend the treatment options of officials in confronting delinquency. Juvenile courts did not appear suddenly as a dramatic or abrupt legal reform without precedent. An 1892 New York statute allowed judges to hear juvenile cases "separately from other criminal cases" (Hart 1910: 70). That same year a "children's court" appeared in Manhattan as a separate part of criminal court. Children's courts were later created in other parts of New York City, and then in 1909 in Buffalo. The state legislature waited until 1922 before establishing specialized juvenile courts throughout New York's less populated areas.

In some respects, relocating juveniles under the age of 16 from New York's general criminal courts to separate children's or juvenile courts did not produce a dramatic breakthrough with past legal procedures. There was a semblance of concern with due process and the right to appeal as expressed in the following section of an act that established Buffalo's Children's Court:

> a judgment upon conviction, rendered by a judge sitting as a court of special sessions, children's court, or magistrate, may be [duly] reviewed by the county court. If a new trial be ordered, it shall be had before a city court judge sitting as a magistrate, a court of special sessions, or a children's court as the case may be, . . . but a judge other than the one sitting for the original trial (Hart 1910: 72–3).

Meanwhile a system of juvenile probation in New York was formally established in 1901. Probation increased the dispositional options of officials and similarly fit the juvenile court's mandate to become a "superparent" in pursuing the "best interests" of juveniles. In the following rhetorical questions, Judge Jullian Mack, who developed Chicago's first juvenile court, emphasized the superparent role of juvenile courts to coordinate and direct the treatment of troubled juveniles.

> Why is it not just and proper to treat these juvenile offenders, as we deal with the neglected children, as a wise and merciful father handles his own child

whose errors are not discovered by the authorities? Why is it not the duty of the state, instead of asking merely whether a boy or a girl has committed a specific offense, to find out what he is physically, mentally, morally, and then if he learns that he is treading the path that leads to criminality, to take him in charge, not so much as to punish as to reform, not to degrade but to uplift, not to crush but to develop, not to make him a criminal but a worthy citizen (Mack 1909: 107).

The stated objective of the juvenile court to act as a parent in treating juveniles merged with the state's interest in predicting and preventing "adult criminality" based on the juvenile's social and mental background. The juvenile court judge in the role of a superparent could then recommend the kinds of services that would be needed to uplift, develop, and to make the delinquent into "a worthy citizen."

It is important also to repeat that the juvenile court did not at this point produce a harsher set of penalties, just a wider array of dispositions and treatment-oriented programs. Although the population labeled *delinquent* increased (Ferdinand 1989), the proportion of juveniles incarcerated in reformatories declined (Hagan & Leon 1977). This could occur because juveniles were more often arrested as delinquents because of more convenient legal avenues for officially defining their deviant behaviors. Police officers were more likely to arrest juveniles, and judges were more likely to adjudicate juveniles as delinquents because of probation.

Mack wrote that "taking a child away from its parents and sending it even to an industrial school is, as far as possible, to be avoided" (Mack 1909: 116). Similarly, Judge Ben Lindsey, who is credited with Denver's first juvenile court, wrote that

> when the juvenile court is considered in its larger aspect, I believe it will be admitted that it is made up of certain principles now recognized in the movement for human betterment. I would say that one of the most important is the principle of probation (Lindsey 1925: 275).

But in the background the house of refuge, reformatory, or training school remained – not as a first resort but as a last resort if the juvenile failed probation or other more inclusionary forms of control. The juvenile court breathed new life into the doctrine of *parens patriae* by legitimating a formal system of probation as another legal avenue in the disposition of delinquents.

The vision of a tightly coordinated juvenile court to treat juveniles initially surfaced in some jurisdictions. For example, in Denver's juvenile court, Judge Ben Lindsey appeared to take a proactive interest in the juveniles who came before him by trying to understand the social context in which they committed their delinquent behaviors. Lindsey is reported to have scolded police officers in their attempt to get other delinquents to testify against each other, because it violated their cultural norms. He allegedly developed the kind of trust and rapport among youth that allowed Lindsey to place delinquents in a reformatory without official escort. He also is described as having regularly visited the juveniles he placed in the local reformatory, and as an early proponent of "family court" with integrated jurisdiction over divorce as well as delinquency (Levine & Levine 1992).

Although a part of the Ben Lindsey story may be more myth than reality, it fit an idealized vision of what a wise and kind juvenile court judge could do in the role of a "superparent." While the juvenile court could be duplicated, Lindsey's unique style could not be reproduced easily. In the process of institutionalizing the juvenile court, positions are filled often "by those who lack the appropriate human qualities, or the positions themselves are so bureaucratized that initiative and flexibility are lost" (Levine & Levine 1992: 140).

Judge Mack was aware of Judge Lindsey's work and argued that it could not be replicated:

> Judge Lindsey cannot be imitated, because his work depends upon his personality. . . . His real greatness is his work as his own chief probation officer. Now, if a judge happens to be fitted by nature to be the chief probation officer in his community, and if his community is of a size that he can combine the work of the judge and chief probation officer, that community is fortunate. But the lines of our work should not be laid out on the basis that we are going to find that unique personality in any of our communities (Mennel 1973: 138–9).

So, there were too few "personalities" to fill the role of a superparent. And besides, in the more densely populated city of Chicago, juvenile court judges did not have the time to be both probation officers and judges.

Other progressive reformers also recognized that the "cult of judicial personality" could not be replicated in emerging systems of juvenile justice (Rothman 1980: 242). They believed in a juvenile justice system in which there would be a staff of probation officers, psychologists, and other experts to guide the judges' decision making. A complex division of labor was envisioned for juvenile justice systems located in large urban areas where the juvenile court judge would be just one part of the decision-making process. In smaller towns and rural areas, there was less of a need for the work of a professional staff of probation officers and the emergence of complex systems of juvenile justice (Rothman 1980: 243).

Systems of juvenile justice in large urban centers such as New York City also sold because they were administratively convenient. The juvenile court's stated purpose of pursuing the best interests of the juvenile merged with the state's interest in maintaining an efficient legal procedure for dealing with delinquents. Efficiency was often defined in terms of administrative costs. Probation was more convenient than incarceration because it cost less. It was not only the cheaper disposition, but it allowed officials to identify a larger population of delinquents that might otherwise be ignored. For example, Almy (1902) reported that in the first year of Buffalo's newly created juvenile court, the number of juveniles incarcerated was reduced while the number of juveniles arrested increased.

By 1929 juvenile justice in New York appeared to be working so well that at the Seventh Annual Conference of the Judges of Children's Courts, judges proposed to expand its jurisdiction to the most serious delinquents. The judges objected to the exclusion of juveniles charged with capital offenses from the juvenile court:

> It is the opinion of this Committee that the Chautauqua Court Act contains, in this regard, the most progressive provision to be found in any of the three sets of laws which we are here comparing. We believe that the children's court should have jurisdiction over any and all delinquent acts committed by a child, that regardless of the type of offense charged, he is entitled to the full care and protection of the state (Proceedings of the Seventh Annual Conference of . . . New York Judges 1929: 68).

In 1948 the New York legislature finally responded to increased pressure to decriminalize all juvenile offenses, including the capital offense of murder. The situation was the reverse of the more recent embarrassment that juvenile justice officials faced in having to prosecute Willie Bosket as a delinquent. Instead, criminal justice officials complained that they were forced at times to deal with 14-year-old juveniles in criminal court. A district attorney's comments reported in the *New York Times* reveal the extent to which juvenile courts were seen as the only appropriate legal setting for juveniles.

> The job of getting the Legislature to move in that direction [elimination of the capital offense exception] should now be undertaken and assumed, in part at any rate, by those who have been horrified at the sight of the people of the state of New York proceeding against a fourteen-year-old boy in a criminal court (*New York Times*, May 8, 1946, as originally cited in Tappan 1949: 174).

Note that the above comment is not that of a probation officer or a juvenile court judge but that of a district attorney who might 30 years later make the opposite call for returning juveniles to criminal courts, especially those charged with murder.

In New York, decriminalization peaked when in 1948 the age of criminal responsibility for homicide was increased to 15. In 1956 it was increased to 16, so that no juvenile below the age of 16 could be convicted in criminal court for any type of offense. This might be referred to as the golden age of decriminalization in New York, when legal decisions by the state's highest court, the Court of Appeals, confirmed the juvenile court's operating principles of informality, secrecy, and state intervention in the name of *parens patriae*.

There was little in the way of legislative activity during the post–World War II period. The public and its officials were concerned about juvenile delinquency and crime, but attention was directed toward factors other than systems of juvenile justice. There were complaints about the media and the influence of movies and violent comics on the moral behavior of juveniles (Gilbert 1986). It seemed that the juvenile justice system was well insulated and resistant to political complaints about its inability to prevent and to control juvenile crime.

Criminalization

In the early 1960s, criticism of juvenile justice by academics and practitioners produced an impetus for juvenile justice reform. Essentially, they complained that the juvenile courts' denial of basic constitutional rights to juveniles subjected them to treatments that were not necessarily in their best interests. David Matza (1964) explicitly linked the determinants of delinquency to the juvenile court's informal procedures; the juvenile court "created a setting which is conducive to the sensing of rampant inconsistency" (115). Juveniles who were brought to the court for a minor offense might become serious offenders because of the arbitrary manner in which they were adjudicated delinquent.

The legal injustice that juveniles might experience in a nonadversarial juvenile court was not only the concern of sociologists but also that of child-saving organizations. In 1960 New York's Citizens' Committee for Children commissioned Charles Schinitsky to investigate the lack of legal representation for juveniles in juvenile court (Prescott 1981: 61). Schinitsky wrote that

> an essential function of the court is to establish an atmosphere of fairness in
> its dealings with those persons appearing before it. Vital to the creation of

this atmosphere is that an accused parent or child, without funds, know they may have counsel to guide them through their difficulty (Schinitsky 1962: 24).

But there was also a degree of administrative convenience in the conclusion of Schinitsky's argument for the legal representation of juveniles.

An attorney or group of attorneys assigned to the Court on a permanent basis to represent indigent respondents would complement the Court. They would protect respondents' legal rights. They could work with probation officers in the disposition of cases and their sphere of activity would extend beyond the courtroom to religious organizations, the school authorities, settlement houses, temporary shelters and institutions (Schinitsky 1962: 25).

But legal representation for juveniles is just one part of criminalization. The other part is the narrowing of the population of juveniles subject to treatment in juvenile courts. Diversion in a sense "decriminalized" status offenders so that they were no longer officially considered part of the delinquent population.

The 1962 Family Court Act. New York's Family Court Act contained the elements of criminalization. First, it required legal representation for all juveniles in delinquency proceedings. Second, it created a separate legal track for status-offending juveniles who would be referred to as Persons in Need of Supervision (PINS). However, there are aspects of the act that suggest a tighter fit with the traditional goals of juvenile justice. As implied by the title of the act, New York's juvenile court became just one part of an integrative system for dealing with a wide range of legal issues that affected the status of families.

The due process requirements of the Family Court Act at first were viewed as an effective way to provide legal representation for juveniles. The act stressed that evidence should be legally "competent" in contrast to the hearsay, rumor, and unsubstantiated reports that characterized traditional juvenile court proceedings (Sobie 1987: 163). The recommendation of "representation by counsel" reinforced the due process component of the legislation. However, according to Sobie, the act's stated objective of producing a unified family court system was never realized in its final legislative form. Although the Act merged the children's court and the domestic relations court producing a single family court, other courts still retained concurrent jurisdiction over some domestic matters (Sobie 1987: 161).

The length of placements that the juvenile court could administer was also revised to reflect its dual concern with treatment and due process. The court was restricted to an initial maximum placement of 18 months. At the end of this initial period, the court could extend the period of placement by an additional year; however, further placement could be determined only after a formal hearing in juvenile court. This hearing would consider a report by the institution on recommendations for further treatment.

Although the Family Court Act restricted initial placements for the vast majority of delinquency offenses, it also provided a unique set of penalties for 15-year-old juveniles convicted of violent felonies. Fifteen-year-olds adjudicated as "delinquents" for serious violent offenses could be committed to a special unit within a state medium security facility for a period of up to 3 years. This unit was designed to house 16- to 21-year-old adult offenders and was operated by the state's adult Department of Corrections (Singer & Ewing 1986: 467).

Despite the liberal reforms of the Family Court Act, by the 1970s New York's training schools had come to be viewed in terms used decades earlier to describe their forerunners, the reformatories. As Martin Guggenheim (1976) put it, training schools were institutions

> structured according to the same basic model as for adult felons – large, rurally located, undifferentiated structures which provide no help for the youngsters . . . backward and unqualified remedial education . . . no meaningful vocational training and no treatment services for individual children on any significant scale (554).

The sorry state of the training schools was blamed on the Department of Social Services. Governor Nelson Rockefeller proposed that DFY be given control of all state facilities for juveniles. Acceptance of this plan contributed to a marked increase in community-based programs for juveniles as well as the closing of many training schools (McGarrell 1988).

Administrative-Judicial Decisions. In 1972, New York Federal District Court Judge Gurfein ruled that a juvenile's due process rights were violated by his 3-year placement in a facility for youthful offenders. In *Murray* v. *Owens*, Judge Gurfein reversed the placement, which followed a juvenile's conviction for a violent offense, because he was not afforded a criminal trial. Although the U.S. Supreme Court did not require a jury trial for juveniles, Judge Gurfein viewed the placement of a juvenile in an institution for youthful offenders as not in the interest of justice:

> I hold, accordingly, that the petitioner was denied due process of law under the Fourteenth Amendment to the United States Constitution when he was sentenced to a term of three years and committed to Elmira Reception Center without benefit of the right to a trial by jury.

New York's juvenile courts did not have the mechanism for providing juveniles with jury trials. As a consequence, juvenile justice officials felt again restricted in their dispositional options particularly for serious delinquents.

Two years later, in 1974, the New York State Supreme Court's Appellate Division sliced away further at the juvenile court's authority to place repeatedly juveniles for 18-month periods until age 21. The court ruled that any commitment by the court was not mandatory but advisory (In re *Terrance*, New York Supplement, Vol. 357: 97). The appellate court ruled that prior delinquency legislation gives the Division for Youth (DFY) the authority to decide when a juvenile should be released, not the juvenile court judge.

So once more we have the basis for bureaucratic conflict and crisis. New York's juvenile court judges could not dictate lengthy periods of placement for violent juveniles. Judges were confined to mandating indeterminate placements of 18 months. The appellate court viewed the treatment objectives of juvenile justice as taking legal precedence over the last-resort needs of juvenile court judges. And as a consequence, the decision making of DFY was at odds with that of some juvenile court judges.

By the mid-1970s a rapid rise in juvenile crime produced an increasing backlog of cases. The number of delinquency cases in New York City's juvenile court grew steadily from 12,593 in 1975 to 18,291 in 1978 (Office of Court Administration, Annual Reports). Based on observations of New York's juvenile courts, Michael Fabricant (1983) concluded that:

> The delays prior to and between hearings exacted a particular cost upon petitioners. Their efforts to have specific grievances redressed were frustrated by an apparently overworked bureaucracy. The requirement that they appear before the court repeatedly dictated that the complainant miss work days. The emotional and financial cost of sustaining a case frequently persuaded the complainant either informally or formally to discontinue his involvement with the court (129).

Fabricant also observed that legal counsel for juveniles produced new pockets of power.

> The public defenders' effectiveness at having cases dismissed or withdrawn suggests that they are the newest and most dominant gatekeepers to the juvenile-justice network (133).

Another subsystem of juvenile justice thus emerged in New York in the form of legal aid. Although its stated intent was again in the best interests of juveniles, the introduction of legal representation served other interests that in some cases loosened rather than tightened the administration of juvenile justice.[2]

National Trends. Traditional systems of juvenile justice appeared less acceptable to national as well as state policy makers. In 1967 the President's Crime Commission repeated the opinion that the informal procedures of juvenile court may do more harm than good when it stated that

> [T]here is increasing evidence that the informal procedures [of juvenile courts], contrary to the original expectations, may themselves constitute a further obstacle to effective treatment of the delinquent to the extent that they engender in the child a "sense of injustice" provoked by seemingly all-powerful and changeless exercise of authority by judges and probation officers. (U.S. President's Commission on Law Enforcement and Administration of Justice 1967: 85).

The "increasing evidence" that the Commission drew on is confined mainly to a study by Wheeler and Cottrell (1966) in which they argued that incarcerated delinquents sensed injustice because they expected treatment and received punishment. Based on nonrandom interviews with incarcerated delinquents, Wheeler and Cottrell (1966) concluded that

> unless appropriate due process of law is followed, even the juvenile who has violated the law may not feel that he is being fairly treated and may therefore resist the rehabilitative efforts of court personnel (33).

The U.S. Supreme Court further related the view that the informal procedures of the juvenile court perpetuated a sense of injustice among delinquents. In its first decision in what would become a series of due process–oriented rulings for juvenile court, the Supreme Court dealt with a case of judicial waiver involving a capital offense (re *Kent*, 1967). By mandating a more formal waiver hearing for juveniles, the Supreme Court made its first attempt at criminalization:

> There is evidence, in fact, that there may be grounds for concern that the child receives the worst of both worlds; that he gets neither the protection accorded to adults nor the solicitous care and regenerative treatment postulated for children (*Kent v. United States*, 383 U.S. 541, 555 [1966]).

But the Supreme Court's condemnation of a traditional juvenile court stopped short of fully advocating adult due process rights for juveniles. Later the Supreme Court rejected the right to a trial by jury and protection against preventive detention, suggesting that the court wanted the "best" of both worlds in the form of justice and treatment for juveniles (Horowitz 1977: 171–219). Through the assistance of counsel and other legal reforms, the contemporary juvenile court appeared in a better position to satisfy more than one set of emerging bureaucratic interests.

Just as the move to criminalize delinquency and juvenile justice grew out of legal reforms that decriminalized, so too did recriminalization develop from a contemporary juvenile court that diverted status offenders and formalized the legal processing of delinquents. Cressey and McDermott (1973), in one of the first monographs to review the implications of diversion programs, predicted the future shape of juvenile justice. They hypothesized the emergence of more distinct categories of delinquents and legal avenues for identifying their deviant behavior when they stated over 20 years ago that

> there will be a polarization of attitudes and programs: Lawbreaking juveniles are likely to be processed along the lines of the adult model and hence will receive more due process and less humanistic consideration – after all, are they not merely small criminals? Juveniles who have been called "predelinquents," because they can't get along at home or in school, will be diverted (61).

Criminalization? Yes, but perhaps recriminalization also in that the part of the system that treated juveniles like small criminals would not only involve juvenile courts but also would require legislators and other officials to seek criminal courts as ways of dealing with those "small criminals." Criminalization worked to ignore predelinquents, to concentrate on serious delinquents, and in the process to create the kinds of juvenile offenders that soon would find themselves in criminal courts.

Conclusion

Contemporary systems of juvenile justice developed through a history of earlier reforms – reforms that produced the various subsystems of treating juveniles in a variety of institutional settings ranging from reformatories to probation offices. Each newly created legal avenue was justified by a belief in its ability to do good or to provide justice. But the less often stated reason is that reformatories, juvenile courts, probation, due process, diversion, and legal representation developed as convenient legal avenues for doing something about the problem of juvenile crime and justice. They emerged because of political and official beliefs that the system was not operating as well as it could. In the end, each generation of reformers accepted the subsystems of prior generations, not because of their proven ability to reduce juvenile crime but because of their administrative convenience. They helped to loosen, not tighten, the legal boundaries of juvenile justice.

But the story of juvenile violence and juvenile justice reform is specific to densely populated urban areas, such as New York City, where a complex bureaucratic setting produced several layers of legal decision making. The programmed image of a reform became increasingly difficult to implement in urban systems of juvenile justice. So the history of juvenile justice reforms is not an even one; it moved more in one direction than in another depending on the times and places of reforms. The story of juvenile justice as presented is basically one of the problems of urban crime and of legal and social control in cities. If the focus were on the history of juvenile justice in small towns, then a different interpretation would be necessary. But recall that the subway murders did take place in New York City.

Recriminalization on the Move
and Its Legal Rules

THE MOTIVATION TO RECRIMINALIZE DELINQUENCY was not merely a consequence of the ideological bent of several conservative critics of juvenile justice. U.S. Supreme Court judges and distinguished scholars on the President's Crime Commission contributed their share of criticism. By the mid-1970S, public and official complaints about juvenile justice once more threatened the system's political and moral legitimacy. In New York, the stage was set for recriminalization in the shape of its JO law.

The immediate sources of crisis and the legal response at this point will be examined more closely; they are directly related to the manner in which New York was able to create and implement its unique form of recriminalization. I will examine the political and organizational steps leading to the JO law in the way of media stories, an earlier reform, legislative committee reports, and the debates that preceded the JO law.

By media stories I do not mean that they were unrelated to reality. Rather, they presented a version of reality that fit a recurring popular media theme of violent juvenile crime and juvenile justice. They stressed that a segment of delinquents was more violent and more chronic than the delinquents of earlier generations. At the same time, they argued that the juvenile justice system failed to keep up with the more violent behavior of this new generation of violent delinquents. In highlighting the problem of juvenile crime and justice, media stories set the stage for commission reports recommending legal reform.

The media stories that I describe are drawn from the *New York Times*. A more dramatic presentation of these themes could have been presented through less sophisticated popular newspapers. But it is the paper that is probably most frequently read by policy makers and legislators in New York. An increase in the frequency of articles on juvenile justice occurred during the 1976 and 1978 legal reforms. According to Edmund McGarrell (1988), the number of articles critical of juvenile justice increased "from levels of forty to seventy per year during the 1968 to 1971 period, to 107 to 155 during the 1972 to 1978 period" (125).

The 1976 Juvenile Justice Reform Act

The 1976 Juvenile Justice Reform Act (JJRA) produced several of recriminalization's legal rules and was preceded by stories of juvenile justice. A series of articles and editorials appeared in the *New York Times* decrying the violent criminal acts of young people and questioning the efficacy of the juvenile justice system's treatment approach (see, e.g., Tomasson 1976; Treaster 1976). For example, in a *Sunday New York Times Magazine* article titled "They Think I Can Kill Because I'm Fourteen," Ted Morgan described how the current generation of violent delinquents acted as cold-blooded, calculating offenders. He quoted a variety of "experts" who stated that some juveniles

> would kill someone who put them down, and they would feel absolutely no remorse . . . [A]ll over the country they are getting these kids who reflect a social situation in which only power works, where the only transaction is "either you make me or I'll make you" (Morgan 1975: 9).

To try to understand and treat these kids was of little use, according to Morgan, because they lived and died through the use of violence. It was difficult to feel sorry for delinquents who showed no remorse for their actions. They were no longer presented as general and specific victims of poverty or of disorganized families and communities. Moreover, the juvenile courts appeared to make things worse by doing nothing to punish and deter their repeated violent behavior.

Morgan further relied on the opinion of law enforcement officials to tell readers how seriously delinquents viewed New York's juvenile justice system. For example:

> A 14-year-old knows the worst that can happen is 18 months in a training school. . . . He thinks, I can kill a man because I'm 14. So you have murderers and rapists returned to the street in no time. If he's older, his parents come in and lie about his age, and say they can't find his birth certificate. They should knock down the whole age barrier, depending on the type of crime and the past history of the kid involved (1975: 11).

Morgan emphasized not only the availability of lenient penalties but also the inability of juvenile justice agencies and officials to provide meaningful treatment and effective control. He quoted other officials who described the multitude of bureaucratic objectives that prevent the system from monitoring closely the cases of juveniles entering New York's juvenile court.

> The Department of Probation takes the position that once a child is placed, its job is over; so judges have no way of monitoring premature releases or inappropriate placements. The judges have increasing judicial responsibility but cannot provide the required services or impose fixed penalties. The legal-aid lawyers, regardless of a child's need for treatment, see themselves as guardians of his legal rights. The Division for Youth is forced to release juvenile offenders to keep up with intake (Morgan 1975: 31).

In the meantime, Governor Hugh Carey responded to public and official concerns by establishing the Cahill Commission in 1975 to recommend better ways to control violent juvenile delinquents. The Cahill Commission consisted of a broad spectrum of experts and the governor's commissioner of Division for Youth (DFY), Peter Edelman, who took a leadership role in the commission's deliberations. Based on extensive interviews with policy makers, McGarrell (1988: 104–5) reported several aspects of the commission's deliberations. First, some members of the commission wanted to create waiver legislation, but Edelman argued against it. He convinced other commission members that the juvenile justice system was the most appropriate legal setting for differentiating serious violent delinquents. In the end a compromise was created between those commission members who wanted to waive violent juveniles to criminal court and those who wanted to retain them in juvenile court. The commission members agreed to recommend that a separate, designated felony track be established for juveniles charged with serious violent offenses. Youths falling into the designated felony category would be subject to a wider range of minimum and maximum dispositions in New York's juvenile court.

Thus the Cahill Commission attempted to balance the treatment- and punishment-oriented interests of juvenile justice by broadening the dispositional options of juvenile justice officials. By proposing the creation of separate legal labels and tracks within juvenile court, the Cahill Commission responded to an emerging need to see violent delinquents subject to a more punishment-oriented juvenile justice system.

Three aspects of the JJRA paved the way toward recriminalization in the form of the JO law. First, the Act allowed the publicly elected DA to enter the juvenile court. Previously, only an appointed county attorney could represent the state in juvenile court, which is generally the case in civil proceedings. Introducing a public prosecutor in juvenile court for designated felony cases shifted the court's stated function and purpose.

Second, the stated goal of operating in the best interests of the juvenile was modified to take into account a traditional criminal justice objective. The JJRA explicitly restated the purpose of juvenile justice in juvenile court so that

> In *any* juvenile delinquency proceeding under this article, the court shall consider the needs and best interests of the respondent *as well as the need for protection of the community* (emphasis added) (JJRA 1976).

Although the need to protect the community may have always been an implicit part of juvenile justice, the JJRA made it an explicit reason for adjudicating delinquents.

Finally, the JJRA increased the severity of possible DFY placements. It did so by increasing the possible minimum and maximum periods of placement. Depending on the type of designated felony offense, juveniles would face a minimum of 12 to 18 months in a DFY secure institution and a maximum of 3 to 5 years in DFY facilities. The establishment of minimum periods of placement in secure institutions would limit the traditional discretion that DFY officials had had in deciding the appropriate date of release. Instead, time would be served based on a determinate period of placement, as is the case for adult offenders in the criminal justice system.

Administrative reforms accompanied passage of the JJRA. In proposing the legislation, Governor Carey announced that DFY was now required to restrict and to regulate more stringently the release and home visits of juveniles placed in its institutions (Carey 1976: 16). The media reports continued, however, and political mileage was to be gained by continuing to broadcast the problems of juvenile crime and justice.

Between the JJRA and the JO Laws

Despite the JJRA, the problems of juvenile crime and justice reappeared in media stories and legislative reports. Those who advocated passage of the JJRA in lieu of waiver legislation hoped for a decline in public criticism of New York's juvenile courts. After all, the JJRA created a separate track for violent delinquents that could impose more severe dispositions than would be the case for ordinary delinquents. Reporters, commentators, and politicians still continued to broadcast the media stories and to produce the committee reports that questioned the ability of juvenile justice officials to control and to prevent serious juvenile violence.

Step One: More Media Stories. Soon after passage of the JJRA, a series of front-page *New York Times* articles by Anthony Treaster stressed once more the problem of violent juvenile crime and juvenile justice. The articles discussed not only the problem of violent juvenile crime but also its relationship to victimization of the elderly. Although juvenile arrest records are technically confidential, Treaster obtained the arrest and conviction histories of several youths arrested for victimizing senior citizens. He listed the arrest history of one such youth described as "typical" (Treaster 1976: 42):

Offense	Disposition
Burglary	Sent home with warning
Robbery (took bicycle at knife point)	Sent home with warning
Robbery (mugging)	Dismissed (no complainant)
Robbery (mugging)	Dismissed (no complainant)
Robbery (mugging)	Dismissed (no complainant)
Robbery (mugging)	Dismissed (no complainant)
Burglary	Pending, youth failed to appear in court
Robbery (mugging)	Pending; youth failed to appear in court
Robbery (mugging), assault, burglary	Found guilty
Burglary	Awaiting sentence

Clearly something was wrong with a system that produced so many dismissals and nonappearances. Despite the harsher penalties of the JJRA, Treaster's data revealed to the public and its officials that New York's juvenile courts still failed to respond to the serious violent delinquent. According to one police officer quoted by Treaster, New York's juvenile justice system still failed to deter juveniles adjudicated as delinquents for the most violent offenses.

> The whole thing's a joke to these kids . . . . As soon as you grab them they say, "I'm only 14" or 15 or whatever, and "there's nothing you can do to me" (Treaster 1976: 46).

Treaster also told how probation lacked the resources for controlling and treating delinquents.

> With sometimes as many as 100 cases each, probation officers have almost completely stopped making home visits and usually have youths come into their offices. Sometimes the only contact is by telephone, and if a youth drifts off altogether no one goes looking for him (Treaster 1976: 46).

The above observation is not unique to juvenile justice in 1976. Juvenile justice systems never seemed to have all the resources they needed to treat delinquents. But the prestigious *New York Times* caused officials to think twice about effectiveness and about the juvenile justice system's capability for controlling chronic delinquents. Moreover, when defenders of juvenile justice, such as DFY commissioner Peter Edelman were quoted, it was not in a light that could satisfy public and official concerns. For example, Edelman, in responding to the violent offenses of a released DFY youth, stated that

> [it is] not always possible to predict correctly that a release will work out satisfactorily – you cannot be 100 percent right (Silver, *New York Times*, July 22, 1978).

Of course, the risks of treatment were well known to those in the helping professions. But highlighting those risks to the public played into the hands of politicians who advocated even harsher penalties than those contained in the JJRA.

Step Two: More Committee Reports. State legislative committee reports (Marino 1977a, 1977b, 1977c) that preceded the JO law focused not just on juvenile crime but on some of the vulnerable targets of violent juvenile delinquents, such as the elderly. Linking the problem of juvenile justice to the legal system's inability to prevent delinquents from attacking senior citizens served political purposes in making the case for juvenile justice reform. The problem of juvenile crime and justice became even more serious when the public's attention was drawn to the elderly as victims of juvenile violence. Chronic violent delinquents needed to be even more harshly punished because they were now choosing more and more vulnerable victims.

On December 7, 1976, in a televised hearing, the Select Senate Committee on Crime heard opening testimony from Detectives Keegan and Gaffney[1] of the Bronx Senior Citizen Robbery Unit (Marino 1977c). They described the manner in which juveniles attacked senior citizens:

These juveniles would work in a wolf pack – three, four, five at a time. It was not uncommon to have a ten-year-old placed in a bank to watch people cashing checks. When he found a likely victim he would go outside and signal the older kids. They in turn would follow this woman until she went to her apartment, with the hopes of pushing her in (2).

The detectives later emphasized the elderly's vulnerability to crime and how delinquents saw senior citizens as good targets for victimization. They further testified that more lenient treatment of juveniles encouraged delinquents to repeat their victimization of senior citizens.

The juveniles tell us it [robbery] is a very "good" crime to commit. The elderly victim will have difficulty identifying [an offender], particularly a juvenile. We are prohibited by law from photographing a juvenile offender. If an arrest is made, they tell the people during the crime, "We know where you live, we will come back" (4).

Difficulty in identifying juveniles who rob? The ability to attack senior citizens without fear because they cannot be photographed? These are questions that focused on New York's inability to identify and apprehend violent delinquents.

The elderly were naturally afraid of retaliation, but juvenile court appeared to do little to calm that fear, according to the following testimony:

The number one fear of an elderly person is retaliation. They [juvenile delinquents] have that going for them. They say it is a very good crime. "If arrested I will not be convicted. If convicted, I will be in Family Court," and it's a joke and they will be out on the street. Whether they are found innocent or guilty, they are going to be out on the street; so why are we wasting our time even going through this procedure (4)?

The image presented so far at the committee hearing was that of a legal process in which the victims were more afraid of the court than the offenders.

[W]hen I tried to get him [the victim] to court, I had a real problem. He was frightened. He couldn't understand why, when they were going to let him [the offender] out. I had a lot of talking to do to finally get him there. When I finally got him there it was adjourned five different times. I had to take this man out of his house and out of his surroundings, had to take him over to Family Court, sit him in a corridor where there are hundreds of people there, relatives of the defendant, and he has to be confronted by these people in this hallway. And so it's quite . . . quite difficult for him (3).

The testimony then shifted to how law enforcement officials viewed the treatment of the "hard-core" delinquent. In this exchange with the testifying detective, the chairman of the Committee, Senator Ralph Marino, revealed his view toward the treatment orientation of the juvenile justice system.

DETECTIVE: Well, we found . . . from conversations with certain people within the Family Court System, that when they come across a hard-core juvenile and they place him in an institution, if that hard-core individual becomes a problem up in that institution, he is practically immediately released as . . . and found to be . . .

SENATOR MARINO: Rehabilitated?

DETECTIVE: . . . rehabilitated.

SENATOR MARINO: Which is a joke.

DETECTIVE: I have had people tell me that it's almost impossible to place a juvenile who is arrested for arson because nobody wants him and they are afraid the facilities will be burned down. I don't know if that's a fact, but this is what they told me (5).

In the next exchange, Senator Marino solicited a response that stressed New York's juvenile justice system's failure to produce placements or sentences that could prevent chronic delinquents from repeating their offenses.

SENATOR MARINO: Has it been your experience that when you were able to make an arrest, you were arresting basically young people?

DETECTIVE: Yes. And not only that, we were arresting the same person over and over again. We would take him to Family Court, we would insist upon going to a judge. After court delays, maybe six or seven appearances, we got before the judge and we had a trial and the person was found guilty or, in Family Court, a finding of fact, we would leave the court convinced that the juvenile offender has now been prosecuted, found guilty, and will be dealt with by the Court . . . [But] it was not uncommon to run into that same juvenile on the street a week later, and we had to ask him what happened in court. We have had cases where he was found guilty and sent home pending placement with the New York State Division for Youth. There was no room for him. So now he's out on the street. They tell him to come back in one month. What they have actually done is given that juvenile immunity. Any crime he commits in that month he will get no more punishment than he would originally (2).

Other testimony emphasized the need to place chronic juvenile offenders in a more punishment-oriented system. Law enforcement officials further complained that they could neither identify nor control a small segment of the delinquent population believed responsible for a large proportion of violent crime.

> I would say that there are a small group of juveniles that are doing this . . . but if you get 50 or 60 kids in a borough and they are completely recycled out into the street for violent crimes like robbery or rape and murder, well, those 60 kids can put a crime pattern out there that would be 1,800 to 2,000 cases of robbery (4).

Others asserted that the juvenile court also was incapable of identifying the chronic delinquent in New York City.

> Record-keeping by the Family Court is incredible. If you are arrested 20 times as a juvenile in the Bronx and for some reason are arrested in Queens, as far as Queens is concerned that's your first arrest as a juvenile. And it is uncommon for these courts to get together (7).

Finally, the following testimony, which recommended adult processing for juveniles as young as 14 in felony cases, anticipated the future shape of the JO law.

> I am heartily in favor of that [fingerprint bill]. In my personal opinion, for a long time these juveniles should be fingerprinted, and I am heartily in favor of dropping the age limit down to 14 or 15 for these felony cases. I believe, in this day and age, the children, or juveniles, are much more sophisticated than they were years ago when this line of demarcation was established. They are exposed to the media, violence; they are much more, I would say, smarter and streetwise than the kids were years and years ago. They are familiar with weapons, which the kids didn't have years ago. So that the line of demarcation of 16 years I think is outdated and, as has been suggested, I think should be lowered to include anybody over the age of 13, in felony cases (9).

The next witnesses were juvenile delinquents themselves (Marino 1977c). Their staged appearance in front of television cameras dramatized their status as serious delinquents. The juveniles entered the legislative chamber wearing hoods, supposedly so that their identities would not be publicly revealed. But by not seeing their young faces, the delinquents who testified appeared less like juveniles and more like adult criminal offenders.

The testimony fit their anonymous image as serious offenders. They were rational perpetrators of crime, as exemplified by the following description of a mugging incident:

usually one person, . . . would get on the elevator with the lady, see what button she pressed . . . if she pressed the fifth floor, he will press the fourth . . . . The rest of us would be . . . in the stairway, he would holler up what floor, . . . we would all just run up to the floor she's getting off . . . . As soon as she opened the door, just walk behind, push her on in, get the money (14).

In the foreground of the delinquents' motivation to commit robbery was a calculated low risk of punishment in juvenile court.

I guess you know, every time you get arrested when you are a juvenile they say you have to be 16 or the record doesn't count. That's what they said, so it didn't matter how many times you got busted as long as you was under 16. . . . So it was easy money, you know, as long as you was a juvenile, so that's why everybody did it (13).

The gathered testimony set part of the stage for lowering the age of criminal responsibility. An organizational interest emerged in a lower age of responsibility if legal reform enhanced the ability of Senior Citizen Robbery Unit detectives to respond to violent juveniles. Moreover, by describing delinquents as sophisticated criminals, more resources could be devoted to the police.

Another volume (Marino 1977b) of the committee's reports stated that the elderly are frequently the target of "indoor robbery victimizations." However, the report lacked data on the elderly's victimization for other types of offenses, which led readers of the report to conclude erroneously that the elderly were overrepresented in all acts of robbery.[2] Although the report showed that felony arrests of juveniles in New York City increased from 3,111 in 1966 to 7,438 in 1975, the report neglected to mention the possible impact of the police on recorded arrests. For instance, the number of New York City police officers increased from 27,000 in 1965 to 30,600 in 1975.[3] Moreover, the increase in the number of juveniles arrested for victimizing the elderly might also be attributed to the diligent efforts of the police working in senior citizen robbery prevention units. Yet from the public's point of view, it may have made little difference whether arrests were equal to crime. The system seemed incapable of handling the increasing number of juveniles identified as delinquents.

The media stories, the JJRA, and commission and committee reports set the political and organizational stage for Willie Bosket to enter and trigger immediate calls for waiver legislation. By the time 15-year-old Willie Bosket murdered his victims, juvenile justice had already lost a substantial amount of credibility. Legislators were no longer willing to say again to the public that violent juveniles, such as Bosket, could be dealt with in juvenile courts. The public and its officials wanted something more than just get-tough legislation that appeared to rearrange the existing penalties of juvenile courts. They now wanted legislation that would punish juveniles for their violent behavior in criminal court and not in juvenile court. But administrative convenience would also play a hand in maintaining the legitimacy of juvenile justice and in producing a more complex return to the days in which juveniles were sentenced exclusively in criminal courts.

The 1978 Juvenile Offender Law

The JO law came in the form of an amendment to the 1976 JJRA (New York State Crime Package Bill of 1978). It was based on the same set of violent designated felony offenses. For juveniles charged with these offenses, it shifted the court of initial jurisdiction from juvenile court to criminal court. Criminal justice officials instead of juvenile justice officials were required to make legal decisions on the status of eligible juveniles. As a consequence, it produced the legal label of juvenile offender for those juveniles charged with certain designated offenses.

In criminal court, juvenile offenders are technically treated like adult offenders. They are eligible for all the due process rights of adult defendants. For instance, juveniles as juvenile offenders in New York can receive a trial by jury in criminal court, but a jury trial is not an option for delinquents in juvenile court. Moreover, the processing of juveniles in criminal court is open to the public, unlike juvenile courts.[4] For convicted juveniles, the JO law also meant a possible criminal court record, which could mark them for life in their pursuit of employment and higher education.

Although the actual length of sentences is not as severe as those for adult offenders, maximum penalties are substantially greater than what juveniles could have received for the same offenses in juvenile court. For example, the JO law increased the maximum length of imprisonment for murder to life in prison from a maximum of 5 years under the JJRA. Moreover, the minimum period of incarceration in secure facilities for juveniles convicted in juvenile court was 12 to 18 months for a designated felony offense followed by 12 months in nonsecure residential facilities. The JO law requires the entire length of a juvenile offender's sentence to be served in secure facilities.

Table 3.1 lists the range of possible sentences by offense type for juveniles convicted of designated felonies in criminal court. The legal definitions of eligible designated felony offenses are listed in Appendix A. Note

Table 3.1. Juvenile Offender Law: Offenses and Penalties

Designated Felony	Sentence Length	
Class A	**Minimum**	**Maximum**
Murder	5–9 years	life
Arson, Kidnapping	4–6 years	12–15 years
Class B		
Manslaughter 1,		
Rape 1, Robbery 1,	1/3 of max.	3–10 years
Sodomy 1, Burglary 1,		
Arson 2, Attempted		
Murder 2, Attempted		
Kidnapping 1,		
Aggravated Sexual		
Abuse		
Class C		
Burglary 2,	1/3 of max.	3–7 years
Robbery 2,		
Assault 1		

that the minimum sentence for juvenile offenders convicted of B felonies can be as low as one year based on a maximum sentence of three years. As with adult offenders, criminal court judges are granted considerable discretion in determining the exact minimum and maximum length of sentence for juvenile offenders. This makes it possible for a juvenile offender sentenced by the criminal court for a B and C felony ultimately to serve less time in a DFY facility than a juvenile delinquent placed by the juvenile court for the same designated felony offense. Moreover, the JO law did not eliminate juvenile justice for juvenile offenders at the point of incarceration. Secure placement is not with the state's adult Department of Corrections (DOC) but with DFY where juvenile offenders must receive "educational" and "rehabilitative" services. The JO further requires the transfer of incarcerated juvenile offenders to DOC on the exact date of their twenty-first birthday, although they may face transfer anytime after the age of sixteen at the discretion of DFY officials.

The JO law did not mandate the criminal court as the only possible court of jurisdiction for eligible juveniles. Juveniles could be transferred from the criminal court to the juvenile court in what is commonly referred to as a *reverse waiver* procedure. The reverse waiver rule produced an additional legal avenue in which criminal justice officials could return jurisdiction over violent juveniles to juvenile court. For juveniles accused of mur-

der, first degree rape, sodomy, or armed robbery, the JO law required that
the removal process be based on one or more of the following elements:

(i) mitigating circumstances that bear directly upon the manner in which
the crime was committed; (ii) where the defendant was not the sole participant in the crime, the defendant's participation was relatively minor although not so minor as to constitute a defense to the prosecution; or (iii)
possible deficiencies in the proof of the crime.

If the charge against an eligible juvenile involved something other than
class A designated felonies, such as robbery or assault, the legal requirements were less explicit, and the conditions allowing for transfer to juvenile
court were relatively vague. In determining removal, however, the law directed officials to consider "individually and collectively" all of the following factors:

(a) the seriousness and circumstances of the offense; (b) the extent of the
harm caused by the offense; (c) the evidence of guilt, whether admissible or
inadmissible at trial; (d) the history, character and condition of the defendant; (e) the purpose and effect of imposing upon the defendant a sentence
authorized for the offense; (f) the impact of the removal of the case to the
family court on the safety and welfare of the community; (g) the impact of
the removal of the case to the family court upon the confidence of the
public in the criminal justice system; (h) where the court deems it appropriate, the attitude of the complainant or victim with respect to [transfer]; (i)
any other relevant fact indicating that a judgment of conviction in the
criminal court would serve no useful purpose.

If the case of an eligible juvenile was removed to juvenile court, the criminal court had to "state on the record the factor or factors upon which the
court's determination was based [and] give its reasons for removal in detail
and not in conclusory terms." Where removal required the consent of the
District Attorney, the JO law mandated a statement detailing the reason for
consenting to removal. These transfer or removal provisions were undoubtedly intended to provide the needed "safety valve" that Zimring (1991)
related as a requirement of legislative waiver.[5]

The JO law returned legal discretion over violent juveniles to what it was
in the period before New York's juvenile courts. It empowered the district
attorney with the ability to do something about violent juveniles in the legal
decision to charge a juvenile as an adult offender. As is the case with adult
offenders, the decision is subject to negotiation and dependent on circumstances that go beyond general legal categories. However, for adult defendants, decisions to reduce the severity of arrest charges lead to less severe

penalties in criminal court, while for juvenile offenders a reduction in arrest charges lead to nondesignated felony offense charges and a different organizational setting for their adjudication, the juvenile court.

In short, the get-tough reform proposed by the governor shifted the sources of legal discretion over violent juveniles from juvenile justice officials to criminal justice officials. It did so at various stages of the legal process. Criminal justice officials would initially decide if the juvenile was an appropriate candidate for criminal court. Criminal court judges, not juvenile court judges, would be the first to see juveniles identified as offenders. If convicted and sentenced to incarceration as a juvenile offender, DFY officials could not decide the exact date of release. As is the case with adult offenders, a parole board would decide the date on which a juvenile could be released after serving the minimum sentence.

The Legislative Debates

In the midst of their reelection campaigns and summer vacations, New York's state legislators returned to Albany in July 1978 to pass the JO law by an overwhelming majority in both houses of the legislature. The Senate vote was 50–2 for the JO law. The vote in the Assembly was similarly skewed; 125 favored and only 10 opposed the bill. It was signed into law on July 20, 1978 (Thorpe 1979).

Clearly the vote reflects the fact that legislators needed to do something about violent juvenile crime and juvenile justice. The legislative debates highlighted the political concerns and interests that led to passage of the JO law. Part of those concerns are reflected in expressions of confidence and doubt about the ability of the JO law to reduce violent juvenile crime. In the following sections, I will detail part of the debates to highlight the conflict that existed in the minds of legislators.[6] The debates also illustrate particular ideologies as "a map or grid" that shaped the JO law (McGarrell 1989: 169).

The Senate Debate. Senator Franz S. Leichter was one of the two senators to vote against the JO law. He voiced frustration at the insufficient amount of time available to examine the particular details of the bill. In explaining his negative vote, he emphasized the rush atmosphere in which he was being asked to support the JO law.

> It is sheer madness to come up with a bill like this, of – I don't know – some 70, 80 pages at 12:15 and to demand that this bill be passed at this hour.

Now, I realize that many of the provisions in this bill have already been considered, some have been passed into law, but certainly insofar as the treatment of juveniles is concerned, there are many provisions here that are totally new, that are going to have a devastating impact, as I see it, on the criminal justice system and not to hold hearings on this, not even to reflect on it or for that matter not even to give the members a chance to read the provisions I think is a very great disservice . . . (472).

The second dissenting vote, by State Senator Carl McCall, complained that the JO bill was pure politics and that it bypassed the usual committee hearings needed to consider intelligently juvenile justice reform. He stated that

this bill is really a hoax. I think we were called back here because the people that we represent really expected us to do something about crime. They are concerned about crime, rightfully so. They are very frightened and we have a responsibility to deal with that fright, to deal with that concern. And I think that what we are doing here tonight hardly addresses that. . . . We have a bill before us at the last moment. I think for all those people who are here who have to vote on it, I doubt very many of them have had an opportunity to read this entire bill. There have been no hearings. There are groups throughout the state that ought to be heard from that ought to give us their opinions, their judgments about how this is going to work . . . (482–3).

Even those senators who ultimately voted for the JO law expressed resistance to the idea of treating juveniles in criminal courts. From Senator Jeremiah Bloom's remarks, we might incorrectly assume his opposition. He openly expressed his frustration at having once more to do something about violent juvenile crime.

[R]eading this bill makes me realize this is an election year, and we go through these paces every four years in an election charade. Most of the features of this bill have been on the books as bills introduced since 1975 [JJRA 1976], but here in this last moment we are supposed to make the people of our great state secure. . . . We have solved all the problems of crime and now we are going to tell the people, "You are now safe" (489–90).

Some Republicans saw the JO law as a political ploy by Democrats to sponsor a bill that they had earlier proposed. In announcing his vote for the JO bill, Republican Senator Douglas Barclay stated that Democrats were finally seeing the Republican position on crime.

Now, the interesting thing to me is that we really could have done this much earlier, much sooner, but it has taken this length of time to get the Governor and the Assembly to agree that the Republican position should be adopted in this state for a strong crime bill (454).

Democratic Senator Seymour Halpern, who represented the borough of Queens in New York City, also voted for the bill and said he preferred the more traditional route of waiver in which the transfer process could begin in juvenile courts.

In the juvenile area I still believe that the better approach would be to permit waiver from the Family Court to the adult court insofar as the Juvenile Justice Reform Act of 1976 and the amendments which were passed and signed into law earlier this year seem to be having a very positive effect . . . (464–65).

In defense of the JO bill, its co-sponsor, Senator Manfred Ohrenstein, a Democrat from New York City, responded that the JO law reflected a shift in public attitudes and tolerance for juvenile violence, though it is not clear when serious acts of juvenile violence were ever tolerated by the public.

To those who criticize this effort I would like to say this: I think there was one thing left out in some of the remarks that were made and that is that there is a context to what is occurring here and there is a context to why this very extensive, very pervasive bill is before us, and that is that this State has been swept by revulsion against the things which are happening in the streets of our urban areas (498–500).

Another co-sponsor of the proposal, Senator Warren Anderson, a Republican who represented less populated upstate counties, argued that the JO bill would make people feel safer because juveniles would be forced to "pay the penalty." Theories of deterrence or retribution as the justification for the JO bill were implicit in much of the support behind it. Senator Anderson stated that the bottom line was retribution and deterrence. This is what the average citizen wanted:

The people we represent want those who are convicted to pay the penalty. The people who we represent want to be able to walk along the streets, want to be protected, and this is what this bill is about. I would just have to say that it is only one phase of our responsibility but it is a very real phase, and I don't think we should back away from that. I think that we can support this bill wholeheartedly, and hopefully, it will play a major part in making this State a little better place in which to live (508).

But other legislators were less clear about how to make New York a better or safer place to live. On the one hand, they thought it might work, and, on the other hand, they had a feeling they would be back to reform once more what was already reformed. Take, for instance, this confused statement of Senator Abraham Bernstein, a democrat who represented the Bronx in New York City:

> I think it does have an opportunity to work, particularly if we can effectuate the other things that we mentioned, and I will be darned if I want to go back without saying we have done something. . . . You know, we have passed much legislation. Sometimes we pass legislation that we have come back and corrected, but unless you do something you cannot correct anything, and this may be the impetus for a better and more effective legislation (475).

Senator Leichter could not contain himself and reiterated the political interests that were driving Bernstein's favorable vote:

> Senator [Bernstein], I thank you because you have stated, I think as well as anyone has, why we are passing . . . [the JO bill], because you and some of the Senators and the Assembly and the Governor are going to be darned leaving here tonight without having done something, so we are going to do something . . . . we are sort of reacting here in a panic fashion without real understanding and real thought . . . (476–8).

The Assembly Debate. Like their colleagues in the Senate, several Assembly legislators complained about the hurried atmosphere of the session. They too felt pressured to do something about juvenile crime by passing the JO law. Assemblyman Woodrow Lewis of Brooklyn, one of the ten Assembly members to vote against the JO bill, questioned the politically charged atmosphere that would lead the state to sentence a 13-year-old juvenile to prison for a period of 9 years to life.

> You have gotten yourselves in this box, where you must do something. I agree, you must take the criminals, juvenile or adult, off the streets. The answer is not putting them in there and saying, "Well, look, forget it, we are not concerned when you come out. This is our true methodology, you stay there until we can better our system of finding out what we are going to do with you." Well, that is a bad reflection on society in 1978 that has not yet found out what to do with 13-year-olds but put them in prison for life . . . . But for God's sake, don't rush to this kind of judgment that you think you have to imprison a 13-year-old for life, because it is a reflection on you and me and not on the 13-year-old (115–16).

Similarly, Assemblyman Frank Barbaro, who also opposed the bill and was from Brooklyn as well, claimed that his fellow liberal, Democratic party colleagues were abandoning their principles and the past efforts to reject automatic waiver provisions.

I stand here and I hear people who I considered to be liberals capitulating. Capitulating to the hysteria that is in the street, and it is a justified hysteria. People are frightened, and they have a right to be frightened because crime is running rampant (129–30).

The black and Hispanic caucus leader of the Assembly, Arthur Eve of Buffalo, pleaded with his fellow legislators not to vote for the bill. He argued that the JO bill would not have just a symbolic effect. It would have serious repercussions on juveniles.

We have gone almost mad. We have gone the process of dehumanization. I believe we have reached the point where the juvenile justice system literally will not exist anymore. You are taking children and you are going to treat them like adults. You are going to mete out very, very serious punishment (81–2).

Assemblyman Eve rejected the idea of deterrence or incapacitation as the real reason for proposing the JO law. Instead, he stressed that

this bill is here because of the political situation. Some of my colleagues have talked about how the people out there want this kind of legislation. The papers have done an excellent job . . . . My colleagues, I wish you could vote against this bill, to have the courage to say no. This is not the route for us to go in. Let's sit down and really deal with the problem, let's try to prevent kids from getting into that system, because that is the real, ultimate conclusion . . . . We must deal with both simultaneously, because if we don't, all we are saying is when that old lady is ripped off or that young person is shot, our only response is, "I am going to take care of that kid who did that to you, who took your life." And, we wait until after the crime is done and then we respond. That is not being responsible legislators, my colleagues (84–9).

Eve wanted his colleagues to move beyond the media presentation of the facts and to reconsider prevention and the purpose of juvenile justice. Assemblyman Albert Vann, another member of the black and Hispanic caucus, similarly argued that there is a reason for treating juveniles in a legal process separate from adults.

Mr. Speaker, it seems to me that there is a reason why we have had different sets of laws for children and adults. It seems to me that we have realized that a child is not capable of making certain decisions or a certain level of maturity, incompetence and the like. It is very difficult for me to understand, Mr. Speaker, that at this point in time we have reached the conclusion that we must treat children as we treat adults. Perhaps that would not be so bad, if we believed that the adult criminal justice system was working (116–17).

Why would the adult criminal justice system work any better than the juvenile justice system? In a heated exchange between Assemblymen Edward Sullivan and Howard Lasher, the ability of the adult criminal justice system to deter juvenile crime was questioned. Assemblyman Sullivan argued that publicity for juvenile offenders would expose them to a public criminal label and, consequently, lead them into more serious criminal behavior. In contrast, Assemblyman Lasher defended the initial presumption of criminal responsibility for juvenile offenders, and he defended the public criminal label as contributing to the deterrent value of the law.

ASSEMBLYMAN SULLIVAN: So, if this law passes, as no doubt it will, and is signed into law, as no doubt it will, then the laws of the State of New York will say, in effect, that a person under the age of 18 is incapable because of, perhaps, a lack of judgment, of conducting business on his signature, but a person of the age of 13 is capable of defending himself in a Criminal Court where he might possibly receive a life sentence . . . . Now, what do you think the effect on young people will be, of that releasing of names? When a young fellow sees the name of his friend on page 3 of the *Daily News*, what do you think the effect will be?

ASSEMBLYMAN LASHER: It will act as a deterrent for anybody else to commit the same crime.

ASSEMBLYMAN SULLIVAN: Why will it be a deterrent?

ASSEMBLYMAN LASHER: If he knows a friend of his may be going away to jail for a long period of time, if I was any friend of his, I would not want to be with him.

ASSEMBLYMAN SULLIVAN: He knows that now, doesn't he, because the word "if he is a friend of the fellow," he would know it anyway. What will be the effect generally of the publicity? Don't you think this glory of being in the *Daily News* might have some effect of actually leading people to crime?

ASSEMBLYMAN LASHER: No. And the reason I don't think so with respect to this type of bill is that the sentences that can be, and probably will be, handed out under this bill will not say to somebody else, "Go ahead and do it, you will get your name on page two or three." It will say to him, "If you do it, you're very, very capable of going away for a long period of time, and if you have any smarts at all, you won't commit the crime." Under the prior system, I had my doubts when you had the juvenile system in the Juvenile Court, I had my doubts whether we should publish names because of the notoriety you talked about, but when the penalties are so severe –

ASSEMBLYMAN SULLIVAN: Excuse me, Mr. Lasher. The penalty hasn't been decided yet. The fellow has just been arrested and arraigned; there is no penalty yet. He has been arrested on murder or whatever the crime is, and now he is arraigned and his picture is on the front page of the paper.

There is no penalty yet, is there? He hasn't been sentenced yet, has he?
ASSEMBLYMAN LASHER: No.
ASSEMBLYMAN SULLIVAN: How many months later would he be sentenced, would you guess?
ASSEMBLYMAN LASHER: It won't matter.
ASSEMBLYMAN SULLIVAN: Ten months, 12 months?
ASSEMBLYMAN LASHER: If you want to speak about reality, it won't matter because at the time that the information is determined by the district attorney's office, the sentences that will go along with the article that will appear with his name, will be a long sentence. So and so can be convicted of a life sentence for murder (101–6).

Mr. Lasher also defended the JO bill on the basis of its symbolic value, recognizing that the publicity associated with the penalties would play a crucial role in calming public concerns and fears. The stated penalties would show the public, including potential juveniles, that the system was prepared to do something to punish juveniles for violent crime, whether or not the punishment in criminal court was actually more severe than what the same juveniles could receive in juvenile court.

Republicans expressed political frustration that the Democrats were playing politics through the bill by pretending to get tough on juvenile crime right before an election. In explaining his vote for the JO bill, Assemblyman Mega expressed Republican frustration at the Democrats' refusal to consider earlier legislative attempts to lower the age of criminal responsibility.

We could have had legislation like this without the pressure, without being under the gun. In January we could have worked it out. We had similar legislation which Mr. Lasher would not put out of his Committee, and that was brought out on a debate. Why do we have to act under this pressure and put out the legislation – because it's politics (137).

Just as some in the Senate expressed a desire to debate and consider alternative waiver legislation, some Assembly members expressed their preference for a system of waiver that would begin in juvenile court. Assemblyman Jerold Nadler, a Democrat representing part of Manhattan, voted for the JO bill despite his preference for judicial waiver legislation. He warned that the JO bill contained too many opportunities for transfer back to juvenile court in overloaded criminal courts.

I would prefer it to be the other way around, if we would have it in the family court system and waive particularly vicious cases up into the adult system. But, political compromise dictated otherwise, and so we are now facing a bill which says we are going to waive them, put them in the adult system, and we are going to provide three different opportunities for a waiver procedure to waiver down in each case. This is going to help clog the courts further than we have done already . . . (127–8).

Most legislators in the Assembly, like their colleagues in the Senate, justified voting for the JO law because they wanted to "do something" about violent juvenile crime, not because the JO law was their optimum response to violent juvenile crime. Assemblyman Owen Johnson, a Republican from Long Island, first stressed that his constituents were most afraid of crime and wanted to see something done. He then expressed his doubts about the JO law's fairness and its ability to prevent juvenile crime. In the end, the fear and concerns among constituents led to his positive vote.

> I represent a constituency that find themselves very much prisoners of the daylight, and at sunset we find people scurrying into their homes. I represent a constituency that cries out for some sign from the Legislature that we are, in fact, going to try to provide them some element that will deal with the fear under which they live. . . . I am very, very much dissatisfied with many aspects of this bill. I find it abominable that in our civil law we have a concept of a guardian *ad litem* wherein a person under the age of 18 who is unable to manage his or her affairs has, appointed by the court, someone who can properly represent their interests. The crime package we are voting on today does not have a guardianship provision, as pointed out by Mr. Sullivan. I find it very, very much distressing and just echo the concerns of Mr. Eve that if, as Mr. Duryea stated, it was a Republican bill, that they cannot convince their colleagues from the Senate to pass some sort of preventive package wherein the sources of crime could, in fact, be stopped before the commission of the crimes. At the same time, the greatest force to which I am going to respond is a constituency that is scared, a constituency that is crying out for this bill, a constituency that calls asking for passage of this bill today (134–5).

Johnson also warned that the JO law would soon be viewed as a political product that would follow the fate of other draconian legislation, such as the Rockefeller drug laws.

Doubts were also raised by legislators as to why they were considering legislation triggered by the violent behavior of one juvenile when recent reports showed a decline in violent juvenile crime.

> I also want to observe in recent years, probably the last 18 months, according to an article in the *New York Times*, crime has actually decreased – violent crime in our Country, and in our State and in New York City. I understand

crime against the elderly in New York City has dropped 18 percent. There are many factors given as the cause of this reduction, but crime is still foremost in the minds of our people, and crime still exists at levels we cannot tolerate (139).

But crime rates did not really matter. In the end it was the credibility of juvenile justice systems that was at stake in producing support for the JO law, as Assemblyman Angelo Orazaio went on to state further.

The issue is not in this bill whether or not it's a preventive, whether or not it's a deterrent, whether or not we have, by this legislation reduced or will reduce crime. The issue is how we can at this point, admitting our own guilt, the failure of this society to do better, how we can defend ourselves against the crime that exists, and we see at this point no other alternative than to support this kind of legislation that . . . by some miracle . . . will reduce crime in the future (139–40).

The political ramifications of opposing the bill were also bluntly expressed by Assemblyman Arthur Kremer:

They asked me, what was I as a Legislator doing to make the streets safe. That they were afraid to walk in the streets in the same community that I live in; that they were afraid of being ripped off by young people who – their impression of them was young people who know more about the law than the lawyers, and the D.A.s, and the judges do, and who know how to get out and who know that you don't go to jail, and who know that you can put a knife to a guy's throat, and with 13 years of age, and nothing is going to happen to you (93–4).

It is important also to bear in mind that there were many legislators who stated their confidence in the JO law's ability to deter and incapacitate violent juvenile crime. They were crystal clear in the stated reason for their vote, as expressed in the comments of Assemblyman Oliver Koppell, a Democrat representing parts of the Bronx:

Meting out measured punishment is something that will, in fact, deter . . . . Every time a young person reads he committed murder and he is subject to a mandatory sentence of 18 months, that says to that unsophisticated mind, "Well, it couldn't be very bad. All it was, was 18 months." . . . The law must say to that person, yes, this is very bad (125).

And, indeed, the JO law did say violent juvenile crime was very bad. But in the rush to pass the JO law, legislators were back the next year to modify the JO law so that it would be not only "tough on juvenile crime," but also more administratively convenient. The JO law needed to be less determinate and more open to the complexities of criminal justice.

Legal Modifications

The 1978 JO law neglected to provide juvenile offenders with the legal right to Youthful Offender (YO) status. As previously noted in Chapter 1, New York's 1943 Youthful Offender Statute allows criminal court judges to grant juveniles between 16 and 18 YO status. Although it cannot be granted for persons charged with murder, YO status allows older juveniles for other violent felonies to receive probation or shorter periods of incarceration. Moreover, YO status "seals" an offender's record so that it remains technically confidential. However, it is noted on subsequent arrests so that persons can only receive YO status once.

Although the 1978 JO law attempted to restrict the discretion of legal officials by setting more determinate penalties for juveniles charged with violent offenses, it made the possible penalties for 14- and 15-year-old juveniles potentially harsher than for juveniles between 16 and 18. Without the availability of YO status for juvenile offenders, the JO law produced initially a more severe legal process for younger juveniles than older juveniles charged with the same set of designated felony offenses. In short, it was clear to many officials that after less than a year of working with the JO law, procedural modifications were needed.

The 1979 Juvenile Offender Amendment. In 1979 the legislators were back to amend the JO law to allow for a juvenile's conviction to be sealed as a YO and juvenile offender.[7] So the 1979 amendment created an additional avenue of legal discretion. With a unanimous vote in the Senate, and only four dissenting votes in the Assembly, there was general agreement that the JO law should be modified. Yet the official story as it appears in the debates, and then in solicited letters of opinion, reveals aspects of how the JO law was viewed one year after its implementation. Assemblyman Eve, who voted against the 1978 bill and its 1979 amendment, stated:

> This is not going to help anybody. Yes, it is going to add some other sections to the law that other kids can be charged with. There may be some improvements that I might consider. . . . People who have to go through this process certainly felt we have not made any improvement, we have not dealt with the problem of young people and how we are going to stop them from getting themselves into problems (9706).

Other legislators, such as Republican Senator Owen Johnson, complained that they were forced yet again to consider legislation without any indicators of success:

> We have not had presented before us publicly, nor would I venture to say, if any of us had presented to us privately one statistic, one fact, one piece of indisputable data to see a benefit that has been derived from this bill . . . (9707–8).

But crime rates did not really matter, as the Senator quickly recognized. What counted most and what remained from the political heat of summer 1978 was the need to do something about violent juvenile crime. Assemblywoman Gerdi Lipschutz said:

> I have a predominant amount of senior citizens, in fact the entire County of Queens in my own District. Those senior citizens are still the easy prey of, unfortunately, the kind of things young people are accused of and arrested for, this kind of crime. They are still afraid. They still lock themselves into their homes, and are afraid to travel about once the sun sets in the evening. I am voting for this bill, although I do have some reservations about some of its provisions (9720–1).

Before Governor Carey signed the 1979 JO amendment into law, his office solicited comments from various interest groups. This was a time for legal aid and child welfare organizations to voice their opposition to the JO law. The 1978 emergency session surprised these agencies and left them with little opportunity to mobilize their constituencies. The executive director of the Citizen's Committee for Children of New York recommended that the 1979 JO bill be vetoed:

> We urge your veto of *S6357 A8003*. The bill further confuses some provisions of the Juvenile Offender Law and places impossible conditions on the removal hearings. Rather than a patch-up, you should demand more staff work and public hearings before any changes in the bill are made (Bernard C. Fisher, executive director, Citizens' Committee for Children of New York Inc., June 26, 1979).

Other letters recommending a veto stated that the criminal justice system was an inappropriate legal setting for juveniles and would just contribute to further delay in official decision making. In their view, the JO law was much too inefficient and ineffective in meeting its stated objectives. According to a letter written to the governor by the executive director of the Federation of Protestant Welfare Agencies:

The cumbersome, wasteful procedures this bill forces onto the Criminal Courts only serve to delay justice. One of the first jury trials under the new law took five months from arrest to conclusion. In addition to the increasingly heavy caseload the criminal system must handle, the children are not getting the proper placement or treatment while they are going through the judicial process.

This bill will only highlight the delays and inconsistencies in rendering Juvenile justice and the overcrowding in the criminal system caused by the 1978 Juvenile Offender Law. We therefore urge you to veto the above bill and to take leadership in beginning a comprehensive study of the juvenile justice system, taking into account the public, the court system, and the professionals who deal with children in trouble (Berkeley Johnson, Federation of Protestant Welfare Agencies, June 9, 1979).

District attorneys were unanimous in their support of both the existing JO law and the 1979 amendment. They argued that it was a workable solution to the problems they faced in their routine handling of juvenile offenders. But the following letter co-authored by Charles Schinitsky, whose 1962 article made the case for legal representation for juveniles, provided a different perspective on the JO law. Polsky and Schinitsky suggested that the JO law had added to delay and increased procedural inefficiency in the case processing of juveniles.

> Eleventh hour changes in this joint effort have undermined this initial purpose and, regardless of the merit or lack of merit of various substantive changes, have created a procedural morass which gravely inhibits the ability of the court and its counsel to respond. Perhaps more significant, although directly related to the procedural problems, is the absolute certainty that juveniles for whom removal is ultimately granted will spend substantially longer periods within the criminal justice court and detention systems than is now the case. . . . We urge the disapproval of *A.8003/S.6357* and respectfully suggest that the 1978 Act be reconsidered at the next Session . . . (Leon B. Polsky, The Legal Aid Society, Attorney-in-Charge, Criminal Defense Division, and Charles Schinitsky, Attorney-in-Charge, Juvenile Rights Division, June 26, 1979).

The 1979 JO legislation fit the bark and bite pattern of criminal justice reforms (Casper & Brereton 1984). The bark was contained in the initial 1978 JO law, which criminal justice officials adapted to meet the needs of a loosely coupled criminal justice and juvenile justice system. Criminal justice officials, namely prosecutors, had difficulty in meeting the more determinant harsh penalties of the JO law. YO status provided a new legal avenue in which to convict juveniles as offenders. The 1979 amendment reproduced a familiar story of reform within reforms that expanded the dispositional options of legal officials.

The 1982 Cost-Sharing Amendment. Another important, but less known, legal modification to the JO law occurred in a 1982 amendment. The amendment modified the formula for determining the juvenile's county's cost for incarcerating convicted juvenile offenders. For juveniles placed as delinquents through the juvenile court, the juvenile's county of jurisdiction shared 50 percent of the fiscal cost of placement. However, the JO law shifted that expense to the state when incarceration as a juvenile offender occurred through criminal courts. The 1982 amendment eventually made the cost of institutionalization to counties equal for juveniles regardless of whether they were placed by juvenile courts or sentenced by criminal courts,[8] gradually increasing the county's cost of incarceration for convicted juvenile offenders from 12.5 percent in 1983 to 50 percent in 1986. Although the 1982 amendment is a relatively obscure piece of legislation, the amendment is important in understanding the JO law's creation and implementation.

Conclusion

Recriminalization in the form of New York's JO law was not merely a product of Willie Bosket and a governor's election campaign. The political and organizational concerns and interests go deeper than the stated reasons for doing something about crime. Certainly deep-seated concerns and fears needed to be addressed in the everyday interpretation of juvenile violence and juvenile justice. The media stories and committee reports expressed a lack of public and official confidence in a traditional juvenile justice system.

Legislators were frustrated by the lack of alternative legal routes to pursue in getting tough on juvenile crime and juvenile justice. Many who voted for the JO law would have preferred judicial forms of waiver in which jurisdiction over juveniles initially remained with juvenile justice officials. They would have preferred proposals for treatment-oriented programs that might work in reducing violent juvenile crime. But in the end, legislators expressed their distrust for the juvenile justice system and its various subsystems for controlling chronic violent delinquents.

Criminal justice became the legislators' last resort after trying harsher penalties in juvenile court through the JJRA. Like earlier juvenile justice reforms, the JJRA appeared ineffective in preventing and controlling serious violent delinquents, such as Willie Bosket. The availability of harsher penalties in juvenile court affected only one part of the juvenile justice system. Recall that Bosket was released prior to his maximum possible placement by DFY officials. Official distrust for juvenile court as the place to punish violent juveniles led legislators to criminal court and the criminal justice system in the hope that it would be a more determinant legal avenue for controlling violent delinquents.

This is not to suggest that a theory of deterrence did not play in the minds of legislators and other officials. But at the same time they quickly realized that the get-tough provisions of the JO law needed to be modified. Flexibility was the cornerstone not only of juvenile justice systems but also criminal justice systems. By adding the possibility of YO status, the get-tough provisions of the JO law were lightened to allow for decision making on juvenile offenders in a more loosely coupled system of criminal justice.

But real reasons for waiver legislation, as the history of juvenile justice reforms repeatedly tells us, are linked to the temporal and jurisdictional needs and concerns of officials located within particular organizational settings. It is temporal in that a prior history of reforms are necessary for juveniles charged with murder to be labeled officially as delinquents. It is jurisdictional in that the motivation for reform stems from more general problems of urbanization and violence. It was on the New York City subways that Bosket killed his victims, and it is in densely populated urban areas that loosely coupled juvenile justice systems need to be continually revised and reinvented. Not only Willie Bosket, but also disorganized, impoverished environments in New York City, triggered the JO law. Residents of New York City were not only concerned with juvenile justice but the problems of living in a city where the very poor are in close proximity to the rich and not so rich, and where public transportation is a routine part of urban living.

Yet the specific direction of reforms cannot be predicted solely on the basis of general concerns and fears about crime. "Doing something" does not tell us anything about the specific timing and content of reforms; "doing something" is not just a reaction to violent crime but also to a prior history of reforms. The JO law and legislative waiver would not have occurred if it were not for the JJRA and New York's attempt to get tough on juvenile crime in juvenile courts. Nor would New York be unique among the vast majority of states which always had some form of waiver if not for its already low age of general criminal responsibility at age 16.

The JO law and legislative waiver emerged in New York in a form that did not eliminate the need for juvenile justice. Rather, maintaining the credibility of juvenile justice systems demanded another legal avenue, which would on the one hand be organizationally convenient, and on the other hand be able to identify and monitor violent delinquents in the adult criminal justice system. The JO law produced that legal route through legislative waiver. In 1979 an amendment led to a further modification, which produced another legal avenue through which New York's criminal justice system could assign criminal responsibility to juveniles. In other words, there is nothing simple about criminal or juvenile justice systems and their process for convicting juveniles in criminal court.

A complex set of processes are at work that are less rational or instrumental than that which would be suggested by a simple vision of a society consisting of either offenders or nonoffenders. The assignment of criminal responsibility is not just an attempt to divide deserving and undeserving juveniles into criminal and noncriminal categories. Something deeper is happening in an expanding juvenile justice bureaucracy in which new outlets for juvenile justice reforms are being advocated. The simple bifurcation of juveniles into delinquents and nondelinquents, which might have described early analyses of juvenile courts, is no longer appropriate in the wake of contemporary systems of juvenile justice and their efforts to recriminalize delinquency.

Recriminalization presents a paradox: it both eliminates and legitimizes the need for juvenile justice. It legitimates the need for juvenile justice by making the system more complex, and by producing new legal avenues that are less understandable to the general public. In systems of juvenile justice, recriminalization makes it possible for the public and officials to find something for everyone in a system of justice where there is both treatment and punishment.

By creating new legal avenues for treating delinquents as juveniles, recriminalization also eliminates part of the need for juvenile justice. By moving delinquents into the adult legal process, juvenile justice officials are less responsible for their case processing. The system becomes less tightly coupled around the decision making of juvenile justice officials. Criminal justice further loosens the juvenile justice process by creating a less tightly coupled legal system.

Thus, the expanding nature of juvenile justice control, in the shape of reforms that attempt to either decriminalize or recriminalize delinquency, has placed law less in the foreground and more in the background of legal decision making. Reforms are less normative and more regulative (Garland 1985: 235). Recriminalization not only depends on the decision making of traditional experts in juvenile justice (such as psychologists and probation officers) but also that of prosecutors and other criminal justice officials to regulate who is defined as juvenile offender.

The JO law increased the regulative options for dealing with juveniles in systems of juvenile and criminal justice. The law allowed for a more diverse set of legal avenues than those that existed at the time in which Willie Bosket killed his subway victims. Recriminalization generally, and the JO law specifically, produced a more visible legal route for identifying juveniles as criminal offenders. But it also produced even less visible, legal avenues in a negotiated order of justice that exists in the hallways, offices, and criminal as well as juvenile courtrooms of juvenile and criminal justice systems.

It would be a mistake to assume (as many in New York do) that Willie Bosket was responsible for the JO law. Such an assumption relies on the short-term memories of legislators and others who would like to reduce crime and justice to the most simplistic set of events. It would also be a mistake to attribute the JO law exclusively to the political ambitions of legislators and the governor, who were facing election-year campaigns. In other words, the political reasons for waiver legislation are only part of the rationale for repetitive or periodic juvenile justice reforms. The particular shape of waiver in New York is a product of the state's unique history of juvenile justice reforms and its prior inability to assign criminal responsibility to violent juveniles such as Willie Bosket.

Contextual and Legal Reasons
for Identifying Juveniles
as Criminal Offenders

I NOW SHIFT MY FOCUS from the JO law's creation to its implementation. Yet I do not want to shift gears completely because the reasons for the JO law's implementation are similar to those cited for its creation. They are to avoid and to confront crisis. What kind of crisis? Well, the sort of crisis that can suddenly lead officials to create waiver legislation, such as when Governor Carey learned that Willie Bosket was responsible for the murder of subway passengers. But the creators of the JO law are not alone in their attempt to control and avoid crisis. The police, prosecutors, and judges arrest, charge, and sentence juveniles as offenders in criminal court instead of as delinquents in juvenile court, because they want to control and avoid their repeated acts of delinquency and crime. And just as there are political and organizational interests and concerns that lead to the creation of the JO law, so too are there factors that go beyond the offense and offender characteristics to explain the law's implementation.

In the following sections, I first draw on principles that have been used to identify juvenile court decision making to illustrate the legal reasons for assigning criminal responsibility to juveniles. Next I relate part of the context in which juveniles may be considered offenders instead of as delinquents. I then conclude this chapter with several sources of data to explain the context in which juveniles are initially labeled as offenders in the adult criminal justice process.

Principles for Assigning Criminal Responsibility

The assignment of criminal responsibility to juveniles in New York is technically guided by the JO law. Legislative forms of waiver require officials to base their decisions on the criminal responsibility of juveniles according to the "principle of offense" (Feld 1987). Juveniles technically cannot be brought into criminal court for nondesignated violent offenses even though these offenses are also acts of violence that might lead to serious criminal behavior. Moreover, JO offenses must be completed acts, not just attempts (see Appendix A for a list and definitions of eligible designated felony offenses).

Advocates of legislative waiver have emphasized that the determinant quality of offense-based transfer decisions constrains the decision making of legal officials. Instead of prosecuting juveniles as adults for less serious offenses through systems of judicial waiver, Barry Feld (1987) has argued that legislative waiver emphasizes

> the offense-oriented adult sentencing policies of retribution, deterrence, and selective incapacitation. States have accomplished this goal by legislatively narrowing the scope of juvenile court jurisdiction to exclude youths charged with certain serious offenses (Feld 1987: 511).

The principle of the offense meets offense-based objectives in systems of legislative waiver because it is rooted in the legal requirement that criminal responsibility can be assigned to juveniles only for a specific range of violent offenses. Closely related to the principle of the offense is the principle of equality. According to Matza:

> The principle of equality refers to a specific set of substantive criteria that are awarded central relevance and, historically, to a set of considerations that were specifically and momentously precluded. Its meaning, especially in criminal proceedings, has been to give a central and unrivaled position in the framework of relevance to considerations of offense and conditions closely related to offense like prior record, and to more or less preclude considerations of status and circumstances (1964: 114).

In other words, the particular circumstances and individual characteristics of offenders technically do not count in legal decision making that is grounded in the principle of the offense. It is a principle that is closest to the classical view of letting "the punishment fit the crime." Determinate sentencing schemes follow this line of legal discourse; they presume that an objective measure of severity can be reproduced in sentencing guidelines that sharply restrict judicial sentencing options.

While legislative waiver and the JO law restrict the types of offenses for which juveniles may be considered criminally responsible, it leaves to officials the ultimate judgment as to which kinds of juveniles should be treated as adult offenders. Like their counterparts in juvenile court, who must make decisions as to the juvenile's delinquent status, criminal justice officials are required to make some judgment of the "moral character" of eligible juveniles (Emerson 1969 and 1974). The determination of moral character takes place in complex juvenile/criminal justice systems where officials are granted a wide range of violent offenses for which to assign criminal responsibility.

As instructed by the JO law, criminal justice officials must decide which juveniles are more or less deserving of arrest, conviction, and incarceration as a juvenile offender. They are to fit the offense charges and the characteristics of the offender within the stated requirements of the law based on their official perception of the "best interests of justice." What is in the best interests of justice is not necessarily dictated by the mere fact of a 14-year-old who is observed in the act of robbery. The extent of harm inflicted, the quality of evidence, the culpability of the offender, and whether it was the juvenile's first offense are all factors that may enter into the official determination of the best interests of justice.

As is the case with adult offenders, the determination of criminal responsibility for juveniles depends on the decision making of more than one single official. A diverse set of officials must approve each others' decisions at various stages of the criminal justice process. Officials must consider the prior decision making of other officials based on police reports and the reports of other professionals in deciding the legal status of juveniles. Everything matters in these reports so that the principle of "individualized justice" enters alongside of the principle of the offense. In part this is dictated by the JO law when it instructs officials to consider "the history, character and condition of the defendant."

Criminal justice officials must be convinced that juveniles are not amenable to treatment in juvenile court before assigning the JO label or before sentencing the convicted juvenile offender to a secure facility. The criteria for deciding which juveniles are amenable to treatment or to transfer to the juvenile court can appear vague to persons outside of the criminal justice system. Individualized justice is a principle that contains "many more items in its framework of relevance" (Matza 1964: 114–15). It requires officials to consider "a full understanding of the client's personal and social character" (Matza 1964: 115). Yet individualized justice does not preclude consideration of offense characteristics, because it allows officials to use the offense as just one of many aspects of the eligible offender's case. Matza (1964) stresses that

spokesmen for individualized justice do not suggest that offense is irrelevant; rather, that it is one of many considerations that are to be used in
arriving at a sound disposition. Offense, like many other forms of behavior,
is to be taken as an indication or "symptom" of the juvenile's personal and
social disorder (114).

In extreme cases of violence, such as murder, offense becomes especially
relevant; there is little need to look beyond the offense at the juvenile's
characteristics. Discretion is limited by law; for example, juveniles charged
with murder are not eligible for youthful offender (YO) status. In such acts,
officials have no other choice but to charge juveniles in criminal court as
juvenile offenders. In offenses less serious than murder, however, such as
robbery and assaults, which are listed as B or C felonies, individualized
justice is more likely to come into play to assist officials in their determination of criminal responsibility. With these less serious JO offenses, officials
may refer to the juvenile's personal background. Indicators of support in
the family, school, and places of work enter as relevant factors to assist the
official assessment of "moral character" and juvenile offender status. In
other words, legal officials do what countless criminology textbooks recommend in looking to parents and schools as indicators of social control and
future delinquent or criminal behaviors.

Matza suggests that a doctrine of "parental sponsorship" guides the
principle of individualized justice. At the point of sentencing, for example,
offense seriousness and parental sponsorship interact so that

> whether a juvenile goes to some manner of prison or is put on some manner
> of probation . . . depends first, on a traditional rule-of-thumb assessment of
> the total risk of danger and thus scandal evident in the juvenile's current
> offense and prior record of offenses; this initial reckoning is then impor-
> tantly qualified by an assessment of the potentialities of "out-patient supervi-
> sion" and the guarantee against scandal inherent in the willingness and
> ability of parents or surrogates to sponsor the child (1964: 125).

That is, all things being equal, "those with adequate [parental] sponsorship
will be rendered unto probation, and those inadequately sponsored to
prison" (Matza 1964: 125).

In other words, juveniles with someone to say to the judge "I will take
this child and watch him like a hawk" are more likely to avoid conviction
and incarceration than juveniles without parental sponsorship. But other
officials at earlier stages in the legal process may also be exposed to evidence of sponsorship. The police officer may see parental concern and
interest in a mother's assurance that her child will not repeat the offense. A

concerned school teacher might call the prosecutor before the first court appearance to tell of the charged juvenile's excellent school performance. And the list goes on of the many ways in which sponsorship can be invoked at various stages of the legal process to protect juveniles from a criminal label.

But assessments of criminal responsibility and moral character go beyond any direct indicator of sponsorships. Officials do not have the time to investigate all there is to know about a juvenile and the true extent of adult support that he or she has in a household or neighborhood. Decisions must often be made quickly so that the indicators of parental sponsorship are often operationalized in the number of parents in the household. This may extend to race. If black juveniles are viewed as lacking the parental support that officials see as critical to reducing the chances of recidivism, then they may be more subject to harsher penalties. It may not be race per se that dictates legal decision making, but how race is perceived as linked to support, recidivism, and "substantive justice" (Horwitz & Wasserman 1980). Thus, the overrepresentation of black juveniles in the juvenile justice process (Dannefer & Schutt 1982; Landau & Nathan 1983; Sampson 1986; Thornberry 1973) may reflect official perceptions of black juveniles as more threatening and more likely to recidivate than white juveniles (Liska & Tausig 1979; McCarthy & Smith 1986; Tittle & Curran 1988).

Despite the fact that criminal justice officials are well aware of the complex reasons for why juveniles commit violent offenses, officials are restricted by their professional roles in complex, loosely coupled legal systems. Officials will state that they cannot learn everything there is to know about the juveniles they see, especially in large jurisdictions, where decisions often must be made quickly and based on limited amounts of information and experience. Experience is generally confined to the location of officials in a particular jurisdictional setting within a specific geographical area. As a consequence, official judgments about offense and offender seriousness are shaped not only by the individual characteristics of the offense and offender but also by the organizational context in which legal decisions are made.

Contextual Reasons

The contextual reasons for legal decision making suggest that it is not the offense or offender per se that produces the severity of legal decision making but how offense and offender are interpreted by diverse sets of officials within a particular organizational setting (Emerson 1983). The principles of offense and individualized justice are continuously adjusted to suit the concerns and interests of different sets of officials located in different counties of jurisdiction. Legal decision making is not only a product of principles as explicitly or implicitly stated in legal rules but also the types of offenses and kinds of offenders that officials routinely see in their particular legal setting. Robert Emerson makes this point when he states that

> in a variety of social control settings, assessments of the "seriousness" of particular cases (or whatever organizationally relevant dimensions) tend to be made in relation to the kinds of cases regularly encountered in that particular setting (Emerson 1983: 428).

An example that Emerson (1983) cites in support of the subjective quality of offense severity is the seriousness scores attached by respondents to offenses depending on whether they appeared on a nice or nasty list of other offenses. On a nastier list of offenses, the mean severity of a serious offense is rated less severely than the same offense on a nicer list of offenses. So too a holistic perspective of case processing decisions suggests that juveniles in criminal court do not appear as serious offenders in relation to a population of nastier, more chronic, adult offenders. In juvenile court, those same juveniles might appear as more serious than younger, less violent juvenile delinquents. There is no change in the objective characteristics of these juveniles or their offenses that determines seriousness. Rather, it is how seriousness is interpreted in relation to a larger set of other cases that officials routinely see in their legal role in particular jurisdictional settings.

Sources of variation in the mix of cases that officials routinely see in their legal decision making rest on an inter- and intrajurisdictional context (Emerson 1991). I refer to the variation that exists between the kinds of cases officials see in a single county of jurisdiction as *intrajurisdictional.* Intrajurisdictional variation exists when criminal justice officials at distinct stages in the legal process use their discretion to reduce the selected population of offenders. Prosecutors must interpret the seriousness of arrest charges as reported by the police. Although the police in making a designated felony arrest may see the juvenile's behavior as warranting the JO label, prosecutors may not. In the stream of cases that prosecutors see, certain JO offenses may be less serious than what is initially stated in the police officer's arrest charges. Prosecutors screen the arrests of police officers because they want to make a case while the police want to make an arrest (Stanko 1981). Thus intrajurisdictional variation in the organizational context of assigning criminal responsibility to juveniles emerges when prosecutors and judges reduce the initially selected population of eligible juvenile offenders.

Official perceptions of offense and offender seriousness are also influenced by variation in the nature and extent of crime and deviance in different types of jurisdiction. Officials routinely see a nastier list of offenders in the more densely populated counties of New York City than in the more rural parts of New York state. The historical review in Chapter 2 suggests that the problem of juvenile crime and justice was specific to large urban centers. The subway murders, media reports, and committee hearings were confined to New York City. Acts of deviance that are considered serious crimes in small towns may be considered trivial acts of crime in larger, more urbanized areas. For example, nearly all acts of murder in Buffalo attract considerable media attention from arrest to conviction, while in New York City only the most serious acts of lethal violence make it into the media. The daily act of murder in New York City allows officials, the public, and the media to distinguish between types of homicide so that only the most serious, usually involving strangers and theft, appear of general public interest. In Buffalo, no distinction is made in that all acts of murder are reported by the news media. Although all killings are serious acts of violence, their perceived severity by legal officials and the public is most likely a function of the frequency and location of occurrence.

Similarly, in jurisdictions where there are plenty of murders and rapes, the less serious designated C felonies, burglaries and assaults, are more likely to be redefined implicitly as non-JO offenses. In such cases, the label *juvenile offender* (JO) is resisted at both the arrest and prosecutorial stages of decision making. The police as well as prosecutors in those communities confine their assignment of criminal responsibility for juveniles to the most serious, JO offenses.

But contextual reasons for identifying juveniles as juvenile offenders do not negate the importance of legal categories. As previously noted, in the most serious acts of violence, such as murder, the response of officials is a more automatic one; there is nothing or little to negotiate in terms of the juvenile's status as offender. Extreme cases of violence produce little disagreement between the police, prosecutors, and judges within and between counties of jurisdiction on how charged juveniles should be adjudicated and sentenced. In other words, juveniles charged with subway murders are treated as serious offenders whether they are charged in high or low crime rate jurisdictions; pleas as to the juvenile's potential for treat-

ment in juvenile court are resisted because officials see no other choice
except to prosecute such juveniles as juvenile offenders.

Yet among a wide range of the eligible JO offenses, murder is an infre-
quent event. It is a capital offense for which juveniles cannot receive the
more benign Youthful Offender label. Therefore, the legal and organizational context of legal decision making is by law restricted by the principle
of offense. However, less serious JO offenses, such as incidents of rape,
robbery, and assault, which do not receive media attention in the densely
populated jurisdictions of New York City, require a less automatic response
that frequently avoids the assignment of criminal responsibility.

Moreover, the pool of violent offenses varies by location; that is, violent
crime is more prevalent in New York City than it is in less urbanized
sections of New York State. Officials see more violent juveniles in the Bronx
than they do in the less densely populated city of Buffalo. Not only do they
see more offenses, but there are more officials to identify and process
juvenile offender cases. For example, in the densely populated large counties of New York City, prosecutors specialize in charging juveniles arrested
for violent offenses as juvenile offenders. The staff and quantity of cases
allow for routine procedures to emerge for juveniles arrested for JO offenses in New York City, but not in smaller counties where JO offenses are
relatively rare events.

There are other contextual reasons for identifying juveniles as criminal
offenders besides those that can be attributed to size of jurisdiction. These
include the degree to which a community of officials exists in which decision makers at various stages of the criminal justice process act in concert
to label juveniles as offenders. In some jurisdictions, the local legal culture
may act more as a community than in others, producing fewer disparities in
case processing decisions and a more tightly coupled criminal justice system (Eisenstein, Flemming, & Nardulli 1988).

To repeat: It is not just offense and offender characteristics that drive
legal decision making but how those characteristics articulate with particular sets of legal officials. It is how the severity of offense and offender are
perceived among legal officials located in different counties of jurisdiction
at different stages in the criminal justice process that reflect the contextual
reasons for assigning criminal responsibility to juveniles.

Prior Research

Despite the formal judicial waiver hearing mandated in the Supreme
Court's 1966 *Kent* decision, systems of judicial waiver that originate in

juvenile court have been criticized as arbitrary because nonserious delinquents are too often brought into criminal court. Hamparian et al. (1982:
130) found that only 32 percent of judicial waivers in 1978 were for violent
offenses. Osbun and Rode (1984: 199) found that transferred juveniles in
Minnesota included many "juveniles whose records do not appear to be
very serious." They argued that juvenile court judges failed "to identify
many juveniles whose records are characterized by violent, frequent, and
persistent delinquent activity" (199). In Minnesota, Barry Feld (1990: 40–
1) found that offense seriousness and prior arrests explained very little (3
percent) of the variance in judicial waiver decisions. Drawing on a sample
of violent juvenile offenders in cities with judicial waiver statutes, Fagan
and Deschenes (1990: 348) noted that "judicial waiver statutes empower
the juvenile court judge to make a transfer decision without applying objective criteria." Based on his extensive review of waiver legislation, Feld (1987:
494) suggested that "judicial waiver statutes reveal all of the defects characteristic of individualized, discretionary sentencing schema."

The empirical research literature on judicial waiver has led Feld to
conclude further that the punishment-oriented objectives of waiver are best
met in states that have adopted legislative waiver reforms (1987: 511).
Bishop and Frazier (1991: 300) also suggest that one way to introduce
"greater equity and predictability to the transfer process would be to look to
the legislature to bring more offenses (or offense/prior-record combina-
tions) within the ambit of the legislative exclusion statute." But the conclusion that legislative waiver eliminates and reduces nonobjective sources of
judicial discretion is based largely on research in states with judicial waiver
procedures. Few studies exist on the implementation of legislative waiver.

As previously noted, legislative waiver does not eliminate official discretion in the initial classification of delinquents as offenders, and it may
duplicate other forms of discretionary decision making. The opportunity
to reduce the offense charges to non-JO offenses or to invoke a reverse
waiver procedure are the unique legal avenues in which the discretion of
juvenile justice officials can be replaced with that of criminal justice officials. If legislative waiver procedures merely shift the official sources of
discretion, then there is little that is automatic about the initial exclusion of
juveniles based on offense categories from the initial jurisdiction of juvenile court. In states with legislative waiver, criminal justice officials may be
just as arbitrary in their determination of criminal responsibility for juveniles as juvenile justice officials in states with judicial waiver. Indeed,
Thomas and Bilchik (1985: 479), in discussing Florida's prosecutorial system of waiver, warned that criminal court prosecutors may produce more

uncontrolled discretionary decisions for juveniles than juvenile justice officials. Similarly, Franklin Zimring (1991) argued that legislative forms of
waiver are no more equitable than judicial waiver procedures because they
merely "reallocate discretion, generally from a juvenile court judge to prosecutors or criminal court judges" (275).

Sources of Data

The story of implementation now begins with case processing data on
juvenile offenders in New York. But it is a story that is limited to available
data; as a consequence, it cannot test or even attempt to model all the
factors that are involved in the case processing of juveniles in juve-
nile/criminal justice systems.[1] Still, there is a process to be described and
analyzed. I begin with a brief overview of the criminal justice process for
juveniles in New York. Then I present qualitative data from recorded interviews with legal officials located in various jurisdictions of New York State. A
more representative sample of prosecutors is surveyed on the likelihood of
prosecuting juveniles as adults based on two types of offense and offender
situations. Finally, quantitative data on case processing decisions on the
indictment of juveniles as juvenile offenders in Buffalo is analyzed. My
consideration of the hypothesized contextual effects in case processing
decisions is examined in the next chapter with a larger set of state agency
data.

The Criminal Justice Process for Juveniles

The legal route in assigning criminal responsibility to juveniles begins with
an arrest.[2] A similar process is in place for adult offenders. There are
exceptions, however, such as the fact that police officers are required to
notify the parent or guardian of an arrested juvenile offender. Like adult
offenders, juveniles as offenders are fingerprinted and charged at central
booking. Then the arresting police officer describes to the prosecutor on
duty verbally and through the officer's paperwork the circumstances of the
charges and the availability of victims and witnesses. A "complaint" is generated only after the prosecutor and the arresting officer make an assessment
of "probable cause" based on available evidence and after they agree on the
charges to be brought before the criminal court. This assessment is not
purely discretionary; it is constrained by law and evidence.

The next step involves an "arraignment" hearing in which an eligible juvenile is charged and the facts of the case are briefly discussed to determine bail. If the juvenile is not in a position to receive or to make bail, then he or she is incarcerated in detention. Currently in New York State, an indictment by a grand jury must be presented within 6 days or else the juvenile is released from detention on recognizance.

As is the case with adult offenders, after the grand jury indicts, the case is then moved to trial court for the determination of a hearing date. At that point, there is usually a bench conference involving the prosecutor, the defense attorney, and the judge. The juvenile's plea of innocence or guilt is considered along with any considerations for the unique circumstances of the juvenile. At the hearing, the juvenile's defense counsel may argue that his client played a minor role in a group offense or that circumstances beyond the juvenile's control led to the offense. The defense counsel at times refers to the juvenile's need for treatment and might tell of the juvenile's troubled family situation. In turn, the prosecutor counters by relating, as required by statute, the severity of the crime, the injuries inflicted, prior record, and the general strength of the state's case.

Qualitative Data

Individualized justice and the particular characteristics of the juvenile are important for less serious JO offenses. When prosecutors are asked specifically what is the most important determinant of the removal process or the decision to charge a juvenile in criminal court, they speak first about offense seriousness and then about the juvenile's prior record. One senior prosecutor stated that offense seriousness is not always more important than prior record.

> When we deal with an offender, we look at his prior record, definitely. We then look at the seriousness of the crime. I don't mean to make some sort of firm priority there. If the crime is bad enough, the fact that he has no prior record is not going to prevent us from indicting him. However, if he does have a record that shows that he has beaten the system, or hasn't profited, the crime could be less serious and he may be indicted.

Prosecutors, in assigning criminal responsibility to juveniles, place JO offenses on serious and nonserious processing tracks. They do not use the word *nonserious* to describe any JO offense but instead the term *ordinary*. Murder and rape fall on a more serious track within the list of JO offenses because they are considered *extraordinary* offenses. In the words of one prosecutor:

> In the ordinary case, when I say ordinary case, it is that case which does not constitute a specific exception: murder, sodomy 1, rape 1, and an armed felony in which the gun is actually operable. If it isn't one of those, then the legislature said the DA alone can now ask for the removal, not the defendant and not the criminal court judge. And the court must grant it if it is in the interests of justice to do so.

It is easier to avoid assigning criminal responsibility to juveniles when the offense is an ordinary JO offense. For extraordinary JO offenses, processing in criminal court is still not necessarily automatic. If prosecutors seek to avoid criminal court for juveniles arrested for extraordinary designated felonies, they must list the set of mitigating circumstances that in their opinion do not mandate criminal court conviction. They then can remove the juvenile's case to juvenile court where the juvenile is charged as a delinquent. But the decision to remove a juvenile's case to juvenile court is technically that of the prosecutor and the criminal court judge. They must agree to the conditions of removal. However, the JO law provides no clear and absolute guidelines as to which eligible juveniles should be removed to juvenile court or sentenced as adults in criminal court.

In ordinary cases – the JO offenses which do not involve murder, rape, or robbery with a weapon – prosecutors look at case circumstances beyond the characteristics of the offense. Officials consider the arrested juvenile's family background and parental support. This is not only the case at the prosecutorial stage but also at the sentencing stage. In recommending incarceration or probation, prosecutors stress that the convicted JO's family background is important.

> We look to see if a JO seems to have a strong supportive family unit. Where there is some potential for rehabilitation from the family unit, then we might consider that as opposed to an individual that is on his own. We have to look at what the ultimate purpose is going to be.

Yet family background is not the only personal characteristic that allows officials to go beyond the offense-related circumstances attached to a JO's case. Officials also like to consider the general demeanor of the JO and how that might influence legal decision making. According to one criminal court judge in the Bronx:

> What counts most is the appearance of these juveniles. Kids who really look like little kids are not likely to be brought to criminal court. I may react with

surprise as to the size of the youth particularly in relation to sentencing adult offenders who are considerably older, tougher looking, and with a much longer sentencing history.

The judge's statement illustrates the importance of age-related characteristics to criminal justice decision making. Although the set of cases may change at each step in the criminal justice process, some juvenile offenders maintain certain adolescent characteristics that readily distinguish them from older, adult offenders – namely, they appear too young to warrant prosecution in criminal court. Moreover, younger juveniles have a shorter chronological time span than older juveniles in which to accumulate a criminal record. For example, in contrast to a younger, 14-year-old juvenile, a 15-year-old juvenile has one more year in which to accumulate JO arrests.

But personal appearance counts in other ways as well, according to one prosecutor:

> I think it is somewhat telling of a person who comes in with a white shirt and a tie who has at least taken that effort to show some respect for the court as opposed to someone who comes in a ripped-up tee shirt and jeans who shows no respect.

If juveniles are less wise than their adult counterparts as to the best way to dress or act for success, then younger offenders may be subject to more harsh penalties than older ones.

As is the case with adult offenders, decision making depends on more than just a few variables. The quality of evidence and legal representation is commonly cited as a factor in case processing decisions. Older, private attorneys appear more willing to negotiate a plea than younger attorneys assigned through the offices of legal aid. Indigent juvenile offenders can be assigned a private attorney who is paid by the state on an hourly basis if there are no available legal aid attorneys. These attorneys are referred to as *18B attorneys*.

> You will see a lot of 18B attorneys and private attorneys more willing to take a plea than the legal aid attorneys. Many of them [legal aid] are young and starting out and they relish in getting involved in legal issues and in many cases, dragging cases on. Dragging them on longer than they really should be because they see a legal issue that they want to litigate and perhaps lose the real focus of the case.

In other words, the quality and type of legal representation can make it more or less difficult to assign criminal responsibility to juveniles as well as to adults.

But recall that the context of legal decision making may vary by jurisdictional and temporal characteristics. Some prosecutors refer to this as the gray area of the law; they involve situations where there is no clear-cut answer as to whether the juvenile should be processed as a juvenile offender instead of as a juvenile delinquent. One chief prosecutor noted that case processing decisions depend more on particular courts and officials and less on the stated legal requirements.

> The only thing that is certain is that the rule may be different tomorrow as far as what people do because the black letter law is itself very vague, but how it's interpreted and how it's put into practice changes from court to court and even sometimes within the court depending on the personnel.

In other words, there is opportunity for legal discretion in that the black letter of the law as interpreted by criminal justice officials is indeed vague.

In conclusion, interviews with officials reveal part of the reasons for the JO law's implementation. They tell of a social as well as a legal construction of criminal responsibility that falls along lines that distinguish types of JO offenses and types of juvenile offenders. Murder and rape fall into serious, extraordinary offense categories, while other designated felony offenses are in a less serious category. But other substantive sources of legal decision making enter case processing decisions. These include the background and personal characteristics of juvenile offenders. Of critical importance is prior offense. Parental support, physical appearance, quality of legal representation, and the best interests of justice all were mentioned as producing a complex picture of decision making that is sometimes more rather than less routine.

Surveyed Perceptions of Offense Seriousness and Prior Arrests

To tap into several critical elements that entered the decision making process for prosecutors, I sent a one-page questionnaire by mail in 1985 to the district attorney (DA) in each of New York State's sixty-two counties. I wanted to know the extent to which prior arrests and the extent of injury inflicted upon victims influenced prosecutorial decisions to define juveniles as offenders in criminal court. DAs were asked to evaluate the likelihood of prosecution based on an 11-point scale (11 indicates very likely while 1 very unlikely) for two types of JO offenses (see Appendix B for questionnaire). Responses were returned by forty-five DA offices; the letter was addressed to the DA, but it said that his or her representative could respond to the items. The DAs who did not return the questionnaire were from smaller upstate counties in which JO cases are relatively rare. DAs in each of the five counties in New York City responded to the survey. On average, surveyed DAs indicated they had 9 years of experience and were 41 years of age. The youngest DA was 24, and the oldest 54.

In keeping with my promise not to identify a respondent's county of jurisdiction, I present only the aggregated results of my analysis of surveyed responses. The first incident for which DAs were asked to evaluate the likelihood of criminal court prosecution consisted of a lethal stabbing of one juvenile by another juvenile.

> A juvenile is accused of stabbing another youth with a knife. As a result, the victim dies. The juvenile claims that the victim was mistakenly assumed to be someone who had earlier threatened the juvenile's life.

The number of prior arrests is varied to estimate the likelihood of prosecution based on the juvenile's first, third, or sixth arrest.

The second incident consisted of a robbery with a knife in which the victim is injured:

> A juvenile steals an elderly woman's purse, with the threat of a knife. In the process, she is knocked to the ground. Upon arrest the juvenile claims that the victim's injuries were not intended.

The extent of harm inflicted is varied to reflect the severity of the offense. The first scenario is one in which the elderly victim suffered minor bruises and required no medical attention. In the second situation, the elderly victim experienced a broken arm and overnight hospitalization. In the third and final situation, the elderly victim received extensive injuries in which a complex fracture necessitated hospitalization for a period of 6 months.

Figure 4.1 displays the mean ratings for the first surveyed incident involving the murder of a juvenile by another juvenile. If it was the juvenile's first offense, several prosecutors indicated that they were uncertain about charging the juvenile as an adult in criminal court. However, the majority of prosecutors (58 percent) were very likely to charge the juvenile as an adult in criminal court even for the juvenile's first offense. This certainty increased from 9.9 to 10.8 for juveniles with two previous arrests. Only seven prosecutors gave scores of less than 11 if it was the juvenile's third arrest. For juveniles who had five previous arrests, the rating of prosecutors was unanimous: all indicated that they were very likely to charge the juvenile as an adult in criminal court.

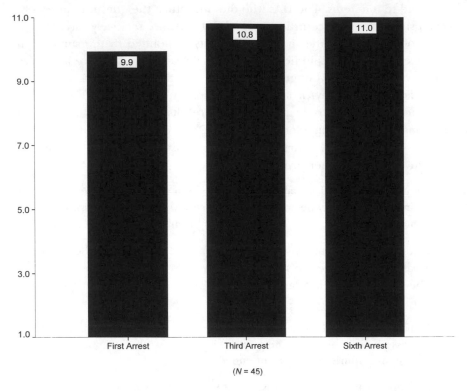

(N = 45)

Figure 4.1. Mean Perceived Likelihood of Prosecution by Prior Arrests

The second incident, in which the extent of injuries inflicted upon the victim varied from minor to serious physical harm, produced greater differences in the likelihood of prosecuting juveniles in criminal court. The second incident is comparable to robbery in the first degree. Moreover, the victim is a senior citizen, which would further heighten the seriousness of the act. Still there was some difference in the likelihood of prosecution based on the extent of injury inflicted upon the victim. Where there is minor injury to the victim, 29 percent of the DAs said they were very likely to prosecute in criminal court; that is, 13 DAs scored the incident as 11 (very likely). Figure 4.2 presents the mean values by type of injury. The average ranking produced a mean score of 9 for minor in contrast to 9.6 for major injury (overnight hospitalization) and 10.4 for 6-month hospitalization. In cases of 6-month hospitalization for the elderly victim, 70 percent of the DAs said they would prosecute the juvenile in criminal court.

Although the two offenses surveyed technically qualify as JO offenses,

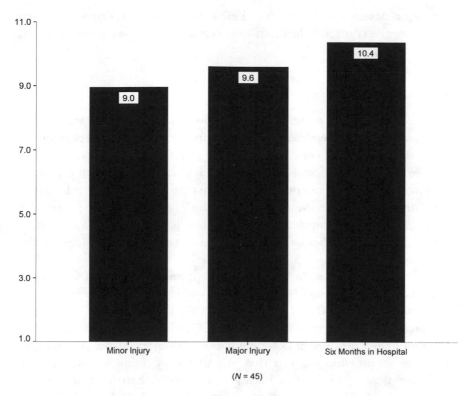

Figure 4.2. Mean Perceived Likelihood of Prosecution by Type of Injury

prosecutors are more likely to believe that juveniles should be treated as adults when they repeat their offenses or commit very serious injuries to their victims. Of course, the crime scenarios do not reflect accurately the detailed information that is readily available to criminal justice officials in their routine preparation of criminal charges. The cases that DAs handle are more complex than that which is presented in briefly stated crime scenarios. Furthermore, the results of the analysis may have looked different if prior arrests were tabulated for the incident involving a purse-snatching with a knife. In other words, I have treated both scenarios as if they are independent events when they clearly are not.

In deciding which cases should be sent where, DAs who responded to the survey appeared to give more weight to prior arrest information. Prior arrests may be interpreted as just another way of determining the moral character and dangerousness of hypothesized juvenile offenders. However, such information is routinely available to criminal justice officials only for the prior designated felonies of eligible juveniles. The extent to which prior juvenile court adjudications are accessed by criminal justice officials remains unclear.

Grand Jury Referrals

I now consider actual prosecutorial decision making at an early stage in the criminal justice process. Between September 1, 1978 and December 31, 1985, the Buffalo city court recorded 103 juvenile offender arrests. As we will see in the next chapter, Buffalo, which is part of Erie County, produced relatively few juvenile offender arrests. The rate of juvenile offender arrest is relatively low in non–New York City counties. Moreover, the proportion of arrested juveniles convicted in Erie County is also relatively low, leading me to focus on predictors of decision making at an early stage in the criminal justice process.

From the case files of Buffalo's arrested juvenile offenders, I was able to code as independent variables three non–offense- and two offense-related characteristics to predict the prosecutor's decision to indict juveniles as criminal offenders. I view the presence of both parents in the juvenile's household as a measure of potential parental support. Matza's doctrine of parental sponsorship suggests that juveniles who reside in single-parent households are perceived as having less support than juveniles in two-parent households and therefore are at greater risk of being labeled as offenders. The race of the juvenile should also be related to indictment decisions especially if minorities are viewed as subject to less support than majority youth.

Legally relevant variables are the extent of injuries inflicted on the victim(s) by the offender and prior felony arrests. Injuries are coded on an ordinal scale ranging in value from 1 to 5 (1 = no injuries, 2 = minor injuries, 3 = treated and discharged, 4 = hospitalization, and 5 = death). Prior offenses are measured by the offender's number of previously re-corded arrests.

Finally, I consider an additional indicator of trouble: whether the juvenile's arrest and name were publicized in either of Buffalo's two daily newspapers that existed at the time (0 = no; 1 = yes). Recall that arrested juvenile offenders are not protected by the juvenile court's traditional requirement of confidentiality. I expect the presence of publicity to relate to the perceived severity of offenses, and to affect the prosecutor's initial decision to charge juveniles as adults.

Table 4.1. Descriptive Statistics for Buffalo Case Processing Data (N = 103)

	Mean	Standard Deviation (SD)
Independent Variables		
Race (1 Non white)	.77	.42
Injuries (1 to 5)	2.56	1.13
Parental Status (1 single)	.85	.36
Prior Arrest (1 prior)	.54	.50
Media (1 publicity)	.48	.50
Dependent Variable		
Grand Jury Referral (1 Grand Jury)	.50	.50

Variable coding in parentheses.

The Characteristics of Arrested Juvenile Offenders in Buffalo. Table 4.1 displays the characteristics of arrested juvenile offenders in Buffalo. Half of arrested juvenile offenders faced indictment by the grand jury, which must take place prior to a conviction in criminal court. The descriptive statistics for the juveniles initially charged as juvenile offenders further show that the majority (77 percent) of charged juveniles are nonwhite, and 85 percent reside in one-parent households. The extent of injuries inflicted upon their victims on average was minor, not requiring the victim's hospitalization. Most of the charged juveniles had a prior arrest, and nearly half had their names publicized in the newspaper along with the JO offense.

Logistic estimates (see Table 4.2) are computed to determine the relative importance of offense and offender characteristics on the prosecutor's referral of eligible juveniles to the grand jury.[3] Missing values reduced the total number of cases to 65. Based on the coefficient to its standard error, there are two variables that are significant predictors of the prosecutor's referral of a juvenile offender to the grand jury: parental status and extent of injuries to the victim. The coefficients for these variables are more than twice their standard error (indicating that they are significant at below the .05 level). The negative effect of parental status reflects the greater likelihood that juveniles from single-parent homes will be referred to the grand jury. The exp (1.996) = 7.36 means that juveniles residing in single-parent households are seven times more likely than juveniles from two-parent households to be referred to the grand jury. The effect of parental marital status reduces the effect of race on grand jury referrals, which would be significant if parental status were not controlled.

The extent of injuries is the only offense-related variable that is statistically significant. The exp (.526) means that for each unit increase in the

Table 4.2. Logistic Estimates of Grand Jury Referrals

Variables	Homicide (N = 65)	Non-Homicide (N = 62)
Race	-.329 (.756)	-.212 (.763)
Parental Status	1.996* (.868)	2.088* (.905)
Extent of Injuries	.526* (.269)	.412 (.289)
Prior Arrest	.663 (.586)	.558 (.593)
Media	.279 (.566)	.173 (.572)
Constant	-.462	-.326
Log Likelihood	152.112	149.424

* P > .05.
Standard errors are in parentheses.

severity of injuries inflicted on their victims, juveniles are 1.7 more likely to be referred to the grand jury.

The effects of prior felony arrest and media coverage are not significant. When the three juvenile offender cases involving homicide are excluded from the analysis, the effect of offense seriousness is no longer significant. The only statistically significant predictor of grand jury referral for non-homicide cases is the number of parents in the juvenile offender's household.

In these logistic regressions, parental status (a non–offense-related variable) is the most important determinant of the prosecutor's decision to refer eligible juveniles to the grand jury. Based on the initial processing of juveniles arrested for serious offenses, the data analysis for Buffalo supports the view that parental support is one way to assess moral character and to assign criminal responsibility to juveniles. In Buffalo, non–offense-related considerations are not eliminated by legislative or automatic forms of waiver. Rather, legislative waiver at the stage of indictment in Buffalo appears to replace some of the discretionary decisions of juvenile justice officials with those of criminal justice officials.

The above findings are compatible with other multivariate research on the case processing of juveniles in contemporary juvenile court. Mark Jacobs (1990) used a multivariate analysis of juvenile court dispositions and found that the strongest predictor of out-of-home placement is parental marital status. He concluded that juveniles "from nontraditional families and children living apart from their parents are at risk of out-of-home placement entirely out of proportion to the risk of recidivism they pose" (Jacobs 1990: 216).

The absence of the possible effect of the media may be a consequence of the more insulated quality of initial decisions at the grand jury stage and how the media variable was coded. I did not provide a measure of the extent of total media coverage. The measure I used was based on newspapers and not on television news, which has a larger audience. Still, the effect of parental status suggests that aspects of individualized justice follow juveniles into the adult criminal justice system. Despite legislative attempts to accomplish the reverse by getting tough on juvenile crime, substantive justice reemerges in the decision making of criminal justice officials. The effect of parental support on Buffalo's initial assignment of criminal responsibility in the form of a grand jury referral provides partial support for the argument that legislative waiver reproduces substantive sources of legal discretion among criminal justice officials (e.g., Zimring 1991).

Prosecutors in Erie County might be correct in their assessment that juveniles in single-parent households are more at risk of trouble than those from dual-parent households. In either case, the significance of parental status and the insignificance of other variables suggest that waiver legislation was implemented in Buffalo in ways that are less determined by the principle of offense and more a consequence of individualized justice.

Conclusion

The reasons for identifying juveniles as criminal offenders are embedded in a complex criminal justice process. They are based on official assessments of offense and offender seriousness for juveniles charged with JO offenses. Such assessments look to the characteristics of the offense and offender as expected in criminal court as well as in traditional juvenile court. In deciding the criminal responsibility of juveniles, the technically more formal procedures of criminal justice officials appear, however, to duplicate the same substantive sources of justice that prior analyses have noted about juvenile justice decision making.

The qualitative data tell of the importance of offense seriousness and individualized justice for officials located in the larger urban jurisdictions within New York State. The Buffalo data point to the importance of individualized justice at one stage in the criminal justice process in one county of jurisdiction. By themselves, these data are of limited value, for they tell us nothing about the assessments of officials at different stages of the criminal justice process in different counties of jurisdiction. It is impossible to see with the Buffalo data inter- and intrajurisdictional variation in the assignment of criminal responsibility to juveniles. From whose standpoint can we say that Buffalo's rate of convicting arrested juvenile offenders in criminal court is high or low?

Other sources of data are needed to determine the degree to which there is inter- and intrajurisdictional variation in the assignment of criminal responsibility to juveniles. In the next chapter, I will examine if the individualized sources of justice in waiver decision are unique to one stage in the criminal justice process and to one particular county of jurisdiction.

The Case Processing
of Juvenile Offenders:
From Arrest to Disposition

THE TASK OF ASSIGNING CRIMINAL RESPONSIBILITY to juveniles takes place within systems of criminal justice. Defining a population of juveniles as offenders instead of as delinquents depends on the jurisdictional and temporal location of criminal justice officials. The implementation of the JO law's legal rules is based on more than just what is technically stated as a JO offense and an eligible juvenile offender. Case processing decisions require the police to make arrests, prosecutors to charge juveniles as adult offenders, and judges to determine the type and length of sentence.

In this chapter, I stress that the assignment of criminal responsibility to juveniles is often independent of offense severity and the personal characteristics of juveniles. Who is arrested, convicted, and incarcerated as a juvenile offender reflects temporal and jurisdictional contexts that go beyond the individual characteristics of a JO case. There is an organizational context that is rooted in the practical concerns and interests of officials to produce what Emerson (1991) refers to as "organizational contingencies." To see the concerns and interests of legal decision makers is to see "a construction that decision-makers themselves use in assessing and showing the practical rationality of specific decisions" (Emerson 1991: 210). For example, in some jurisdictions the police may not want to arrest every juvenile as a juvenile offender for every eligible C felony offense, because they know that prosecutors will routinely dismiss such offenses as not worthy of charges in criminal court. Similarly, prosecutors in certain jurisdictions may not be interested in seeing the charges they make against juvenile offenders routinely rejected by grand juries or dismissed by criminal court judges. In other words, the decision making of one set of criminal justice officials depends in part on the behavior of another set of officials. The criminal justice process in this sense operates as a system of justice in that what the police do influences prosecutors, and similarly what prosecutors do with their cases influences future police arrests (Feeley & Lazerson 1983).

Moreover, decision making takes place in a dynamic criminal justice process where the concerns and interests of officials are subject to change. The JO law is subject to interpretation. Like other criminal justice reforms, it provides opportunities for the official use of discretion in deciding which juveniles are technically criminal offenders. To repeat the words of one prosecutor quoted in the previous chapter:

> The only thing that is certain is that the rule may be different tomorrow as far as what people do because the black letter law is itself very vague, but how it's interpreted and how it's put into practice changes from court to court and even sometimes within the court depending on the personnel.

This does not mean that legal decision making on the status of juvenile offenders is a random process. Rather, political and organizational concerns and interests suggest why the black letter of the law may be more or less vague to one group of officials in contrast to another. Moreover, the advantages of treating eligible juvenile offenders in juvenile court instead of criminal court are not visible based solely on the attributes of a particular case.

Matza notes the organizational context of juvenile justice decision making when he further qualifies the decision making of juvenile justice with the additional doctrine of "residential availability." Like the doctrine of "parental sponsorship," residential availability explains why some juveniles are incarcerated and others are not. When all else is considered equal, the decision to invoke a last-resort sanction, such as incarceration, is qualified in the following way:

> Let us suppose that the judge is faced with a particular case in which choice between probation and prison is exceedingly difficult. In such a case, he may reason that, since the residential facilities are already vastly overcrowded, no purpose would be served by sending yet another juvenile there. The offender would not be helped and the services to the juveniles already in prison would be reduced by the additional client. Thus, the judge is given guidance by the doctrine of residential availability (Matza 1964: 127).

That is, an overcrowded residential facility makes it less desirable to sentence juveniles to custody; therefore probation becomes the more attractive legal alternative. It is not the objective characteristics of the juvenile's case per se that determines his or her incarceration but an organizational contingency in the form of residential space that partially determines incarceration.

Matza's arguments are not confined to decision making in a traditional juvenile justice system. It applies to another juvenile justice last-resort sanction in terms of waiver to criminal court. A shift in the county's cost of incarcerating juvenile offenders may provide the additional organizational incentive for defining juveniles as offenders instead of as delinquents. Recall that in 1983 and subsequent years after, the proportional cost to counties of jurisdiction for incarcerating juvenile offenders gradually increased. As a consequence, officials may have had less of an incentive not only to incarcerate convicted juvenile offenders but also to arrest and convict eligible juveniles as offenders.

Residential availability is just one kind of organizational contingency. There are other contextual aspects of juvenile/criminal justice decision making that influence the waiver of juveniles to criminal court. If juvenile courts in one jurisdiction are seen as a more effective alternative to criminal court for eligible juvenile offenders, then fewer eligible juveniles may be defined as offenders. Such jurisdictions are more likely to see the offenses of eligible juveniles more as acts of delinquency than acts of crime. But again there is no single body of officials that dictates how the black or gray letter of the JO law will be followed.

Also juvenile/criminal justice systems require officials to work in tandem with each other in defining and redefining an eligible population of juvenile offenders. If the police arrest lots of juveniles for a wide range of eligible JO offenses, then they will say they are following the letter of the JO law. Every juvenile they see in the act of any C felony, such as second degree robbery, is booked as a juvenile offender. Similarly, if prosecutors take that same population of arrested juvenile offenders and essentially rubber-stamp the arresting officers' decision, then there is a tight fit between the actions of prosecutors and arresting officers. Finally, if every eligible juvenile arrested for any JO offense is convicted and incarcerated, then officials operate in an even more tightly coupled criminal justice system. In such a system, there is little disagreement between legislators, police officers, prosecutors, and judges in the kinds and types of juveniles who should be arrested, convicted, and incarcerated as juvenile offenders.

On the other hand, if there is considerable disagreement between legal decision makers, then officials are acting as autonomous agents (Emerson 1991). The decisions of one set of officials are loosely coupled with the decisions of another set of officials. If few juveniles who actually commit juvenile offender offenses are arrested and booked as adult offenders, then there is a loose fit between the JO law and what police officials do in enforcing its legal provisions. Similarly, if few juvenile offenders are charged in criminal court, then the decision making of the police is loosely coupled with that of prosecutors. Finally, if judges disagree with the recommendations of prosecutors by incarcerating few convicted juvenile offenders, then the system is further operating in a loosely coupled manner. In short, when officials do more than just rubber stamp each other's decisions, there is variation in the types of offenses for which criminal responsibility can be assigned to juveniles and in the kinds of sentences that can be inflicted upon convicted juvenile offenders.

I do not have the kind of data that allows me to examine all the possible organizational contingencies that go into legal decision making for juvenile offenders. Nor do I have direct measures of tightly and loosely coupled systems of criminal justice. Instead, I suggest that some counties of jurisdiction operate in a more tightly coupled manner than others based on their rates of arrest, conviction, and incarceration. I draw on multivariate techniques of analysis to see if jurisdictional and temporal attributes are independent of offense and offender characteristics.

I begin by describing the state agency data collected by the New York State Division of Criminal Justice Services (DCJS).[1] I then use these data to analyze variation in the assignment of criminal responsibility to juveniles at the arrest, conviction, and dispositional stages of legal decision making. These data are finally supplemented with other state agency data to highlight the organizational reasons for defining juveniles as juvenile offenders.

State Agency Data

In 1985 DCJS provided me with a data tape of its recorded case processing decisions for arrested juvenile offenders. Between September 1, 1978 (when the JO law took effect) and May 30, 1985 (the time when the data were produced as a result of my request), approximately 10,000 juveniles under the age of 16 were arrested and charged as juvenile offenders. At the time, I did not know how valuable the DCJS data would be as the only currently available source of information on the case processing of a very large and relatively young population of juveniles initially waived into the adult criminal justice system. Unfortunately, upon requesting a more recent, updated set of DCJS data in 1992, I was informed that since 1986, DCJS purged the records of arrested juvenile offenders after removal to juvenile court (letter from Marjorie Cohen of DCJS, April 21, 1992). A more current data set then would contain only a fraction of the arrested population of juvenile offenders – that is, those juveniles convicted in criminal court. It would preclude with individual level data an analysis of legal discretion at the police and prosecutorial stages of decision making.

Still, there are serious disadvantages in working with state agency data. They contain few legal and organizational variables of interest. For example, the available DCJS set of data contains no information on whether juveniles reside with one or two parents. This might be considered a serious limitation, especially if we bear in mind that in the previous chapter the marital status of the juvenile's parents is a significant predictor of the grand jury's decision to indict juveniles as offenders. There is also limited information on offense seriousness and other legally relevant variables, such as the quality of the evidence or legal representation. The DCJS data tell us nothing about the role that the juvenile played in a group offense. Nor is there information on the victim–offender relationship, which has been found to be a significant predictor of criminal justice decision making (e.g., LaFree 1989).

Although the DCJS data lack information on the juvenile's family situation, the basic personal characteristics of juveniles are contained in the coded race, age, and gender of juvenile offenders. I assume that these variables provide indirect measures of individualized justice. For example, in the Buffalo data I noted that race is correlated with the likelihood of residing in a single-parent household. Legal decision making that may lead to the juvenile offender label and harsher penalties for minority youth may not be as a consequence of race per se but of the degree of support or parental sponsorship that is attached to the race of juveniles.

The same can be said for age and gender. As noted in the qualitative data, I expect younger juveniles to be viewed as more deserving of treatment and less deserving of criminal punishment. Again, age is only an indirect measure of the degree to which some juveniles appear more as children than as adults; that is, some 14-year-olds look older than 15-year-olds. I also expect gender to relate to individualized justice, because girls are more often viewed as in greater need of treatment and the more benign dispositions of juvenile justice (Chesney-Lind & Shelden 1992: 130).

To measure offense seriousness, I reconfigured the offense-based arrest file to produce an offender file with measures of offense seriousness and prior offenses. The multiple arrest charges attached to each juvenile offender arrest produced my measure of offense seriousness. To measure prior arrests I used the New York State Identification number (NYSID) attached to each arrested juvenile offender to determine whether he or she had a prior juvenile offender arrest. The DCJS data contain information on the type of adjudication and disposition as well as the minimum and maximum length of sentence.[2]

To measure the organizational context of legal decision making by aggregating jurisdictional and temporal indicators of case processing decisions, I first display several measures of the characteristics of counties as an indicator of jurisdictional context. In the multivariate analysis, I then use the population size of county as one indicator of jurisdictional characteristics, producing separate analyses for New York City (NYC) and non–NYC counties. Jurisdictional characteristics are also measured by aggregating each county's rates of arrest severity, criminal court convictions, and length of sentence. The rates are based on case processing decisions for juvenile offenders as computed with the DCJS data. I assume that they reflect one aspect of the organizational contingencies that officials deal with in their case processing decisions. For instance, I expect the mean offense severity of arrest to be related to the rate of conviction, type of disposition, and sentence length.

In presenting the bivariate and multivariate correlates of case processing decisions, I am limited by the number of available variables in the DCJS data. I do not claim to model the complex set of determinants that produce populations of juveniles waived to criminal court. More exact models of legal decision making in the assignment of criminal responsibility will need to await the development of more complete sets of data.

Arrests

I first examined the penal law code numbers attached to each arrest record to ascertain the most serious offense. Researchers typically reduce an incident of crime to the most serious offense charged. This follows the recommended procedure in the Uniform Crime Reporting (UCR) Handbook. The most common JO offenses are displayed in Figure 5.1. They show that most arrests are for robberies in the first and second degree. They constitute over two-thirds of the 9,937 recorded JO arrests. Most robberies in the first degree are incidents in which juveniles are charged with injuring or threatening the victim with a weapon, such as a gun or a knife. The less serious category of robbery in the second degree refers to incidents in which the offender possessed a weapon but did not use it or threaten to use it against the victim.

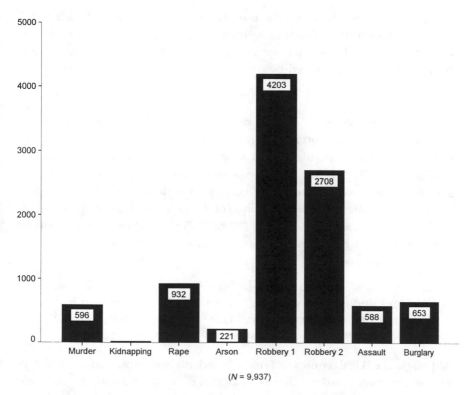

Figure 5.1. Arrest Frequencies for Offense Categories

After robbery the next most common charge is rape/sodomy. Although rape/sodomy offenses constitute a substantially smaller proportion of the UCR index categories of violent offenses, they represent 9 percent of all JO arrests. The fact that the bulk of JO arrest charges are for the most serious categories of JO offenses is reflected in homicide charges. Based on Figure 5.1 the reader might mistakenly assume that murder is as common a juvenile crime as assault and burglary, which is of course not the case. Rather, the distribution of offenses reflects police arrest decisions to charge juveniles as adult offenders for the most serious offense charges. However, offense charges also reflect the legal requirements of the JO law. In New York, juveniles cannot be assigned criminal responsibility for offenses unless they are charged with serious categories of robbery, assault, and burglary. That is, while all robberies in the first degree are designated felonies, not all legal categories of robbery in the second degree are offenses for which juveniles can be assigned criminal responsibility. Although the distribution of offenses is based on the most serious offense charge, incidents of violence more often than not contain several offense charges. These charges are included for an overall measure of the severity of an arrest because they are considered by prosecutors and judges in their case processing decisions.

Offense Seriousness. As critical reviews of official crime statistics have long argued, it is important to go beyond the legal categories and to consider the multitude of charges attached to each arrest (e.g., Sellin & Wolfgang 1964). To count the seriousness of crime, I noted that researchers traditionally have drawn on the UCR definition of what constitutes an index offense. In their critique of the measurement of crime based on legal categories, Wolfgang et al. (1985: 132) relate the manner in which crime is counted based on the following incident drawn from the UCR's recording handbook:

> A holdup man forces a husband and his wife to get out of their automobile. He shoots the husband, gun whips and rapes the wife (hospitalized) and leaves in the automobile (recovered later) after taking money ($100) from the husband. The husband dies as a result of the shooting.

Although the UCR counts offenses based on the most serious offense charges, criminal justice officials in practice rarely deal with a single offense. They often consider from arrest to disposition a multitude of offense charges. In doing so, they draw on the complex elements of an incident to prepare their cases. Prosecutors in the above incident would not restrict their decision making to the UCR category of homicide. They would also consider charging offenders with the acts of rape, assault, and theft.

By employing the UCR procedure of counting only the most serious offense category, researchers frequently miss the other elements of a crime that are routinely associated with case processing decisions, such as the rape and theft in the above incident. To produce a more sensitive measure of offense seriousness, I totaled all the offense charges to provide a measure of arrest seriousness. My measure of arrest seriousness is a composite measure that weights the offense charges by the total severity of all arrest charges. The weights are derived from ratio scores produced in the National Crime Severity Survey (NCSS) (Wolfgang et al. 1985). The NCSS scores are based on a 1977 survey of approximately 60,000 persons that was conducted as a supplement to the annual National Crime Survey of victimization.

The weights assigned to the various designated felony offense charges are listed in Appendix C. Based on the NCSS ratio score attached to an incident in which "a person stabs a victim to death," a homicide is coded as having a value of 36. Manslaughter is 28 using the NCSS description for a wife killing her spouse. Attempted murder is scored at 19 based on an NCSS incident in which

> a person intentionally shoots a victim with a gun. The victim requires treatment by a doctor but not hospitalization (Wolfgang et al. 1985: 49).

Other JO offense charges are similarly weighted based on the NCSS ratio scores to derive a total measure of offense seriousness.

Yet the NCSS ratio scores are based on a surveyed dimension of offense severity. Other dimensions of offense severity include the stated punishment attached to various offense charges and the perceived severity of crime among prosecutors rather than among the general public. However, the research on offense seriousness weighting suggests that there is considerable convergence in the popular public view and the official view of offense seriousness (Wolfgang et al., 1985). Moreover, when I measured offense seriousness, according to the ordinal legal categories of A, B, and C felony designations, the results are similar to that of my interval level measure based on the NCSS ratio scores.

I prefer the NCSS transformed scores to measure variation in severity within the ordinal legal categories of felony offenses. The NCSS weights capture a dimension of seriousness that says a B felony charge of rape is more serious than a B felony charge of burglary. With an ordinal level of coding, both the rape and burglary offenses would receive weights of 2, while with the NCSS ratio scores, the rape would be more heavily weighted than the burglary. To repeat, my internal measure of offense seriousness from this point on is based on the *weighted total* arrest charges, not just the most serious incident. But in illustrating bivariate relationships between case outcomes and the various variables of interest, I will look at the most serious felony level of offense charges.

Offender Characteristics. Most juveniles arrested as juvenile offenders are nonwhite boys. The average age of arrest is slightly over 15. Only 732 of the 9,937 juveniles arrested as juvenile offenders are girls. Over two-thirds of arrested JOs are black juveniles. Slightly more Hispanic juveniles are arrested as juvenile offenders than white juveniles – 1,573 compared to 1,513. The overrepresentation of minority youth in the population of arrested juvenile offenders is not surprising based on UCR arrest data.

There is considerable variation in the types of offenses for which juve-

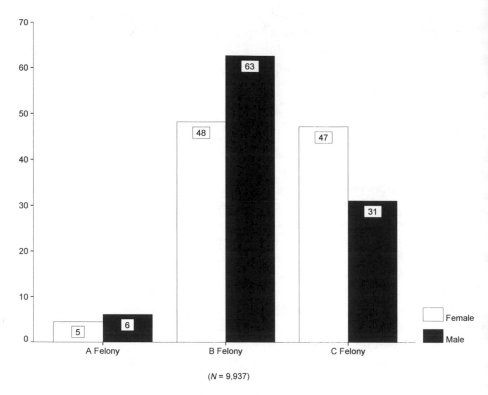

(N = 9,937)

Figure 5.2. Felony Type by Gender in Percents

niles are charged by race and gender. Figure 5.2 shows that girls are more
often charged with C felonies, while boys are charged more often with B
felonies. Note that class A felonies are the most serious crimes on the book,
and class C felonies are less serious than class B felonies. For example, first
degree robbery is a class B felony while second degree robbery is a class C
felony. For the most serious category of offenses, class A felonies, there is
only a slight difference in the percent of boys and girls charged.

Variation in the type of arrest charges for B and C categories of offense
may represent differences not only in the incidence of behavior but also in
the decision making of officials. With the available data, I cannot tell if the
type and seriousness of arrest charges is a reflection of the actual incidence
of designated felony offenses or a tendency on the part of officials to
charge males with more serious offenses.

Figure 5.3 shows that black juveniles are more often charged with less
serious juvenile offender offenses than white and Hispanic juveniles. The

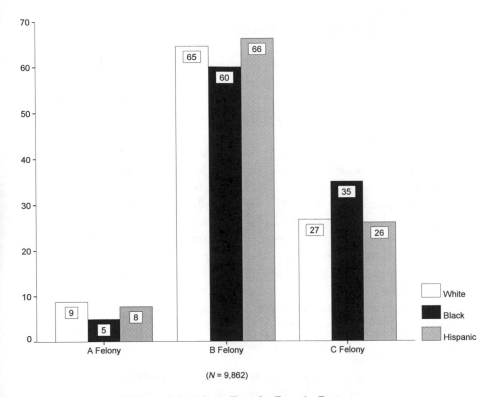

(*N* = 9,862)

Figure 5.3. Felony Type by Race in Percents

largest difference in the percent arrested emerges in the C felony category. C felonies are the most serious arrest charge for 27 percent of white juveniles and 26 percent of Hispanic juveniles, while they are the most serious charge for 35 percent of black juveniles. In contrast, 9 percent of white juveniles are charged with A felonies compared to 5 percent of black juveniles.

The most feasible explanation for the greater representation of black juveniles in less serious juvenile offender offenses is that officials are less inclined to assign criminal responsibility to white and Hispanic juveniles. There is no reason to believe that white and Hispanic juveniles commit more violent offenses than blacks. Rather, the categorical data in Figure 5.3 provides convincing evidence that the reasons for charging juveniles as juvenile offenders are not based only on offense severity. This is further confirmed by the interval level seriousness scores for white and black juveniles. The mean severity of arrests for white juveniles is 20.1 compared to

18.7 for black juveniles. In other words, if white juveniles enter the criminal justice process as juvenile offenders, it is for the more serious violent offenses.

As an additional measure of offender characteristics, I recoded prior JO arrests. The NYSID numbers attached to each case record allowed me to sort the file so that I could determine which juveniles were arrested as juvenile offenders more than once. The last arrest is used to determine prior offense status. Recall that the data set is limited to a short time interval of several years because JO status ends at 16. To qualify for a prior arrest, a juvenile would have had to commit two or more offenses between his or her fourteenth and sixteenth birthday (or thirteenth for homicide).

In reformatting the DCJS data into an offender-based file, a total of 8,755 arrested juveniles produced 9,975 incidents. Among those arrested more than once, about 17 percent experienced three or more arrests. Recall that eligible arrests cover juvenile offender offenses that occurred while juveniles were under the age of 16. Among the 12 percent of juveniles arrested more than once, 8 percent faced arrest for A felonies, 63 percent for B felonies, and 30 percent for C felonies. Juveniles with a prior arrest are only slightly less likely to face an arrest for a C felony, as illustrated in Figure 5.4.

Jurisdictional and Temporal Context. Table 5.1 displays the frequency, rate, and mean seriousness of arrest charges and rate of conviction in criminal court for the twelve largest counties within New York State. The four largest counties are located in New York City (NYC) and account for 85 percent of JO arrests. Brooklyn alone produced over one-third of JO arrests. Erie County, which includes the state's second largest city, Buffalo, recorded little more than 1 percent of the total JO arrests, although the county's population of nearly one million is comparable to other downstate counties where JO arrests are more common. Similarly, rates of arrest based on the county's juvenile populations are substantially lower in non–New York City (non–NYC) counties.

The mean arrest seriousness by jurisdiction is related in part to the frequency of arrests. The mean offense severity rates for Erie and Monroe counties are 24.2 and 23.2, respectively, compared to 18.7 for Brooklyn. The substantially higher mean seriousness scores for the western part of New York State suggest greater selectivity among Erie and Monroe county officials in the arrest and the initial assignment of criminal responsibility.

Table 5.1 indicates that within New York City (NYC) and non–NYC counties, Manhattan is the county with the highest rate of arrests and the

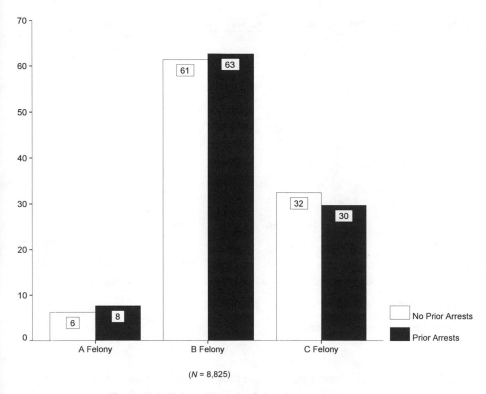

(N = 8,825)

Figure 5.4. Felony Type by Prior Arrests in Percents

lowest arrest severity score. In the capital county of New York State, Albany, officials seem to follow the letter of the JO law by charging a larger proportion of juveniles for less serious juvenile offender offenses. Albany's mean seriousness of arrest is 16.9 compared to 24.2 for Erie County. Among NYC counties, Bronx officials charge juveniles on average with more serious arrests. Among New York City counties, Richmond and Manhattan produced the lowest mean offense seriousness scores, 17.9 and 18.1, while the Bronx recorded the highest mean severity of arrest, 20.4.

But rates of seriousness by county of jurisdiction are not merely a product of variation in rates of crime. There is no reason to believe that juveniles commit more serious violent offenses in Buffalo (Erie County) or Rochester (Monroe County) than in other parts of New York State. Moreover, there is no reason to believe that citizens of Albany are so fortunate that they are victimized by only the least serious of violent juvenile offender offenses.

Table 5.1. Frequency, Rate, Severity of Arrest, and Conviction Rate by Large Jurisdictions

	Frequency[a]	Rate[b]	Offense.[c] Severity	Conviction[d] Rate
New York City Counties				
Brooklyn	3,490	460.8	18.70	.23
Queens	1,155	205.9	18.86	.22
Manhattan	2,134	683.8	18.07	.27
Bronx	1,668	384.1	20.42	.29
Staten Island	167	124.6	17.93	.19
Non–New York City Counties				
Nassau	168	33.6	18.45	.29
Suffolk	256	46.0	18.40	.23
Erie	129	35.4	24.22	.07
Westchester	185	59.4	18.45	.24
Monroe	119	47.2	23.20	.12
Onondaga	101	60.0	19.63	.32
Albany	84	92.1	16.85	.39
Other Counties	281	250.6	22.02	.18

[a] Frequency of arrests.
[b] Rate of arrest per 100,000 14-15-year-olds in county.
[c] Mean severity of arrests.
[d] Rate of conviction in criminal court.

Instead, the most accurate interpretation of the statistics in Table 5.1 is that the frequency and seriousness of offense charges reflect jurisdictional variation in decision making on what constitutes a JO offense. Officials in Buffalo and Rochester appear more inclined to follow the letter of the JO law only for the most serious violent offense charges. In these western New York counties, juveniles who commit the less serious JO offenses are less likely to be arrested as juvenile offenders and are more often charged as delinquents. As a consequence, the cases of juveniles who commit less violent acts of crime may not even enter the criminal justice process. By being more selective about the arrest of juveniles as juvenile offenders, western New York criminal justice officials raise the threshold of offense severity necessary for criminal justice to assign criminal responsibility to juveniles initially.

Variation in how officials identify the types of offenses for which juveniles will be arrested as adult offenders suggests that some counties produce a more loosely coupled criminal justice system for juveniles than other counties. In Erie County (Buffalo), juveniles are only arrested as offenders for the most serious designated felony offenses. In Albany, a more tightly coupled criminal justice system appears to exist whereby the

Table 5.2. Frequency, Rate, Severity of Arrest, and Conviction Rate by Year

Year	Frequency[a]	Rate[b]	Offense Severity[c]	Conviction Rate[d]
1978	596	96.4	17.4	.15
1979	1,600	261.5	18.7	.20
1980	1,533	248.9	18.7	.22
1981	1,657	282.7	19.0	.31
1982	1,454	256.7	19.5	.35
1983	1,266	231.5	19.5	.30
1984	1,287	244.1	19.6	.22
1985	544	107.2	19.8	.07

[a]Frequency of arrests.
[b]Rate of arrest per 100,000 14- to 15-year-olds in county.
[c]Mean severity of arrests.
[d]Rate of conviction in criminal court.

police arrest juveniles for a wider range of eligible designated felony offenses. Albany's tightly coupled systems of criminal justice for juvenile offenders may be a consequence of the get-tough policies of a single judge, while Buffalo's more loosely coupled systems of justice may be a consequence of a desire to keep all but the most serious cases exclusively in the juvenile justice system.

Further support for the more loosely coupled manner in which JO offense status may apply is the relationship between offense seriousness and the frequency of arrests. In Albany more juveniles are arrested as juvenile offenders than in Erie County based on the county's juvenile populations. The rate in Albany is 92 per 100,000 juveniles compared to 35 in Erie County, and their mean seriousness scores are 17 and 24, respectively. In counties where fewer juveniles experience JO arrests, the mean seriousness of arrest is substantially greater. In other words, criminal justice officials in counties where fewer juveniles are arrested appear more selective in their assignment of criminal responsibility to juveniles.

The temporal context of legal decision for juvenile offenders is presented in Table 5.2, where the year of arrest appears to produce variation in case processing in several ways. Recall that beginning in 1983, the county's proportional cost of incarcerating convicted juvenile offenders gradually increased. Over time officials may not only have been concerned with the financial cost of dealing with juveniles as offenders but also may have become more efficient in their case processing decisions. The simple relationship between time and arrest severity is presented in Table 5.2. The mean severity of JO arrests over time increased while the frequency of arrests generally declined. In 1979 (the first complete year of the JO law), there were 1,600 JO arrests with a mean seriousness of 18.7, while in 1984 (the last complete year of data collection), JO arrests declined to 1,287, and the mean seriousness of arrests increased to 19.8. The rise in the mean seriousness of arrests, coupled with a decline in frequency, suggests that the police were gradually becoming more selective in their arrests of juveniles for designated felony offenses.[3]

Jurisdictional Consequences and the Severity of Arrests. I argued that the contextual reasons for legal decision making are contingent on case outcomes at later stages in the criminal justice process. Part of the jurisdictional contingencies that I hypothesized to account for legal decision making at the arrest stage is measured in the jurisdictional probability of a JO conviction in criminal court.

Returning to Table 5.1, the probabilities of conviction in criminal court and the mean seriousness of arrests reflect decision making at earlier points in the legal process. For the twelve most populous counties of New York State, the rates generally show that the mean seriousness of JO arrests is inversely related to conviction rate. Jurisdictions with low conviction rates produced relatively high mean seriousness scores. Similarly, jurisdictions with high conviction rates produced low mean seriousness scores. For instance, Erie County and Albany County produced arrest severity and conviction rates in opposite directions: Albany recorded the lowest mean seriousness of arrests (16.85) and the highest conviction rate (.39), while Erie County recorded the lowest conviction rate (.07) and the highest mean seriousness of arrests (24.22).

Albany's higher rate of conviction for less serious juvenile offender offenses suggests that its criminal justice system is more tightly coupled around the stated legal requirements of the JO law. A larger population of juveniles caught committing JO offenses in the state capital are likely to face charges and conviction as juvenile offenders. In contrast, the criminal justice system in Erie County produces a much smaller proportion of convicted juvenile offenders even for the most serious JO offenses.

Multivariate Analysis of Arrest Severity. I now examine with multivariate techniques of analysis the organizational context in which juveniles are arrested as offenders. One question to be addressed is whether variation in the severity of a county's arrest charges is significant once the personal characteristics of arrested juveniles are statistically controlled. It is possible that differences in the demographic characteristics of juvenile offenders located in different jurisdictions may explain variation in arrest severity rates. Table 5.3 presents descriptive statistics on the arrest and adjudication of the total population of juvenile offenders in New York State analyzed in several regression models. Note that the offender-based file and missing values reduce the total number of cases for analysis to 7,803.

The labels in several of the independent variables in the tables that follow are in need of explanation. *Time* is the month of arrest since the month in 1978 when the JO law went into effect. It is used to measure the temporal context of case processing decisions. *Population* is the county's population transformed to its natural log value. The natural log value reduces the range of the distribution so that values are less skewed toward the four largest counties in New York City. *Severity Rate* is the average mean seriousness of juvenile offender arrests. This is based on the average offense severity of arrest in each county of jurisdiction. Similarly, *Conviction*, *Sentencing*, and *Incarceration Rates* are based on the mean values for each county of jurisdiction. They are based on rates for the case processing of juvenile offenders. I use them to measure the organizational contingencies that were previously argued as having influence over legal decision making at various stages in the criminal justice process.

The dependent variable in this section is *Offense Severity*. It is based on the total offense charges transformed to their NCS severity scores as previously noted. In later sections, the *Offense Severity* variable is measured as an independent predictor of types of adjudication and dispositions as well as sentence length. Also in later sections of the analysis, *Adjudication Severity* is measured as a dependent variable based on whether the arrested juvenile offender's case was dismissed, removed to juvenile court, convicted in criminal court as a juvenile offender with YO status, or convicted in criminal court solely as a juvenile offender.

Descriptive Statistics. Table 5.3 shows that in our offender-based file the average age of juvenile offenders arrested is 15, 92 percent are boys, and 68 percent are black. About 11 percent of arrested juvenile offenders recorded more than one prior juvenile offender arrest. Juvenile offenders

Table 5.3. Descriptive Statistics for Arrested Juveniles

Independent Variables	NY State (N = 7,803) Mean	SD	NYC Counties (N = 6,1722) Mean	SD	Non–NYC Counties (N = 1,081) Mean	SD
Age (13–19 range)	15.252	.563	15.256	.560	15.231	.580
Gender (Boys 1)	.924	.267	.926	.262	.911	.285
Race (Black juveniles 1)	.682	.466	.694	.461	.602	.490
Offense Severity (10–105; dep. & indep.)	19.266	11.453	19.099	11.234	20.303	12.686
Prior (Prior Arrest 1)	.107	.309	.117	.321	.048	.214
Time (Month of arrest;1–80)	41.632	21.535	41.613	21.282	41.747	23.053
Population (Logged 10.95–14.62)	14.198	.523	14.324	.336	13.411	.745
Severity Rate (16.85–32.67)	19.051	1.366	18.888	.810	20.059	2.860
Conviction Rate (.07–.80)	.247	.045	.250	.028	.229	.098
Sentencing Rate (12–80)	33.840	4.762	34.238	2.412	31.361	10.977
Incarceration Rate (.25–.91)	.580	.074	.573	.054	.623	.139
Dependent Variables						
Criminal Court Conviction (Conviction 1)	.257	.437	.259	.438	.243	.429
Removal to Juvenile Court (Removal 1)	.308	.462	.342	.474	.095	.294
Adjudication Severity (0–3)	1.909	.974	1.947	.959	1.672	1.033

Variable coding in parentheses.

faced a 26 percent rate of conviction in criminal court. About 31 percent of arrests were removed to juvenile court. Adjudication severity indicates that the average adjudication is slightly below that of conviction in criminal court with YO status. The county level jurisdictional variables are skewed toward the New York City counties where the vast majority of juvenile offender arrests take place.

To test for interactions, separate estimates are displayed for New York City and non–NYC counties. Recall that juvenile justice reforms and the JO law in particular were related to the problem of controlling juveniles in large urban areas. So we should expect differences in the JO law's implementation between NYC and non–NYC Counties. Table 5.3 further displays descriptive statistics for the variables in the NYC Counties and non–NYC Counties multivariate models. In contrast to non–NYC counties, NYC counties recorded a larger percent of boys, black juveniles arrested as juvenile offenders, and juveniles with prior arrests. The conviction and removal rates as well as the severity of adjudication are greater in NYC than non–NYC counties. For juveniles convicted in criminal court, the rate of incarceration is greater in non–NYC counties: .62 compared to .57. The mean severity of arrests is higher in non–NYC counties than in NYC counties: 20.3 compared to 19.1.

Table 5.4 shows the estimated effects of offender, temporal, and jurisdictional characteristics on offense severity. For the entire state of New York, gender and race are significant predictors of offense severity in the direction previously displayed in Figures 5.2 and 5.3. Black juveniles and boys are charged with more severe juvenile offender offenses than white or Hispanic juveniles and girls.

Temporal and jurisdictional characteristics are also significant predictors of arrest severity. Over time the severity of arrests increased; for each month of arrest, there was a .02 increase in offense severity. Each unit increase in a county's logged population value produced a decrease in the severity of arrest by a factor of .86. The downstream consequence of arrest in terms of conviction is also significant; for each unit increase in the rate of conviction, there was an 8.5 decrease in the severity of arrests.

In separate regressions for NYC and non–NYC counties, Table 5.4 further shows the unique pattern of the estimated effects of the independent variables on severity of arrests. The effects of gender and race are significant at the arrest stage only in NYC counties. Boys and blacks are significantly more likely to be arrested for more serious offenses in NYC counties. Although over time officials in both NYC and non–NYC counties charged juveniles with more severe juvenile offender offenses, the estimated effect

Table 5.4. Regression Estimates of Arrest Seriousness (New York State, New York City Counties, Non–New York City Counties)

Variables	NY State (N = 7,803)	NYC Counties (N = 6,722)	NON–NYC Counties (N = 1,081)
Age	-.178 (.231)	-.149 (.246)	-.374 (.659)
Gender	2.374* (.487)	2.508* (.522)	1.421 (1.341)
Race	-1.287* (.280)	-1.248* (.300)	-1.210 (.789)
Prior Arrest	.136 (.422)	-.019 (.430)	2.899 (1.791)
Time of Arrest	.022* (.006)	.013* (.006)	.071* (.017)
Population	-.858* (.253)	.318 (.472)	-1.302* (.528)
Conviction Rate	-8.524* (2.989)	10.391 (5.779)	-14.386* (3.962)
Constant	33.975	12.223	43.110
R Square	.01	.01	.04

* P >.05.
Standard errors are in parentheses.

of time is greater in non–NYC counties (the difference in the coefficient is significant: T value equals 4.5). The effects of jurisdictional characteristics appear specific to non–NYC counties. Each unit increase in the population of non–NYC counties produced a decrease in the severity of arrest by a factor of 1.3. Similarly, each unit increase in the conviction rate produced a decline in the conviction rate by a factor of 14 in non–NYC counties. On the other hand, the effect of conviction rate is positive on offense severity, although the coefficient based on its standard error is not statistically significant.

The reason the effects of temporal and jurisdictional characteristics appear particularly significant in non–NYC counties may be a consequence of greater variation in the organization of criminal justice outside of New York City. NYC counties and their criminal justice systems are regulated by a single-city government. Despite the fact that county DAs are elected in all counties of New York, greater centralization and organizational uniformity appear within NYC than in counties outside of NYC. In the next section, we will see if the effects of offender and jurisdictional characteristics repeat themselves at the adjudication stage of criminal justice decision making.

Adjudicating Arrested Juvenile Offenders

This section is concerned with the decision to convict, remove, or dismiss those juvenile offenders arrested for designated felony offenses. Initially, juveniles are only charged with designated felony offenses. The ultimate adjudication of guilt is preceded by several important steps in the criminal justice process. For instance, there is an arraignment in which a decision is made to detain or release the juvenile. Arrested juvenile offenders must also face indictment by a grand jury before adjudication in criminal court.

As is the case with adult offenders, juvenile offenders may have their cases dismissed if they are considered not criminally responsible for an alleged offense. For adult offenders, however, the dismissal of all charges eliminates the possibility of any legal sanction. That is not the case for juveniles initially arrested as offenders. If the charges for JO offenses are reduced or dismissed, then arrested juvenile offenders are not eligible for criminal court. They must be treated as delinquents in juvenile court. A more formal legal avenue is removal or transfer to juvenile court for JO offenses through a reverse waiver procedure. This requires officials to agree in writing on the criteria as stated in the JO law for the removal of juveniles from New York's criminal court to its juvenile court.

The DCJS data contained multiple codes for the particular types of adjudicatory dispositions. These categories were collapsed into conviction in criminal court, removal to juvenile court, and dismissal. I classified the various subcategories after consulting with several prosecutors and law professors. I coded a juvenile's case as "removed" to juvenile court if the DCJS data indicated that the juvenile was "transferred," "removed," or "disposed in juvenile court." But, again, formal removal to the juvenile court refers only to the population that is legally diverted from the criminal justice system to the juvenile justice system for designated felony offenses. If prosecutors reduced juveniles' offenses to non–JO offenses, then they are technically acts of delinquency for which juveniles are not criminally responsible.

Bearing the above in mind, the dismissal category combines the following adjudication codes: acquitted, dismissed, no bill, DA declined to prosecute, not arraigned, not considered by grand jury, no jurisdiction, and declined prosecution. The coding of case outcomes based on these adjudication codes indicates that the eligible juveniles were not convicted in criminal court nor removed to the juvenile court.

Conviction in criminal court is based on the juvenile's adjudication as either a YO or juvenile offender. Recall that a 1979 amendment to the JO

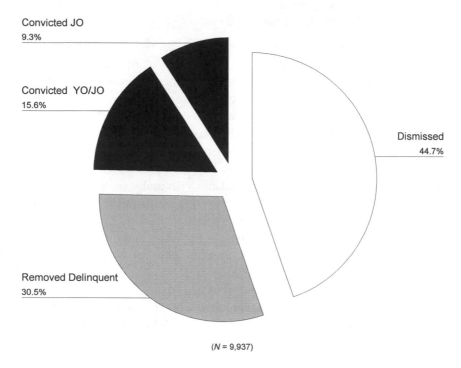

(*N* = 9,937)

Figure 5.5. Adjudication in Percents

law made juveniles eligible for YO status. Technically, such juveniles are still juvenile offenders but YOs as well. Of course, they can receive the juvenile offender label exclusive of YO status. Attached to YO status is the possibility of probation or a reduced term of imprisonment. In contrast to YO status, the conviction of a juvenile solely as a JO produces a public criminal record and longer minimum and maximum periods of incarceration.

   Figure 5.5 shows that nearly one-quarter of all juveniles arrested for JO offenses faced conviction in criminal court. Among those convicted in criminal court, the vast majority received YO status in addition to the juvenile offender label. Only 9 percent of arrested juveniles were convicted in criminal court without the benefit of YO status. The percent of arrested juveniles convicted in criminal court is substantially lower than the proportion of arrested adults convicted in criminal court for the same kinds of offenses. According to other DCJS data for the same period, approximately 60 percent of adults arrested in New York State for the same kind of felonies were convicted in criminal court. The percent of juveniles convicted in criminal court would be comparable to adults if no juveniles had been removed to juvenile court.

In the analysis that follows, I consider adjudication as both a categorical and an ordinal measure of criminal responsibility. As a categorical indicator, I measure the probability of conviction in criminal court, regardless of whether the juvenile was found guilty in the criminal court as a JO or a YO. As an ordinal indicator of criminal responsibility, I measure the degree to which the formal legal labels are applied to eligible juveniles. I assume that the YO label is less severe than the JO label, that removal to juvenile court is less severe than conviction in court, and that dismissal is the least severe adjudication.

Recall that arrested juveniles can be charged with a multitude of offenses for which they can receive more than one type of adjudication. In the analysis that follows, I rely on the most serious type of adjudication. For example, if a juvenile was convicted in criminal court for a robbery in the second degree while the juvenile's first degree arrest charge was dismissed, I counted the juvenile's arrest as a conviction in criminal court.

Offense Type. Figure 5.6 shows a direct relationship between severity of designated felony offense type and the probability of conviction in criminal court as a juvenile offender. One-third of juveniles charged with A felonies were convicted in criminal court, compared to 9 percent for B felonies, and 5 percent for C felonies. Part of the difference in conviction rates is related to the removal category: only 18 percent of juveniles charged with A felonies were transferred to juvenile court compared to 28 percent and 37 percent of juveniles charged with B and C felonies, respectively. The percent of juveniles receiving YO status for C felonies is about the same as that for A felonies. For C felonies, officials appear more inclined just to remove or dismiss arrested juveniles rather than convict with YO status. This is not the case for B felonies, where conviction in criminal court is more likely to produce YO status.[4]

Offender Characteristics. Younger juveniles are more likely to see their cases removed to juvenile court; 34 percent of juveniles between the ages of 13 and 14½ are removed to juvenile court compared to 29 percent of older juveniles. Similarly, the probability of convicting juveniles exclusively as juvenile offenders is greater for juveniles in older age categories than in younger age categories; 11 percent of juveniles over 14½ are convicted exclusively as JOs compared to 7 percent for younger juvenile offenders.

Figure 5.7 displays the relationship between gender and type of adjudi-

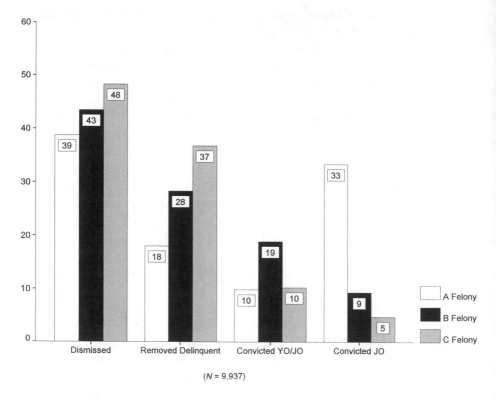

(N = 9,937)

Figure 5.6. Adjudication by Felony Type in Percents

cation. Boys are nearly three times as likely to face conviction in criminal court exclusively as juvenile offenders than are girls. When YO and juvenile offender status is combined, only 16 percent of girls are convicted in criminal court compared to 26 percent of boys. Part of the variation in conviction rates can be attributed to the higher proportion of girls removed to the juvenile court: 36 percent compared to 30 percent. Finally, note that dismissals are slightly more prevalent among girls arrested as juvenile offenders.

White juveniles are more likely to have their cases dismissed than black or Hispanic juveniles. The percent difference is displayed in the first set of bar charts in Figure 5.8. The 9 percent difference in the probability of a dismissal is in part related to the greater probability that black and Hispanic juveniles received a formal sanction in the shape of removal to juvenile court. Although white juveniles who face arrest as juvenile offenders are

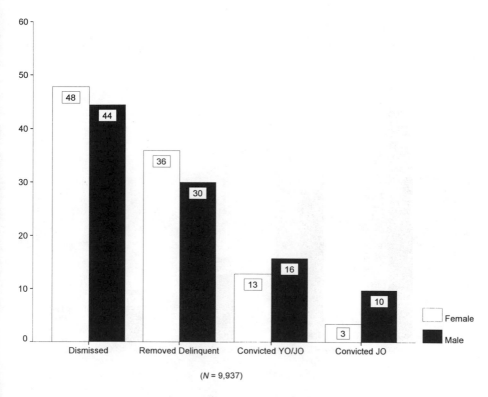

(N = 9,937)

Figure 5.7. Adjudication by Gender in Percents

charged with more serious violent offenses, they face a slightly lower rate of conviction as juvenile offenders in criminal court: 7 percent compared to 10 percent each for Hispanic and black juveniles.

Juveniles who repeated their violent offenses as reflected in another juvenile offender arrest faced a substantially higher risk of adjudication as juvenile offenders. As shown in Figure 5.9, 19 percent of recidivating juvenile offenders were convicted as juvenile offenders compared to 7 percent without a prior arrest. But juveniles with a prior arrest are just as likely to receive YO status as those without a prior arrest. This is not particularly surprising for those within the system, since the first arrest did not necessarily result in a conviction in criminal court; that is, only a prior arrest that results in conviction can disqualify a juvenile for YO status. Still, a large percentage of juveniles, 41 percent, are dismissed from the criminal justice system despite their repeated arrests for violent felony offenses.

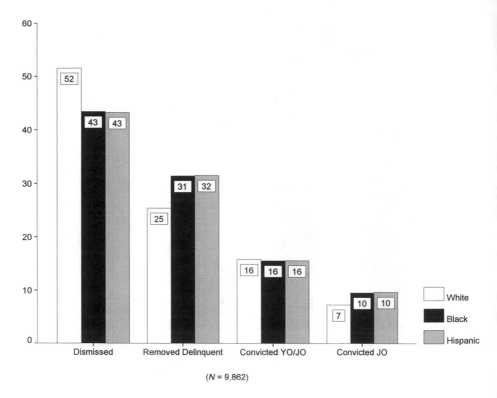

(N = 9,862)

Figure 5.8. Adjudication by Race in Percents

Jurisdictional and Temporal Context. Table 5.5 displays annual rates of
adjudication for the arrested population and disposition for the convicted
population. Note that 1978 and 1985 data are based on less than 12
months. The percent convicted in criminal court peaked in 1982 when 35
percent of arrested juveniles were adjudicated either as YOs or as juvenile
offenders. The percent of juveniles adjudicated as YOs rose steadily from
11 percent in 1979 to 22 percent in 1982, and then declined to 16 percent
in 1984. Similarly, the percent of juveniles adjudicated as juvenile offenders
rose from 8 percent in 1979 to 13 percent in 1982, and then declined to 7
percent in 1984. The rise and decline by year in the percent of arrested
juveniles convicted in criminal court appears to correspond to the 1982
administrative reform in the county's cost of incarcerating juveniles as
offenders in DFY facilities. As the cost of incarcerating juvenile offenders
increased for counties of jurisdiction, the proportion of juveniles convicted
in criminal court declined from its peak in 1982.

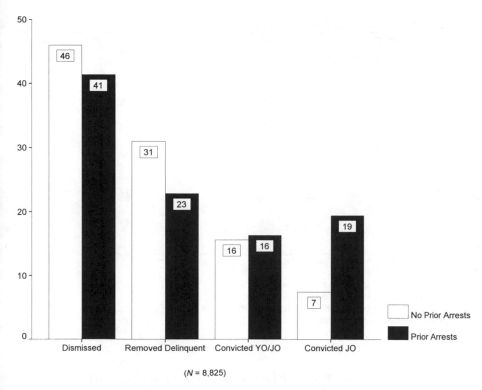

(N = 8,825)

Figure 5.9. Adjudication by Prior Arrests in Percents

Recall that in Table 5.1 the county's average conviction rate appears inversely related to the severity of arrest. For example, Albany recorded the lowest mean seriousness of arrest yet the highest rate of conviction. Similarly, Table 5.6 shows that Albany's higher probability of incarceration and longer mean sentence length followed its high rate of conviction. Apparently, criminal justice officials in Albany produced a tight fit not only between arrest and adjudication but also between adjudication and disposition. Note that mean sentence length is based on the average minimum and maximum date of sentence transformed into expected months served.[5]

Table 5.6 also shows that Erie County has the lowest conviction rate but the highest average mean length of sentence. Another county in the western part of New York State, Monroe County (Rochester), produced next to the lowest conviction rate (.12) and the lowest average length of sentence (18.20). In the densely populated counties of New York City, arrested juve-

Table 5.5. Adjudication and Disposition Rates by Year

Year	Dismissed[a]	Removed[b]	YO/JO[c]	JO[d]	Incarceration Rate[e]	Sentence Length[f]
1978	.45	.41	.08	.07	.64	34.03
1979	.44	.37	.11	.08	.62	37.72
1980	.47	.31	.13	.10	.62	38.37
1981	.38	.31	.20	.11	.61	34.49
1982	.38	.27	.22	.13	.62	34.11
1983	.44	.26	.20	.11	.51	32.31
1984	.51	.26	.16	.07	.49	27.41

[a] Rate of dismissal from the criminal justice process.
[b] Rate of removal to juvenile court.
[c] Rate of conviction in criminal court as a JO with YO status.
[d] Rate of conviction in criminal court as a JO without YO status.
[e] Rate of incarceration for juvenile offenders convicted in criminal court.
[f] Average length of sentence in months.

niles appear more likely to face formal transfer to juvenile court. Brooklyn recorded the highest rate of removal to juvenile court in that 42 percent faced transfer while the Bronx reported the highest conviction rate in criminal court with two-thirds of convicted juveniles receiving a sentence of incarceration. Except for Albany, non–NYC counties produced dismissal rates that were greater than 50 percent of JO arrests.

Multivariate Analysis of Adjudication. I now consider the determinants of both a nominal and ordinal level measure of adjudication. As a nominal level measure, I examine the determinants of convicting juveniles in criminal court either as juvenile offenders or YOs. As an ordinal level measure, my dependent variable is the severity of adjudication on a scale of 0 to 3. Recall that the YO label (coded 2) is less severe than the JO label (coded 3) and that removal to juvenile court (coded 1) is less severe than conviction in criminal court. Dismissal is the least severe type of adjudication (coded 0).

Ordinary Least Square regression estimates for New York State (Table 5.7) support several bivariate relationships observed in the charted figures. Among the juveniles' characteristics, age and gender are significant in the

Table 5.6. Adjudication and Disposition Rates by Jurisdiction

	Dismissed[a]	Removed[b]	YO/JO[c]	JO[d]	Incarceration Rate[e]	Sentence Length[f]
New York City Counties						
Brooklyn	.34	.42	.15	.09	.52	32.52
Queens	.41	.37	.15	.07	.60	30.97
Manhattan	.50	.22	.17	.11	.57	36.71
Bronx	.40	.31	.18	.12	.66	37.10
Staten Island	.70	.12	.12	.07	.68	32.13
Non–New York City Counties						
Nassau	.67	.04	.20	.09	.66	29.71
Suffolk	.64	.13	.18	.05	.49	32.36
Erie	.85	.08	.02	.05	.63	46.40
Westchester	.75	.02	.11	.12	.58	19.09
Monroe	.77	.11	.08	.04	.62	18.20
Onondaga	.59	.09	.23	.09	.61	36.24
Albany	.49	.12	.14	.25	.91	42.90
Other Counties	.68	.14	.11	.07	.63	34.11

[a] Rate of dismissal from the criminal justice process.
[b] Rate of removal to juvenile court.
[c] Rate of conviction in criminal court as a JO with YO status.
[d] Rate of conviction in criminal court as a JO without YO status.
[e] Rate of incarceration for juvenile offenders convicted in criminal court.
[f] Average length of sentence in months.

Table 5.7. Regression Estimates of Adjudication Severity

Variables	NY State (N = 7,803)	NYC Counties (N = 6,722)	Non–NYC Counties (N = 1,081)
Age	.056* (.019)	.042* (.021)	.139* (.053
Gender	.094* (.041)	.065 (.044)	.212* (.108)
Race	.034 (.024)	.017 (.025)	.167* (.064)
Offense Severity	.012* (.001)	.013* (.001)	.010* (.002)
Prior Arrest	.264* (.035)	.265* (.036)	.162 (.143)
Time of Arrest	-.003* (.001)	-.004* (.001)	.003* (.001)
Population	.127* (.027)	.207* (.085)	-.200* (.047)
Severity Rate	-.037* (.009)	.074* (.025)	-.075* (.012)
Incarceration Rate	.488* (.212)	-.370 (.621)	.075 (.279)
Sentencing Rate	.007* (.003)	.023* (.006)	.006 (.003)
Constant	-.822	-3.809*	2.890
R Square	.04	.05	.07

*p < 0.05.
Standard errors are in parentheses.

expected direction. Boys and older juveniles receive more severe adjudications; that is, they are less likely to see their cases dismissed and more likely to face conviction in criminal court. The bivariate relationship noted between adjudication and race drops in significance once other variables are statistically controlled.

The effects of offense severity and prior arrests suggest that the most likely candidates for criminal court or some form of legal control (removal, or YO or JO status) are those charged with the most serious JO offenses and who have a prior arrest. Note that the coefficient for the seriousness of the offense is nearly thirteen times its standard error. Prior arrest is also a highly significant determinant of adjudicatory severity.

Jurisdictional and temporal variables also predict adjudicatory outcomes. For each month since the passage of the JO law, the estimated coefficient shows a slight but significant decline in the severity of adjudication. The parameter coefficient .003 for *Time* over a 3-year period reduced the severity of adjudication on average by one level – that is, from juvenile offender status to youthful offender status, or from youthful offender status to removal. In other words, the longer the law stayed in effect, the more likely juveniles were treated as YOs, removed to juvenile court, or dismissed from the criminal justice process.

The county level variables suggest other contextual effects in the adjudication of juvenile offenders. Juvenile offenders in larger counties face harsher forms of adjudication than those in smaller counties. This confirms the earlier bivariate relationship between formal adjudication in NYC and non–NYC counties. Also important in predicting adjudication severity is the county's average severity of arrests. As the average severity of arrest increased for counties, the severity of adjudication decreased. This is contrary to what we might expect if criminal justice systems were operating in a manner that adjudicated more severely only those juveniles charged with the most serious offenses. However, the incarceration and sentencing rates are directly related to the severity of adjudication. Counties with higher rates of incarceration and longer mean lengths of sentence produce more severe adjudications.

Table 5.7 also displays significant interaction effects based on separate estimates for NYC and non–NYC counties. In NYC counties the only personal characteristic to significantly affect severity of adjudication is the juvenile's age. But in non–NYC counties, age, gender, and race are significant determinants of adjudication severity. However, a t-test of the difference in the unstandardized age coefficients for NYC and non–NYC counties is not statistically significant.

The severity of offense is a more important predictor of adjudication in NYC counties than in non–NYC jurisdictions. Moreover, prior offense is not significant in non–NYC counties, while it is significant in NYC counties.

The effects of temporal and jurisdictional characteristics vary slightly between NYC and non–NYC counties. *Time* has a positive effect on adjudication in non–NYC counties, while it has a negative effect in NYC counties. The size of the county similarly has opposite effects in NYC and non–NYC counties. In non–NYC counties, smaller jurisdictions tend to adjudicate juveniles more severely than do larger jurisdictions. Again this may reflect the difference between larger counties such as Erie County, which rarely adjudicates eligible juveniles as juvenile offenders, and smaller counties such as Albany, which nearly always adjudicates eligible juveniles as juvenile offenders. Similarly, non–NYC counties seem less influenced by the average severity of arrests than are NYC counties. The difference between NYC and non–NYC counties emerges in the downstream consequences of con-

Table 5.8. Logistic Estimates of Removal to Juvenile Court

Variables	NY State (N = 7,803)	NYC Counties (N = 6,722)	Non–NYC Counties (N = 1,081)
Age	-.173* (.046)	-.187* (.048)	-.039 (.182)
Gender	-.342* (.093)	-.314* (.099)	-.669* (.304)
Race	-.009 (.056)	-.033 (.059)	-.139 (.222)
Offense Severity	-.021* (.003)	-.023* (.003)	-.011 (.009)
Prior Arrest	-.490* (.089)	-.565* (.092)	.161 (.494)
Time of Arrest	-.011* (.001)	-.014* (.001)	.019* (.005)
Population	1.681* (.117)	.328 (.254)	-.151 (.158)
Severity Rate	.127* (.009)	.526* (.060)	.001 (.039)
Incarceration Rate	2.464* (.731)	-6.198* (1.514)	.619 (.929)
Sentencing Rate	.007 (.008)	-.077* (.018)	.007 (.012)
Constant	-25.002	-4.919	-.243
Log-Likelihood	-4,490.463	4,317.293	326.997

*$p > 0.05$.
Standard errors are in parentheses.

viction; the average sentence length matters more in NYC than it does in non–NYC counties.

Removal to Juvenile Court. The logistic models of removal to juvenile court in Table 5.8 display a similar pattern of severity. Younger juveniles are more often removed to juvenile court than are older juveniles. Girls are more likely to be removed, controlling for other important offense and jurisdictional variables than boys. The odds ratio indicates that boys have a lower risk of being removed to juvenile court.

The effects of offense severity and prior arrests are in the expected direction. Each unit increase in offense severity or prior arrest decreases the probability of removal to juvenile court. As expected, juveniles charged with more serious offenses or who have a prior offense face a lower likelihood of removal to juvenile court. The temporal context is also strongly correlated with removal in that the transfer of arrested juvenile offenders to juvenile court gradually becomes a less viable option. Recall that for the entire population of arrested juvenile offenders, the probability of removal to New York's juvenile court was .30. However, the determinants of removal appear less clearly linked to the personal characteristics of juveniles than to the county of jurisdiction. This is reflected in the positive coefficient for the size of the county of jurisdiction's population, which is more than fourteen times its standard error, reflecting the degree to which county of jurisdiction is an important determinant of removal to juvenile court. Indeed, the descriptive statistics demonstrate that for NYC counties 34 percent of arrested juveniles are removed compared to 10 percent of juveniles adjudicated in non–NYC counties.

The organizational context of legal decision making is again revealed in the removal process in that the severity of arrests and the probability of conviction, as well as sentence length, influence the removal process. There is an inverse relationship between the mean severity of arrests and the likelihood of removal. This may appear counterintuitive, but removal reflects some form of legal control. Recall my earlier argument that juvenile justice and juvenile courts remain under waiver in the background as another means of dealing with violent juvenile offenders. This formal legal avenue is invoked more frequently in counties where juveniles are arrested for more serious violent felony offenses. A county's average rate of incarceration also has an effect on the probability of removal; counties with higher incarceration rates tend to remove a larger proportion of eligible juveniles to juvenile court. This again reflects a unique organizational contingency: criminal courts are more likely to be reserved for those juveniles in counties where they are at greater risk of longer terms of incarceration.

Table 5.8 further shows the separate logistic models for NYC and non–NYC counties. While age and prior arrests remain significant among NYC counties, they are not significant in non–NYC counties. The month of arrest or the temporal context of decision making has an opposite effect of that which exists in NYC counties. Over time in non–NYC counties, there was on average a 2 percent increase for each month in the risk of juveniles being removed to juvenile court in contrast to a decline in NYC counties over time in the use of removal. In NYC counties case processing rates are significant predictors of removal.

At this point we might ask what these data tell us about the removal process for arrested juvenile offenders. First, it appears that a more tightly coupled system of waiver is at work in NYC jurisdictions, where offense characteristics are important predictors of removal. In non–NYC jurisdictions other nonspecified variables are determining removal to juvenile court. The criminal justice system in these non–NYC counties seems to act in a more loosely coupled manner, because rates of arrest seriousness, incarceration, and sentence length appear unrelated to removal. Of course, there is significant variation, as noted earlier in the rates of adjudication within non–NYC counties (for example, Albany compared to Erie County).

Conviction in Criminal Court. I now shift to the correlates of conviction in criminal court. Recall from Figure 5.7 that 16 percent of girls were convicted in criminal court compared to 26 percent of boys. Table 5.9 shows that gender remains as a significant predictor of conviction for juveniles even after controlling for other important variables; exp (.406) indicates that boys are 1.5 times more likely than girls to be convicted in criminal court. Similarly, older juveniles face a greater likelihood of being convicted in criminal court even after controlling for prior arrests and charge severity.

Still, prior arrests and offense severity are the strongest correlates of conviction in criminal court. Those with more serious offenses and a longer history of prior offenses are most likely to be convicted in criminal court. The effects are highly significant in that their coefficients are more than seven times their respective standard errors. The odds ratio for prior offense shows that juveniles with a prior offense are 1.8 times more likely to be convicted in criminal court than those without a prior offense.

Among the contextual variables, the county's population, average seriousness of arrests, and mean length of sentence are significant predictors of conviction in criminal court. Smaller counties convict more often than large counties, and those counties with lower average seriousness of arrests convict more often than counties with higher average seriousness of arrests. This partially reflects the difference between such counties as Albany and Erie, since Erie County convicted fewer juveniles for more serious offenses than Albany County. The effect of the average mean length of sentencing suggests that there is a greater risk of conviction in criminal court in those counties where juveniles are subject to longer periods of incarceration.

The jurisdictional context in which criminal responsibility is assigned is further highlighted in separate logistic models for NYC and non–NYC counties. Recall that race is an important predictor of conviction in criminal court for the entire state. However, when we look at race in non–NYC counties alone, it is clear that it has a strong and significant effect. Black juveniles in non–NYC counties are 1.45 times more likely to be convicted in

Table 5.9. Logistic Estimates of Conviction in Criminal Court

Variables	NY State (N = 7,803)	NYC Counties (N = 6,722)	Non–NYC Counties (N = 1,081)
Age	.187* (.048)	.156* (.052)	.395* (.130)
Gender	.406* (.111)	.318* (.120)	.767* (.308)
Race	.058 (.058)	.046 (.063)	.372* (.160)
Offense Severity	.026* (.002)	.028* (.002)	.019* (.006)
Prior Arrest	.577* (.079)	.619* (.082)	.212 (.322)
Time of Arrest	.000 (.001)	-.001 (.001)	.004 (.003)
Population	-.154* (.068)	.490* (.237)	-.417* (.109)
Severity Rate	-.126* (.023)	-.088 (.062)	-.187* (.033)
Incarceration Rate	.620 (.520)	2.910 (1.629)	-.448 (.645)
Sentencing Rate	.016* (.007)	.089* (.016)	.010 (.009)
Constant	-1.225	-14.450	.558
Log-Likelihood	-4,308.364	-3,711.729	-599.789

*$p > 0.05$.
Standard errors are in parentheses.

criminal court than whites after controlling for offense seriousness and the temporal and jurisdictional context of adjudication. The difference in the likelihood of conviction between whites and nonwhites is not significant for NYC counties.

Table 5.9 further reveals that the population and case processing decisions of NYC and non–NYC counties vary in their relationship to the probability of conviction in criminal court. Among NYC counties, larger boroughs, for example Brooklyn, are more likely to convict juveniles than are smaller boroughs, such as the Bronx and Staten Island. On the other hand, smaller non–NYC counties, for example Albany, have higher conviction rates than do larger counties, such as Erie. Other differences between NYC and non–NYC counties appear in the effects of the jurisdictional consequences of average county rates of offense seriousness and conviction in criminal court. The average length of sentence is significant only in NYC counties, while the average severity of arrests affects only the likelihood of

conviction in non–NYC counties. Counties with severe arrests in non–NYC
counties on average produce a greater likelihood of conviction in criminal
court. This illustrates again the effects of small and large upstate counties
such as Albany and Erie on the likelihood of conviction in criminal court.

**Legal and Contextual Reasons for Adjudicating Juveniles as Of-
fenders.** The analysis of adjudication allows us to conclude several aspects
of the JO law's implementation. First, the majority of juveniles arrested for
offenses in which they are criminally responsible are dismissed or removed
from the criminal justice process. Only 25 percent of juveniles arrested as
offenders are ultimately convicted in criminal court. If those convicted in
criminal court with YO status are eliminated, then only 10 percent are
convicted strictly as juvenile offenders.

But is the JO law more bark than bite? Yes and No! It all depends on
offense, offender, temporal, and jurisdictional characteristics. This leads to
the second major finding of the analysis. The principle of offense is at work
within categories of JO offenses. Juveniles who are charged with more
serious offenses face a higher probability of conviction in criminal court
and a lower probability of YO status, removal, or dismissal. Third, the
principle of individualized justice is also at work in that older juveniles,
boys, and minority youth are more often adjudicated as juvenile offenders.
Finally, organizational contingencies are also at work. Temporal and jurisdictional context are important in that the year of arrest and county of
jurisdiction are related to the risks of conviction in criminal court, removal
to juvenile court, and dismissal from the criminal justice process.

The results of the multivariate analyses illustrate the importance of organizational context in adjudication severity and the risks of conviction in
criminal court as well as the risks of removal to family court. The context of
case processing decisions for juvenile offenders is further highlighted by
the significant interaction effects that emerged in the assignment of criminal responsibility for NYC and non–NYC counties. For instance, white juveniles are significantly less likely to face conviction in non–NYC criminal
courts than are black juveniles. Based on the logistic estimates for conviction in criminal court, NYC officials appear more colorblind in their decision making than non–NYC officials.

The significance of temporal and jurisdictional context suggests again
that the assignment of criminal responsibility to juveniles occurs within a
negotiated order of criminal justice. The organizational route to convicting
juveniles as adult offenders is not the same from month to month, nor
from county to county. The assignment of criminal responsibility is more

often negotiated in some counties than in others. The higher seriousness of arrest charges in Erie County produces a different negotiated order than the lower seriousness of arrests in Albany County. But contrary to what might be expected in Erie County, even those juveniles who face relatively severe JO offense charges face a low probability of conviction in criminal court. In contrast, juveniles charged on average with less severe designated felony offenses in Albany face a higher probability of conviction in criminal court. The assignment of criminal responsibility to juveniles is a negotiated one for sure, but it is not uniformly negotiated across counties of New York State.

Dispositions

The negotiated order of criminal justice persists for convicted juvenile offenders at the sentencing stage of decision making. For those arrested juvenile offenders who are not removed from the criminal justice process, this is the final stage of decision making. Recall that in Table 5.5 convicted juvenile offenders in Albany faced a greater than 90 percent chance of receiving a sentence of incarceration. Bear in mind that Albany's juveniles are likely to face a maximum secure facility even for offenses that are generally less severe than in other parts of New York State. In contrast to Albany, Suffolk County incarcerated slightly less than half of juveniles convicted in criminal court.

This section shifts the analysis to how offense, offender, and jurisdictional characteristics relate to the likelihood of incarceration (secure placement) and length of sentence. Are the race, gender, and age of juveniles more important determinants of their probability of imprisonment than the county and time of arrest? In particular, is the probability of imprisonment related to jurisdictional context as reflected in the county's population size and by a county's average seriousness of arrests and length of sentences? To answer how the assignment of criminal responsibility to juveniles in criminal court is reproduced in the form of criminal punishment, I now focus on the population of juvenile offenders convicted in criminal court. Note that the convicted population of juveniles includes juveniles who are also officially designated as YOs.

Offense Type. Figure 5.10 shows that the majority (58 percent) of convicted juvenile offenders receive a sentence of incarceration. The remaining 42 percent are sentenced to probation. A further breakdown of disposition type by felony category (Figure 5.11) shows that 87 percent of juveniles

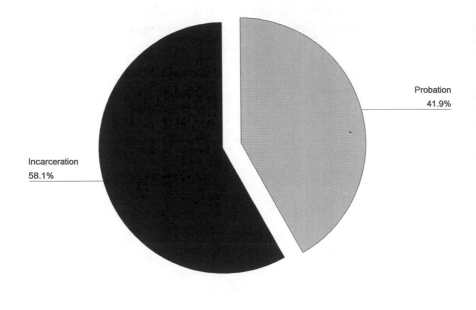

(*N* = 2,376)

Figure 5.10. Disposition in Percents

convicted of A felonies are sentenced to incarceration compared to 56 percent and 52 percent of B and C felonies, respectively. Technically, juveniles convicted of A felonies are not eligible for YO status and probation. Although the A felony is the most serious arrest charge, it is not necessarily the one for which the juvenile is ultimately convicted.

Offender Characteristics. Sentences of incarceration are slightly higher among juveniles in the oldest age category; 60 percent over the age of 15½ are incarcerated compared to 55 percent and 57 percent in younger age categories. However, recall that part of the population in the youngest age category can only be convicted of homicide; therefore, the risk of incarceration for a 13-year-old is heightened by the severity of the offense.

The relationship between gender and sentence type is displayed in Figure 5.12. The majority (59 percent) of boys convicted in criminal court are incarcerated compared to only 39 percent of girls. This may reflect the fact that girls are more often charged with less serious designated felony offenses, and that officials perceive girls as more deserving of treatment, and, therefore, sentences of probation.

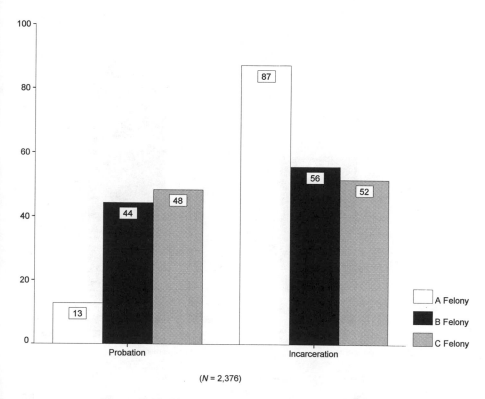

(N = 2,376)

Figure 5.11. Disposition by Felony Type in Percents

Although white juveniles were treated similarly to Hispanic juveniles at earlier stages in the criminal justice process, Hispanic juveniles are just as likely to face incarceration as black juveniles (Figure 5.13). Recall that white and Hispanic juveniles shared approximately the same average seriousness of arrests and risks of adjudication as juvenile offenders. However, at the sentencing stage in the criminal justice process, Hispanic and black juveniles have a similar risk of incarceration. The majority of white juveniles are sentenced to probation (51 percent), while the majority, 60 percent and 59 percent, respectively, of convicted black and Hispanic juveniles are incarcerated.

As expected, the prior felony arrest of convicted juvenile offenders appears related to the likelihood of incarceration (Figure 5.14). Eighty percent of juveniles with a prior designated felony arrest were incarcerated compared to 52 percent without a prior arrest. The reason again for why the effect of prior arrest might not be even stronger at the disposition stage

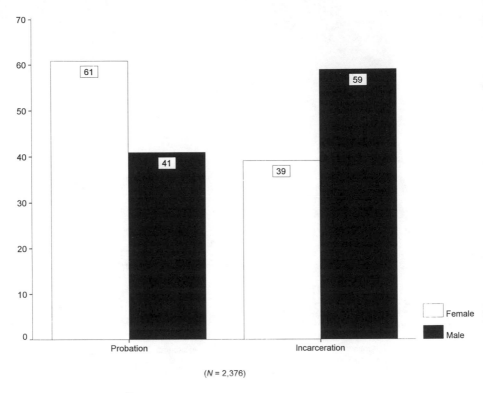

(N = 2,376)

Figure 5.12. Disposition by Gender in Percents

is that the arrest does not necessarily produce a conviction, and if the arrest took place outside of the county jurisdiction, officials may be unaware of its prior occurrence.

Returning to Table 5.5 shows that after the implementation of 1982 legislation, which increased a county's cost of incarcerating juvenile offenders, a larger percent of convicted juvenile offenders received probation. Between 1982 and 1983, the percent of incarcerated juveniles decreased from 62 percent to 51 percent. This is convincing evidence that the temporal context of legal decision making is an important organizational reason not only for assigning criminal responsibility to juveniles but also for ultimately mandating criminal punishment in the form of imprisonment. I will return to the rise and decline in rates of incarceration later with more current sets of state agency data.

The Multivariate Analysis. I produced several logistic and regression models to disentangle the relative importance of offense, offender, and

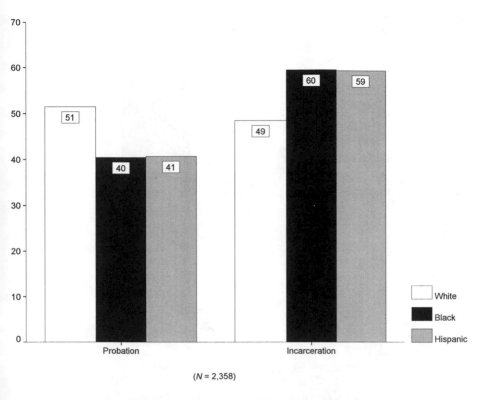

Figure 5.13. Disposition by Race in Percents

jurisdictional characteristics on dispositions. I now confine the analysis to
the proportion of juveniles convicted in criminal court. Missing values
further reduce the total population of convicted juvenile offenders in New
York State to 1,988.

Descriptive statistics are presented in Table 5.10. Note that I recoded the
race variable to reflect its bivariate distribution with type of disposition. I
combined Hispanic and black juveniles to produce a nonwhite racial category.[6] Table 5.10 also shows that the temporal variable is now based on the
month in which the 1983 cost-sharing amendment was first implemented.

Logistic Estimates of Incarceration. Among the personal characteristics
of convicted juvenile offenders, Table 5.11 shows that at the sentencing
stage of decision making, gender and race remain statistically significant
predictors. For nonwhites, on average, the likelihood of incarceration is
1.71 (exp .538) times greater than that of whites. This suggests that race
still has an effect on type of sentence even after controlling for variation in

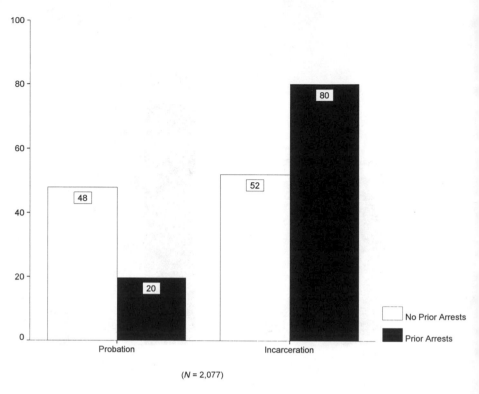

(N = 2,077)

Figure 5.14. Disposition by Prior Arrests in Percents

the severity of arrests. Gender is also significantly related to the likelihood of custody; boys are 1.92 (exp .538) times more likely to be incarcerated than girls.

The strongest predictors of incarceration are offense-related variables. There is a direct and highly significant relationship between offense severity and the likelihood of incarceration. Moreover, a prior designated felony arrest increases the likelihood of incarceration by more than 4.41 times that of juveniles without a prior felony arrest.

Temporal and jurisdictional variables are also important at the disposition stage of decision making. The law variable indicates a temporal effect based on the period before and after implementation of a legal change increasing the county's cost of incarceration. The coefficient for the law variable indicates that the administrative change reduced the risk of incarceration for juveniles.

The county level jurisdictional variables are significant for population

Table 5.10. Descriptive Statistics for Convicted Juveniles

Independent Variables	NY State (N = 1,988)		NYC Counties (N = 1,727)		Non–NYC Counties (N = 261)	
	Mean	SD	Mean	SD	Mean	SD
Age (14–19)	15.304	.544	15.301	.541	15.320	.567
Gender (Boys 1)	.947	.225	.946	.226	.950	.216
Race (Non-white 1)	.852	.356	.875	.331	.707	.460
Offense Severity (10–94)	21.948	13.263	21.951	13.126	21.927	14.169
Prior (Prior Arrest 1)	.155	.362	.169	.375	.061	.240
Law (Arrests after 5/1/83=1).	.237	.426	.232	.422	.276	.448
Population (10.95–14.62)	14.176	.527	14.305	.311	13.327	.806
Severity Rate (16.85–32.67)	18.986	1.262	18.928	.865	19.369	2.653
Sentencing Rate (12–80)	34.086	4.464	34.558	2.415	30.958	10.112
Dependent Variable						
Disposition (Incarceration 1)	.535	.499	.521	.500	.625	.485

Variable coding in parentheses.

Table 5.11. Logistic Estimates of Disposition

Variables	NY State (N = 1,988)	NYC Counties (N = 1,727)	Non–NYC Counties (N = 261)
Age	-.019 (.089)	.022 (.096)	-.241 (.258)
Gender	.654* (.219)	.674* (.238)	.649 (.616)
Race	.538* (.139)	.499* (.158)	.730* (.318)
Offense Severity	.034* (.004)	.033* (.004)	.049* (.014)
Prior Arrest	1.483* (.153)	1.465* (.156)	2.478* (1.065)
Law	-.474* (.114)	-.494* (.124)	-.533 (.320)
Population	-.627* (.104)	-.551* (.239)	-.328 (.196)
Severity Rate	-.057 (.045)	.045 (.064)	-.128 (.692)
Sentencing Rate	.023* (.011)	.021 (.030)	.040* (.0166)
Constant	7.738	4.145	7.750
Log-Likelihood	-1,245.460	-1,088.66	-148.642

*$p > 0.05$.
Standard errors are in parentheses.

and sentencing rate. The population variable indicates that juveniles in larger counties are at less risk of incarceration than juveniles in smaller counties. A jurisdiction's average length of sentence increases the likelihood of incarceration. Apparently, the sentencing of a juvenile to prison is considered more feasible for counties that produce longer lengths of sentences.

Separate logistic models for convicted juveniles in NYC and non–NYC counties also show that offense seriousness and prior arrests are significantly related to incarceration. However, there are some differences in the significance of personal and jurisdictional characteristics. For example, gender is significant in NYC counties but not in non–NYC counties. This might be an artifact of the fewer number of female juvenile offenders in non–NYC counties as reflected in the large standard error in relation to its coefficient.

Differences in organizational context appear in that the law variable and population size were significant only for NYC counties. Among NYC counties, there was a decrease in the proportion incarcerated after the 1982 change in the cost of incarcerating juvenile offenders. Moreover, larger counties of New York City produced a lower risk of incarceration for juvenile offenders. Finally, the mean jurisdictional sentence length is significant in non–NYC counties, while it is not significant in NYC counties. A county's average length of sentence is directly related to the risks of incarceration. This means that when non–NYC counties incarcerate, they do not use it for relatively short sentences.

Sentence Length. At this point we can move to the final step in the criminal justice process for those convicted juveniles who received a sentence of incarceration. Within the minimum and maximum sentences listed earlier in Table 3.1, there is a determination of sentence length. Sentence length should be directly related to offense seriousness. Recall that the mean sentence length is based on minimum and maximum dates of incarceration transformed into expected months served.

Table 5.12 presents the descriptive statistics for only those juveniles who were sentenced to prison for their designated felony offenses. The means for NYC and non–NYC counties show that 90 percent of incarcerated juveniles in New York City are black compared to 75 percent in non–NYC counties. Also among the incarcerated proportion of juveniles, the percent with a prior offense in non–NYC counties is substantially lower than in NYC counties (9 percent compared to 25 percent). The temporal variable (LAW) shows a higher rate of incarceration in non–NYC counties to NYC counties, .24 to .19, after the 1982 legislative change in the county's cost of incarceration.

Approximately 10 percent or 1,000 of the nearly 10,000 juveniles arrested as juvenile offenders were sentenced to prison. The multivariate analysis of sentence length examines those juveniles at the tail end of the criminal justice system. It is a selective pool of offenders that has been reduced substantially by criminal justice decision making at earlier stages in the legal process.

To reduce some of the possible effects of selection bias on the estimated regression parameters, I first followed the two-stage least-square procedures that Berk (1983) recommends to control for the probability of offenders reaching the final stage of decision making. Length of imprisonment may not be a function of only the linear combination of independent variables but of a "hazard rate" that also accounts for the risk of being incarcerated. Ordinary regression procedures that fail to take into account sample selection bias risk producing inconsistent estimates (see Hagan 1988, p. 80). However, the computed sample selection bias estimates that I

Table 5.12. Descriptive Statistics for Juveniles Sentenced to Incarceration

Independent Variables	NY State (N = 1,063)		NYC (N = 900)		Non–NYC Counties (N = 163)	
	Mean	SD	Mean	SD	Mean	SD
Age (14–19)	15.31	.54	15.32	.54	15.28	.55
Gender (Boys 1)	.96	.19	.97	.18	.96	.20
Race (Non White 1)	.88	.33	.90	.30	.75	.43
Offense Severity (10–94)	24.21	15.17	24.22	15.13	24.15	15.45
Prior (Prior Arrest 1)	.23	.42	.25	.43	.09	.29
Law (Arrests after 5/1/83=1)	.20	.40	.19	.39	.24	.43
Population (10.95–14.62)	14.13	.56	14.28	.31	13.27	.79
Severity Rate (16.85–32.67)	19.03	1.36	18.98	.90	19.28	2.76
Dependent Variable						
Sentence Length (1–144)	37.08	24.65	36.97	24.35	37.66	26.31

Variable coding in parentheses.

Tables 5.13. Regression Estimates of Sentence Length

Variables	NY State (N = 1,063)	NYC Counties (N = 900)	Non–NYC Counties (N = 163)
Age	2.709* (1.234)	3.626* (1.314)	-2.565 (3.505)
Gender	4.233 (3.581)	6.753 (3.881)	-7.606 (9.376)
Race	5.232* (2.076)	2.391* (2.401)	14.582* (4.537)
Offense Severity	0.784* (0.045)	0.798* (0.047)	0.708* (.0131)
Prior	4.825* (1.630)	4.618* (1.662)	6.749 (6.805)
Law	-1.293 (1.686)	-0.318 (1.837)	-1.455 (4.450)
Population	-1.900 (1.281)	-0.405 (2.427)	-3.687 (2.599)
Severity Rate	-0.981 (0.521)	-0.300 (0.842)	-1.581 (.0810)
Constant	16.689	-34.265	142.61
R Square	.24	.26	.23

*$p > 0.05$.
Standard errors are in parentheses.

obtained were not significantly different from the uncorrected regression estimates.[7] So for simplicity of presentation, I confine my analysis to the uncorrected ordinary least-square estimates.

For New York State, Table 5.13 shows that as the age of juvenile offenders increases, on average the expected length of sentence increases by three months. However, the effect of race is in the opposite direction from that contained in models of decision making at earlier stages in the criminal justice process. The positive coefficient for race indicates that whites on average receive sentences 5 months longer than minorities receive. This is because fewer white juveniles are defined as juvenile offenders for less serious designated felony offenses. When they are convicted for designated felony offenses as juvenile offenders, they receive longer sentences for more brutal or violent felony offenses.

Offense severity and prior arrests are also significant predictors of sentence length. Each incremental increase in offense severity contributes to a juvenile offender's sentence. A prior arrest on average adds about 5 months to sentence length.

None of the contextual variables is significant in both the corrected and uncorrected estimates of sentence length. This is not surprising. The lack of significance of law, population size, and average offense seriousness on sentence length suggests that these variables have an impact at earlier stages in criminal justice decision making. They predict whether juveniles are convicted in criminal court and receive a sentence of incarceration, not the specific length of sentence.

Differences in the last stage of criminal justice decision making again emerge between NYC and non–NYC counties (Table 5.13). Among NYC counties, race is not significantly related to sentence length, while it is significant among non–NYC counties. Indeed, race and offense seriousness are the only variables to have significant effects on sentence length in non–NYC counties. But the longer sentences noted in the statewide regression for white juveniles seem to be specific to non–NYC counties. There the longer sentences of white juveniles produce on average sentences of 15 months longer than that for minority juveniles. As previously noted, this reflects greater filtering in criminal justice decision making at earlier stages in the legal process so that black and Hispanic juveniles are more often adjudicated and incarcerated for less serious offenses. To repeat: If white juveniles are ultimately incarcerated for JO offenses, it is for the most serious types of designated felonies, resulting in longer periods of imprisonment.

Contextual Reasons Revisited

Recall that the DCJS data were limited to case processing decisions from 1978 to 1985. Although it was not possible to obtain individual level data for the period after 1985, DCJS and DFY provided me with aggregate level data on the rate of conviction and incarceration from 1978 to 1991. I now shift my analyses to these data and to DFY data on the rate of imprisonment for juvenile offenders.

During 1979, the first full year of JO law implementation, less than 4 percent of eligible juveniles were incarcerated (Table 5.14). The incarceration rate increased until 1983 when it peaked at .21. In 1984, a year after the cost-sharing formula for counties of jurisdiction kicked in, the percent of juveniles incarcerated started to drop. I suggested earlier that the rate of incarceration for juvenile offenders may have peaked because officials became aware of the higher county cost of imprisoning juveniles through criminal court. The 12.5 percent that counties were required to pay for the incarceration of a criminally responsible juvenile offender was substantially

Table 5.14. Incarceration Rates for Arrested Juvenile Offenders by Year

Year	Arrests	Number Incarcerated	Rate Incarcerated
1979	1,475	66	0.04
1980	1,444	166	0.12
1981	1,568	218	0.14
1982	1,388	254	0.18
1983	1,190	253	0.21
1984	1,180	157	0.13
1985	1,173	152	0.13
1986	1,171	142	0.12
1987	1,046	107	0.10
1988	1,479	89	0.06
1989	1,826	127	0.07
1990	1,954	147	0.08
Total	16,894.00	1,878.00	0.11

less than the 50 percent cost sharing that year for a juvenile delinquent incarcerated through the juvenile court.

As the county's proportional cost of incarceration gradually increased to the same level that exists in juvenile court, fewer juveniles were imprisoned through criminal court as juvenile offenders. The higher cost of criminal prosecution for juvenile offenders can also be related to fewer juvenile offender arrests. Note that the number of arrests for designated felonies declined from 1,475 in 1979 to 1,180 in 1984. By the time the cost of incarceration increased to the full 50 percent in 1988 for New York State counties, the rate of incarceration plunged to 6 percent of juvenile-designated felony arrests. Between 1983 and 1984 the number of juveniles sent to prison declined from 253 to 157. The number and rate of imprisonment reached its lowest point in 1988 when 89 convicted juvenile offenders were sent to prison, producing an incarceration rate of .06.

I estimate that incarcerating convicted juveniles at $80,000 per year cost $8 million per 100 individuals prior to 1986. After 1986, when the counties collectively began to pay 50 percent of this cost, there would be a $4 million savings for each reduction of 100 incarcerated juvenile offenders. Thus New York City counties, which contain 85 percent of juvenile offenders, might have saved about $3,400,000 (4,000,000 × .85 = 3,400,000.).[8]

At this point, it is important to bear in mind that I have no direct indicators of the possibility that officials in making decisions about juvenile offenders are aware of the county's dollar costs of incarceration. I view the effects of the administrative legal change as another organizational contingency centering on the costs of incarcerating juveniles as juvenile offenders. As the history of juvenile justice reforms in Chapter 2 repeatedly showed, administrative costs are a critical variable in past and present attempts to control delinquency and crime.

It is also important to stress that the decline in the rate of incarceration for eligible juvenile offenders occurred despite no apparent change in the offense seriousness of arrest charges (Table 5.15). The percent of juveniles arrested for homicide increased in 1988 to 6.6 percent, the year in which juvenile offenders experienced the lowest rate of imprisonment. Moreover, there was no discernible change in the rate of rape during this period. Arrests for the least serious offense category, burglary, declined from over 4 percent in 1982 to less than 3 percent in 1989. The slight increase in the rate of imprisonment in 1990 may be due to a comparable one percent increase in the number of homicides.

Table 5.16, which was produced from DFY annual reports (New York State Division for Youth 1980–1990), provides further evidence as to the risk of incarceration for juvenile offenders convicted in criminal court. Despite a drop in the number of juveniles initially sentenced to maximum security institutions, the population in secure facilities actually increased over time. Contrary to what a lower rate of incarceration might lead one to believe, the number of juveniles placed in maximum security DFY institutions gradually increased from 121 to 964 juveniles. The percent of juveniles in secure facilities in 1980 during the early years of the JO law consisted of less than 5.5 percent of the juvenile population. By 1990 that figure increased to 39 percent. Yet note that the percent of juveniles in secure facilities more than doubled between 1985 and 1986.

The increase in the population of juveniles in secure facilities was not just a function of the small proportion of juveniles sentenced to long terms of incarceration. If that were the case, the increase would be more gradual. Also, as previously noted, the increase cannot be attributed to more juve-

Table 5.15. Number and Percent of Juveniles Arrested by Type of Offense and Year

Year	Assault	Homicide	Rape	Kidnapping	Burglary	Arson	Robbery	Total
1979	35* 2.4**	40 2.7	153 10.4	2 0.1	64 4.3	39 2.6	1,142 77.4	1,475 100%
1980	49 3.4	74 5.1	111 7.7	0 0.0	61 4.2	34 2.4	1,115 77.2	1,444 100%
1981	45 2.9	93 5.9	113 7.2	3 0.2	67 4.3	32 2.0	1,215 77.5	1,568 100%
1982	44 3.2	75 5.4	114 8.2	1 0.1	60 4.3	26 1.9	1,068 76.9	1,388 100%
1983	44 3.7	72 6.1	107 9.0	3 0.3	54 4.5	20 1.7	890 74.8	1,190 100%
1984	32 2.7	61 5.2	122 10.3	1 0.1	37 3.1	22 1.9	905 76.7	1,180 100%
1985	58 4.9	64 5.5	161 13.7	1 0.1	21 1.8	27 2.3	841 71.7	1,173 100%
1986	63 5.4	63 5.4	112 9.6	1 0.1	26 2.2	16 1.4	890 76.0	1,171 100%
1987	77 7.4	67 6.4	107 10.2	2 0.2	32 3.1	24 2.3	737 70.5	1,046 100%
1988	85 5.7	98 6.6	146 9.9	6 0.4	49 3.3	15 1.0	1,080 73.0	1,479 100%
1989	84 4.6	108 5.9	116 6.4	2 0.1	51 2.8	12 0.7	1,453 79.6	1,826 100%
1990	82 4.2	139 7.1	98 5.0	4 0.2	35 1.8	7 0.4	1,589 81.3	1,954 100%
Number Total	802 4.2	1059 5.6	1557 8.2	27 0.1	609 3.2	302 1.6	14,524 76.9	18,880 100.0

* Number   **Percent

Table 5.16. Number and Percent of Admissions to Division for Youth Institutions by Year

Year	1980	1981	1982	1983	1984	1985	1986	1987	1988	1989	1990
Secure[a]	121	267	399	334	297	296	731	690	749	887	964
%	5.5	11.2	16.2	13.9	13.2	12.2	32.9	35.6	36.9	37.2	39.0
NonSecure[b]	684	673	759	700	759	872	486	382	424	632	778
%	30.9	28.1	30.8	29.2	33.6	36.0	21.9	19.7	20.9	26.5	31.5
Community[c]	1,035	962	775	692	569	646	396	318	214	198	103
%	46.7	40.2	31.4	28.9	25.2	26.7	17.8	16.4	10.6	.08	.04
Voluntary[d]	375	490	532	669	631	610	606	546	641	669	625
%	16.9	20.5	21.6	27.9	28.0	25.2	27.3	28.2	31.6	28.0	25.3
Total	2,215	2,392	2,465	2,395	2,256	2,424	2,219	1,936	2,028	2,386	2,470
%	100	100	100	100	100	100	100	100	100	100	100

[a] Residential facilities with maximum security.
[b] Residential facilities involve minimal security.
[c] Community based non-residential programs.
[d] Cooperative, voluntary and alternative agencies.

niles sentenced to longer periods of incarceration by criminal court judges. Rather, the increasing frequency and rate of juveniles in secure facilities reflects the complex direction that decision making takes in contemporary juvenile justice and criminal justice systems.

The reason for the decline in judicial rates of incarceration and the rise in the DFY secure population of juveniles reflects another complex aspect of the waiver process. The practical, organizational reasons for criminal punishment persist past the point of disposition for convicted juveniles. An initial sentence of probation may allow criminal justice officials to track a segment of juveniles into secure facilities whether through criminal or juvenile courts.

Qualitative evidence to support the possible effects of probation on resentencing to a secure facility comes from defense attorneys who relate that probation is not necessarily a milder disposition. They will sometimes recommend to their clients to "bite the bullet" with a 1-year sentence rather than to stay on probation for 5 years. According to one defense attorney, adult offenders are often "savvy" enough to see that it is better to serve a minimum amount of time rather than to stay on probation for an extended sentence. However, juvenile offenders may be less aware of the risks of probation as well as the diverse legal avenues through which they can enter Division for Youth secure facilities.

It is important to bear in mind that with the rise in secure facilities in New York State, there was a substantial reduction in the population of juveniles in nonsecure facilities. In fact, McGarrell (1988) highlights this shift in DFY resources from community-based corrections to secure institutions. Apparently, recriminalization has touched criminal justice and juvenile justice systems in a diverse set of legal agencies and avenues.

Conclusion

The case processing data on juvenile offenders in New York's adult criminal justice system suggest that contextual reasons are significant determinants of legal decision making. Jurisdictional and temporal context are related to the arrest, conviction, and sentencing of juveniles as offenders. Organizational context helps to explain why the risks of being labeled a juvenile offender vary from county to county and from one set of criminal justice officials to the next. In other research on juvenile justice decision making, jurisdictional characteristics have also been noted to be important predictors of case outcomes (Hassenfeld & Cheung 1985; Sampson & Laub 1993).

Moreover, the personal characteristics of offenders matter; officials use their legal discretion to distinguish between arrested juveniles whom they see most at risk of repeated violent behavior. However, I have produced no direct measure of moral character or the degree to which officials view a juvenile offender's case as particularly serious. Instead, in this chapter I have relied on state agency data as a measure of official reactions to juvenile offenders at distinct stages in the criminal justice process. My analysis is based not only on the individual case but also on the county of jurisdiction and the time of arrest. The combination of aggregate and individual level data in the analysis is for the purpose of providing insight into inter- and intrajurisdictional sources of variation in legal decision making.

Sources of variation in legal decision making are further related to the concept of loosely and tightly coupled legal systems. First, offense seriousness tightened criminal justice decision making. The more serious the total designated felony offense charges, the more likely juveniles are to be convicted without the benefit of YO status. Total offense seriousness also affects the probability of incarceration, and, of course, the length of sentence.

Another significant finding is the effect of the race of juvenile offenders on case processing decisions. Race reflects the principle of individualized justice in the official assignment of criminal responsibility. Black juveniles face a greater chance of being arrested, convicted, and incarcerated as juvenile offenders. The significance of race is not the same across jurisdictions. Moreover, the effect of race might be explained by variables that are not contained in the available state agency data.

However, when white juveniles are ultimately sentenced in criminal court to a secure facility, their sentence lengths will exceed those of black juvenile offenders. I have suggested that this is the case because of filtering at earlier stages of legal decision making so that even after controlling for the seriousness of offense, white juveniles who remain in the tail end of the criminal justice system are subject to longer sentences than black juveniles.

In short, decision making is not made purely on the objective characteristics of the offense but is based on a form of individualized justice that others have noted to exist in juvenile court decision making. The research findings lend support to the hypothesis that systems of legislative waiver, like judicial waiver, maintain individualized sources of legal discretion (Zimring 1991).

Does the punishment of eligible juvenile offenders fit the crime? Perhaps. But justice appears to depend also on the jurisdictional and temporal context in which juveniles are assigned criminal responsibility for their behavior. Although legal decision making is based on state law, offense and offender characteristics are interpreted within particular jurisdictional and temporal settings. The manner in which the JO law is implemented is different in New York City from that of less populated counties of New York State. That difference persists at each stage of decision making. For example, the risk of being arrested, convicted, and incarcerated as a juvenile offender is substantially greater in Albany than it is in Buffalo.

Finally, organizational concerns and interests in the assignment of criminal responsibility to juveniles reflect administrative change in the rules of recriminalization. One practical consequence of treating juveniles as adult offenders is the cost of criminal justice. In increasingly complex systems of juvenile and criminal justice, success is not merely a consequence of low crime rates and high conviction rates but the ability of officials to maintain the legal process at a minimal level of cost.

To understand the emergence of recriminalization and its impact on legal decision making, it is important that increasing attention be placed on the determinants of structure and context. This is difficult to do because waiver to criminal court deals with juveniles located in systems of juvenile and criminal justice. But greater attention to structure and context with more complete sets of data should increase our understanding of what too often may appear as a random, loosely coupled system of recriminalizing delinquency.

Recriminalization and
Organizing for Deterrence

THERE IS A BOTTOM-LINE QUESTION that policy makers often ask when considering legislative waiver. It is the question of deterrence and whether legislative waiver affects the rate of juvenile crime. In New York State, the question can be asked specifically in terms of the JO law. Did it actually lower the rate of violent juvenile crime? Recall from the legislative debates the comment of Assemblyman Koppell in support of passage of the JO law:

> Meting out measured punishment is something that will, in fact, deter. . . . Every time a young person reads he committed murder and he is subject to a mandatory sentence of 18 months, that says to that unsophisticated mind, "Well, it couldn't be very bad. All it was is 18 months." . . . The law must say to that person, yes, this is very bad (125).

But, as detailed in the previous chapter, charged juvenile offenders may discover that the risks of criminal punishment are relatively low, especially for less than the most serious violent offenses. They may discover that the JO law is more bark than bite as a result of their experiences in the criminal justice system.

Yet in its simplest form, a theory of criminal deterrence proposes that it is the *threat* of legal punishment that will prevent criminal behavior. Deterrence theory takes on a general form when it refers to the impact of the threat of punishment on everyone in a particular group, such as persons between 13 and 16. It is more specific in shape when it refers to the impact of punishment on particular persons, such as chronic delinquents being warned by juvenile court judges that if they progress to designated felony offenses they risk a conviction in criminal court.

Specific deterrence draws on an offender's singular experience and consequently heightens his or her subjective probability that punishment will follow continued criminal behavior. In other words, if juveniles charged as juvenile offenders do not repeat their offenses because they realize from their initial appearance in criminal court that there is a greater risk of punishment, then indeed the JO law may have reduced the incidence of future offenses. Or if high offending juveniles are incarcerated for lengthy periods of time because of the JO law, then the law may have an incapacitative as well as a specific deterrent effect in preventing juveniles from repeating their offenses while incarcerated.

A critical link between punishment and behavior, however, may be the interaction between organizational context (which reflects differences in enforcement activities) and criminal sanctions. In the evaluation of the possible deterrent effects of legal sanctions, little attention has been devoted to the effects of legal reforms that emphasize organizational change along with an increase in the severity of punishment. For instance, Lempert (1982) stresses the importance of organizational characteristics in understanding the deterrent effects of legal sanctions when he states:

> Organizational characteristics help determine what threats are communicated and so affect how threats are perceived. Indeed, within the range of natural variation, it is possible for organizational differences to be more important than sanction rate differences in determining how legal threats are perceived in different populations (535).

Indeed, automatic waiver legislation represents the official desire to couple increased penalties with an organizational change in their legal administration.

For instance, the JJRA of 1976 provided for an increase in the severity of punishment for juveniles within juvenile court. Critics of the JJRA dismissed its possible deterrent effects because juvenile justice officials decided the appropriate level of punishment. Harsher penalties within the same organizational setting may not have conveyed the notion that violent juvenile crime "is very bad," as suggested by Assemblyman Koppell. However, unlike the JJRA, the JO law mandated an organizational shift in the processing of juveniles – that is, from juvenile court to criminal court and from juvenile justice officials to criminal justice officials as legal decision makers.

Although I stressed in the previous chapter that only a small proportion of eligible juveniles are convicted in criminal court and receive the maximum stated penalties, the court's actual rates of adjudication and disposition may not in themselves be relevant for the law to have a deterrent effect. Recall Lempert's (1982: 535) assertion that "it is possible for organizational differences to be more important than sanction rate differences in determining how legal threats are perceived." That is, the threat of punishment may be more effectively communicated through the adult criminal court, regardless of whether the juvenile's arrest actually results in a criminal trial that produces more punitive sentences.

There is some evidence to suggest that juveniles are indeed aware of the criminal laws that apply to them in general and the JO law in particular (Bucci 1985). The news media alerted New York's juveniles as to the existence of the JO law and acquainted them with its provisions. The National Council on Crime and Delinquency distributed pamphlets to high-school students explaining the law and emphasizing its severity. Moreover, delinquents appear aware of the exact age at which they are criminally responsible in criminal court for their offenses (Glassner et al., 1983). Based on interviews with juveniles in New York, they conclude that

> most of the adolescents studied reported that they curtail involvements in criminal activities at age 16, because they fear being jailed if apprehended as adults. They treat the period prior to age 16 as one for experimenting with criminal behaviors, while viewing late adolescence as a time for giving up such involvement unless one is ready to make a long term commitment and face substantial risks in so doing (Glassner et al., 1983: 221).

Of course, many juveniles are wrong about the exact age at which they can be treated as adult offenders. They are expressing legal ignorance when they speak of the specific age of transfer or the heightened risk of criminal punishment. Still, the bottom-line question of the JO law's deterrent effects needs to be addressed.

Research Design

To evaluate the impact of the JO law on crime, David McDowall and I used an interrupted time-series research design, which compares the levels of a time series before and after an intervention is introduced (Singer & McDowall 1988). The time-series data consist of monthly juvenile arrests between January 1974 and December 1984.[1] Each arrest time series is analyzed using the methods of Box and Jenkins (1976; McDowall et al. 1980). The main hypothesis is that if the law is effective in reducing crime, arrests should decrease following its introduction.[2]

Arrest series are computed for juveniles between the ages of 13 and 15 for each of five violent index offenses: homicide, rape, robbery, assault, and arson. The monthly arrest numbers are derived from UCR data tapes for NYC and non–NYC counties where significant differences in the implementation of the JO law appeared between NYC and non–NYC counties. The analysis of non–NYC counties is based on all jurisdictions that reported monthly juvenile arrests continuously over the study period.[3]

In general terms, the procedure starts with the development of a "noise model" to account for seasonality, nonstationarity, and autocorrelation in a time series. These characteristics are predictable sources of within-series variation and must be controlled prior to the impact analysis. After an appropriate noise model has been developed, an "intervention model" is added to represent the effects of the law. If there is a change in a series following the beginning of the law, it is reflected in the estimates of the intervention model.

For each series, three types of intervention models are considered. One of these was an abrupt and permanent change model, which assumed that the law produced an immediate and constant effect lasting through the entire postintervention period. The second model assumed a gradual and permanent change, in which the effect of the law increased over time. Finally, the third model assumed an abrupt but temporary change, in which an immediate effect of the law decayed back to the preintervention level as time went on.[4] While more complex models are possible, these three are reasonable and do not require elaborate assumptions about impact patterns (McDowall et al. 1980). The permanent change models presented the strongest effects and therefore are presented as the most appropriate for each series.

Despite the simplicity of the interrupted time-series design, Cook and Campbell (1979) have pointed out that it is among the strongest quasi-experiments, controlling for most threats to the validity of inferences drawn from it. The strength of the design is a result of the fact that each series is measured many times before and after the intervention. Because of the repeated measurements, the effects of variables other than the intervention cannot explain a postintervention change unless these other variables are themselves systematically altered at the time the intervention is introduced. For example, the level of juvenile crime is partly determined by the number of juveniles in the population. However, unless there was an unusually large change in the number of juveniles at exactly the time the law was introduced, this factor cannot account for an observed effect. Also, the 1982 administrative change in the county's cost for incarcerating sentenced juveniles was gradually implemented in 1983 and cannot be expected to be a factor in juvenile offender arrests during earlier years.

The most notable threat to validity not controlled by the basic interrupted time-series design is the possibility that some other causal variable did change in an unusual way at the time the intervention was introduced – a possibility that Cook and Campbell call the *threat of history*. In order to reduce the possibility of mistakenly attributing the effects of historical change to the law, control series are presented for each crime during the same time period for New York's adult offenders and Philadelphia's juveniles. The next oldest age group of juveniles, arrests of 16- to 19-year-olds, in New York City and non–NYC counties is analyzed. Juvenile arrests in Philadelphia of 13- to 15-year-olds are analyzed by crime and month. Neither control series was subject to a change in legal policy during the period of the analysis, so older New York youth and Philadelphia juveniles should have been exposed to influences similar to those affecting New York's juveniles.

If NYC juvenile arrests decreased following the intervention but did not decrease for the control series, then it can be concluded that the law affected crime rates. If arrests decreased both for NYC juveniles and for at least one of the control series, then it can be concluded that historical events were responsible for the effect. For juveniles in non–NYC counties, the control series is arrests of non–NYC 16- to 19-year-olds. Of course, the use of control series cannot completely rule out the possibility of historical threats. However, the controls do imply that any historical explanation would have to be quite complicated, and such an explanation would therefore be relatively implausible.

Besides history, a second possible set of problems for the design relates to the use of arrests as a measure of crime. The major advantage of the arrest data is that arrests provide age-specific information on crime patterns. A corresponding difficulty with these data is that the volume of arrests is only imperfectly related to the volume of crime and, as noted in the previous chapter, may be influenced by the behavior of police officers. The imperfect relationship between arrests and crimes will undermine the validity of the analysis, as historical threats might, only if this relationship changed at the time the law was introduced. That is, time-series designs can tolerate some bias in the measurements if the amount of bias does not itself change systematically at the point of intervention.

The possibility that there was in fact a systematic change in the measurement process at the time of the intervention corresponds to what Cook and

Campbell call the *threat of instrumentation.* Although there are several ways in which an instrumentation threat could operate, one possibility is particularly worthy of consideration: the police may have changed their arrest practices as a result of the law. For instance, the police might have started to charge juveniles with relatively minor nonindex or nondesignated felony offenses in order to avoid subjecting them to the rigors of criminal court. In both cases a drop in arrests would not truly reflect an actual decline in the incidence of crime.

As with history threats, instrumentation threats cannot be completely dismissed. However, instrumentation effects large enough to influence the findings appear to be quite unlikely. Changes in arrest practices would have to be systematic and widespread to affect the analysis, such as a formal policy shift or the individual activities of many police officers. Moreover, there was no dramatic change in arrest practices according to official accounts and to interviews with police administrators.

Although instrumentation effects are possible, there is no reason to believe that they exert more than a trivial influence on the findings. Also recall that only a minority of juveniles charged with designated felony offenses are actually convicted in criminal court. The fact that the implementation data show that not all eligible juveniles were charged under the law appears to vitiate the argument that the police would feel compelled to change their arrest practices to avoid subjecting minor offenders to adult prosecution.

A final possible problem for the time-series design is related to the fact that some UCR index arrests are not chargeable under the JO law. The JO law applies to 13-, 14-, and 15-year-olds for homicide, but only to 14- and 15-year-olds for the other four crimes. In contrast, *all* of the arrest series include 13-, 14-, and 15-year-olds. Furthermore, not all assaults, robberies, rapes, and arsons are eligible to be charged under the law, but all arrests for these crimes are included in the series analyzed. Therefore, only for homicide does the arrest series correspond perfectly to the law; the other series include some "irrelevant" cases.

Compared to other sources of bias, irrelevant cases will not systematically distort the results, as long as the proportion of these cases is approximately constant throughout each series. The "irrelevant" cases do produce another sort of problem, however. Juvenile crime and arrest rates are affected by a variety of random factors, and the purpose of the statistical analysis is to determine if there is a postintervention change distinct from this random noise. The "irrelevant" cases will be influenced by random factors of their own and will therefore contribute noise to the analysis. This additional noise will in turn make it more difficult to separate random variation from a systematic change and so will reduce the chances of finding an effect for the law. The "irrelevant" cases are thus a problem because they decrease the statistical power of the analysis.

Although statistical power is a concern for our analysis, it does not appear likely that an effect of reasonable size could be missed. The statistical methods used for the analysis have been shown to be quite powerful and should be able to detect any intervention of meaningful size. The random error resulting from the inclusion of some arrests not chargeable under the law implies that the analysis will be on the conservative side, however, and it is conceivable that extremely small effects may be attributed to chance.

Overall, the interrupted time-series design is a strong one. Although it is not possible to rule out completely all threats to validity, the analysis should detect an effect of the law on any of the five types of violent JO offenses in either New York City or upstate New York.

Findings

A summary of the results is presented in Table 6.1 for New York City and its control series, and in Table 6.2 for upstate New York and its control series. The main conclusion to be derived from the analysis is that there is little evidence that the introduction of the JO law was followed by a systematic decline in arrests. Most of the series were unaffected in the postintervention period, and where the effects are in the expected direction, similar patterns are evident for at least one of the control series.

Given the observed pattern of results, is there any theory that could be used to interpret the data as evidence that the JO law influenced the level of crime? To begin with, the results for homicide provide no support upon which to build such a theory. In New York City, the change in the rate of homicide was not statistically significant. Homicides for the targeted population of 13- to 15-year-olds declined by 26 percent. However, there was an even greater drop, 58 percent, among 13- to 15-year-olds in the homicide rate in Philadelphia. Note that the drop in homicides and assaults was statistically significant. In upstate New York, homicide arrests remained stable.

Moreover, while no change in assaults could be detected among the targeted population of juveniles in NYC counties, Philadelphia arrests declined significantly. The JO law appeared to have less of its intended effect

Table 6.1. Mean Numbers of Juvenile Arrests per Month, According to Jurisdiction and Offense, Before and After the Implementation of the JO Law (New York City and Control Series)

Type of Offense	Before the Law (No./Mo.)	Change after the JO Law (No./Mo.)	Standard Error	Percent Change	T-Statistic
Homicide					
NYC, 13 to 15	3.80	-1.00	0.59	-26	-1.62
NYC, 16 to 19	18.70	2.00	1.32	11	1.55
Philadelphia, 13 to 15	1.20	-0.70	0.24	-58	-2.71
Assaults					
NYC, 13 to 15	*	0.02	.03	.81	.81
NYC, 16 to 19	271.30	-21.35	14.30	-08	-1.49
Philadelphia, 13 to 15	24.04	-4.75	1.43	-20	-3.32
Robberies					
NYC, 13 to 15	290.30	16.00	22.43	06	.63
NYC, 16 to 19	*	-.88	.65		-1.35
Philadelphia, 13 to 15	63.00	7.41	3.79	12	1.95
Rapes					
NYC, 13 to 15	14.00	-4.16	1.33	-30	-3.12
NYC, 16 to 19	31.82	-6.41	2.04	-20	-3.14
Philadelphia, 13 to 15	5.19	-.58	.62	-11	-.92
Arsons					
NYC, 13 to 15	9.54	-5.52	.88	-58	-6.27
NYC, 16 to 19	8.73	-2.91	.76	-33	-3.85
Philadelphia, 13 to 15	4.43	-1.03	.58	-23	-1.76

* Indicates the series is nonstationary and therefore lacks a mean.

Table 6.2. Mean Numbers of Juvenile Arrests per Month, According to Jurisdiction and Offense, Before and After the Implementation of the JO Law (Non–New York City and Control Series)

Type of Offense Jurisdiction, and Ages	Before the Law (No./Mo.)	Change after the JO Law (No./Mo.)	Standard Error	Percent Change	T-Statistic
Homicide					
Upstate, 13 to 15	.30	-.01	.11	-03	-.37
Upstate, 16 to 19	2.09	.00	.34	0	.00
Assaults					
Upstate, 13 to 15	12.89	4.42	1.00	34	4.42
Upstate, 16 to 19	*	-.02	.32		-.08
Robberies					
Upstate, 13 to 15	19.88	2.62	1.89	13	1.38
Upstate, 16 to 19	50.61	9.99	2.91	20	3.08
Rapes					
Upstate, 13 to 15	1.25	.42	.31	34	1.34
Upstate, 16 to 19	4.76	.85	.61	18	1.39
Arsons					
Upstate, 13 to 15	6.16	-.45	.81	07	-.55
Upstate, 16 to 19	6.23	.46	.66	07	.71

*The trend parameter for this model was statistically insignificant and so was dropped.

in upstate New York where assaults actually increased significantly by 34 percent.

For methodological purposes, homicide is an especially important crime because the level of implementation of the JO law was high for homicide cases, and homicide is the only crime for which all the arrests are covered by the law. Therefore, we might expect any effect of the law to stand out clearly for homicide arrests, and the failure to find such an effect is noteworthy.

Rape and arson arrests for 13- to 15-year-olds in NYC did decrease significantly following the implementation of the JO law. Rape declined by 30 percent and arson by 58 percent. Rapes, with a mean of 14.0 per month in New York before the law was implemented, declined to a mean of 9.8 thereafter. However, there was a similar drop in arrests for both crimes among NYC 16- to 19-year-olds, and there was a decrease in arson arrests for 13- to 15-year-olds in Philadelphia. The decrease in rape and arson arrests is thus not specific to juveniles in NYC and appears to be part of a general decline that affected other groups as well. The logic of the research design requires that such an effect be attributed to historical events unrelated to the JO law. In upstate New York, juvenile rape and arson arrests did not change following the introduction of the law. It thus seems most reasonable to conclude that the law did not affect rapes or arsons either in NYC or upstate.

The conclusion that New York City juvenile rape and arson were unaffected by the law is not completely satisfying, because both series did decrease. However, the analysis indicates that this decrease is more general than would be expected if the JO law were responsible. Further evidence against an effect of the law on rape is provided by an inspection of the time-series plots, which indicate that rape arrests for both 13- to 15-year-olds and 16- to 19-year-olds in NYC declined most in the period between 1974 and 1976. In fact, if the first 3 years of each series are dropped from the analysis, the effect of the intervention is statistically insignificant. The decrease in NYC rape arrests therefore appears to have been completed well before the JO law went into effect.

It is not possible to dismiss completely an effect of the JO law on rapes and arsons in NYC as was the case for homicides and assaults. However, the evidence against an effect of the law on these crimes is much stronger than the evidence in support of an effect. Perhaps the strongest case for an effect of the law can be made for robberies.

Robbery arrests of 13- to 15-year-olds in both New York City and in upstate New York increased insignificantly following the introduction of the law. However, there were statistically significant increases in two of the control series, arrests in Philadelphia and 16- to 19-year-olds in upstate New York. It is thus possible to argue that the JO law stopped an upward shift in juvenile robberies that would otherwise have occurred. That is, although the JO law did not reduce juvenile robberies, it may have prevented an increase in both upstate New York and in New York City.

Although this argument is not completely implausible, it is quite spec-ulative. In the first place, the increase in the control series is not uniform, because arrests of 16- to 19-year-olds in NYC decrease insignificantly in the postintervention period. The pattern of results is thus not one of a clear increase in all of the control series but only in two out of three.

Further, in both NYC and upstate, arrests of 13- to 15-year-olds are insignificantly higher following the intervention. The general tendency of the series is therefore upward, significantly so for two of the control series and insignificantly so for the two experimental series. The point estimates for the effect of the law are an increase of seven arrests per month for 13- to 15-year-olds in Philadelphia and of ten arrests per month for 16- to 19-year-olds in upstate New York. In contrast, the (statistically insignificant) point estimate for upstate 13- to 15-year-olds is an increase of three arrests per month. In substantive terms the differences between the experimental and control series are therefore extremely small, and it seems unwise to place much stress on them.

Overall, the pattern of results favors the conclusion that the JO law had little measurable effect on juvenile crime, either in NYC or in non–NYC counties. The results of the analysis are complex, but they are clearly inconsistent with a model in which juvenile arrests uniformly declined following the introduction of the law. Indeed, in only two of the experi-mental series (five each in New York City and in upstate) were there statis-tically significant decreases in arrests of 13- to 15-year-olds.

Although it is possible to construct a theory that would account for the results and still attribute some effect to the law, such a theory would have to be very complex. The theory would require that the decreases in arson and rape arrests for New York City juveniles be attributed to the law, but that the decreases in arson arrests for Philadelphia juveniles and in arson and rape arrest for 16- to 19-year-olds in NYC be discounted. On the other hand, the theory would require stressing the increase in robbery arrests of Phila-delphia juveniles and of 16- to 19-year-olds upstate as evidence of the law's preventive effect.

This analysis with its limited set of data cannot reject such possibilities, and they should be regarded as interesting speculations, subject to further examination and testing. However, the most parsimonious explanation is that the JO law was ineffective in reducing juvenile crime.

Conclusion

There are at least two general explanations for the apparent failure of the JO law to reduce juvenile crime in New York. The first explanation is that the law was too weak an intervention to produce a measurable effect on crime patterns. Although the implementation data tells an uneven story of the risks of punishment, they show that since 1977 the number of juveniles confined in New York has more than tripled. This suggests that there was a substantial increase in the risks of punishment. Although even higher levels of punishment may successfully reduce juvenile crime, these levels may have to be greater than any currently envisioned. In theory, enforcement could be expanded, but in fact considerations of justice and the costs of imprisonment may limit the application of waiver statutes like the JO law. If the law failed for lack of implementation, a level of implementation sufficient to influence crime may be simply unattainable in practice.

Despite the fact that the JO law was a major attempt to organize the legal system to reduce violent juvenile crime, it failed to influence crime rates because juveniles were not responsive to its provisions. That is, serious juvenile offenders may not have been deterred by even a marginal increase in the certainty and severity of punishment promised by the law. This explanation is compatible with the possibility that JO law was insufficiently implemented, but it emphasizes the response of juveniles to the law rather than the organizational context as the reason for the no-effect finding.

Part of the reason why the JO law appears to have minimal impact on violent juvenile crime is its implementation in loosely coupled systems of juvenile and criminal justice. The loose fit between crime and punishment for juvenile offenders in criminal court runs contrary to an important principle in a theory of deterrence that stresses the certainty of punishment. The threat of sanctions may be further loosened by the fact that New York's juvenile court is not without power to sanction serious offenders based on the 1976 Juvenile Justice Reform Act. Although most juveniles appearing before New York's juvenile courts have received relatively little punishment, the probability of a punitive disposition is certainly not zero. The additional, harsher penalties of the JO law may not have appeared significant enough to daunt potential offenders. The message that the New York State legislature intended to send to violent juvenile offenders may thus have gone unheeded.

Thus a switch in legal setting and an increase in the severity of punishment does not necessarily lead to a reduction in violent juvenile crime. I do not mean to indicate that there are no long-term consequences as a result of the JO law, which may eventually lead to a reduction in violent juvenile crime. Yet these long-term effects cannot be predicted based on the available evidence and a theory that indicates a short-term intervention. Future research particularly directed at the possible lag effects associated with criminal justice reforms should tell us more about the relationship between crime and punishment in the context of any attempt to organize the legal process for deterrence.

The results of the analysis further suggest that proponents of criminal punishment for juveniles may be as overly optimistic as have been advocates of treatment in the ability of legal reforms to reduce juvenile crime. Moreover, the expected impact of the JO law is not just in terms of rates of violent juvenile crime. There are more visible forms of impact based on the institutions that were created to house the increased population of juveniles sentenced to maximum security DFY facilities.

Convicted Juvenile Offenders
in a Maximum Security Institution

ALTHOUGH IT IS DIFFICULT TO SEE the impact of the JO law on rates of crime, the effect of recriminalization is most visible at the hard end of the system. Among the nearly 17,000 juveniles arrested as juvenile offenders in New York State between 1979 and 1990, about 11 percent were incarcerated. Among those incarcerated, a proportion of convicted juvenile offenders received sentences that were substantially longer than what they could have received in juvenile court. And recall that since passage of the JO law, the population of juveniles incarcerated in New York's maximum security institutions increased substantially (see Table 5.16 in Chapter 5).

This chapter is about one of the secure Division for Youth (DFY) facilities that was created as a consequence of the JO law. The JO law requires that sentenced juvenile offenders initially be incarcerated in maximum security prisons operated by DFY. Those secure facilities are to provide "educational" and "rehabilitative" services as part of their treatment-oriented mandate. In a sense, the transfer of juveniles to the criminal justice system ends at the point of incarceration, when juveniles are returned to the juvenile justice system's divisions for youths and maximum security institutions. But it is a momentary return; after serving the minimum period of incarceration, juvenile offenders are subject to adult parole and to possible transfer to an adult prison system. For juvenile offenders sentenced to a maximum of life in prison for murder, a division for youth secure facility is only a temporary residential setting. However, it seems that if the creators of the JO law wanted to make the process of recriminalization more complete, they would have initially designated the state's adult department of corrections as the agency responsible for the incarceration of juvenile offenders.

The subtle contradiction in punishment and treatment mandates is visible in my observations of a maximum security institution that was created because of the JO law. Soon after passage of the JO law, Assemblyman Arthur Eve lobbied for the placement of a DFY secure facility in his home district, the Masten Park section of Buffalo's east side. Normally, politicians would say "not in my back yard" for any institution that dealt with criminal offenders. But several years earlier, the state had vacated the one-block facility that was at one time a drug rehabilitation center. Assemblyman Eve at the time expressed concern that the abandoned facility would further blight a neighborhood that was already in decline. He wanted to turn the facility into an institution that would be a source for badly needed employment in his district, where jobs were increasingly scarce. Besides Assemblyman Eve could recommend qualified constituents for employment in a state facility, thus providing an important source of political patronage.

Yet Assemblyman Eve was one of a handful of legislators to openly oppose passage of the JO law in debate. In subsequent speeches, he repeated his belief that juveniles have no place in the criminal court and should only be subject to the treatment-oriented objectives of the state. He felt that the JO law would further subject black juveniles to the "institutionalized" forms of racism that lead to their higher rate of incarceration for longer periods of time. At the same time, he was well aware of the fact that new institutions would be needed to house a larger population of juveniles convicted and incarcerated as juvenile offenders.

Soon after passage of the JO law, Assemblyman Eve suggested to DFY officials that the location for one of the planned DFY secure facilities be at Masten Park. He believed that the racial characteristics of the staff should be more in line with those of the resident population of juvenile offenders and, therefore, more in tune with meeting its treatment-oriented goals. Unlike most facilities that are located in more rural parts of the state, Masten Park did attract a large staff of black administrators, counselors, and guards. In fact, Masten Park was DFY's only secure facility located in a largely black, urban community.

Initially built as a convent in the later part of the nineteenth century, it still retained much of its original and elegant architecture. When visiting the institution I was often drawn to the uplifting and graceful shape of its stone-carved windows. Within its high stone walls, Masten Park defied its inner-city location. It occupied an entire city block and seemed to have plenty of outdoor space for recreational activities between two large three-story gray-stone buildings.

Refitting Masten Park as a maximum security institution required the state to invest millions in its reconstruction. One building was gutted and reconstructed to house four units or wings, each containing fifteen rooms in a dormitory-type setting. The new building also housed a school, gym, and workshop facilities. Masten Park's administrative facilities, as well as two additional wings, a gym, and the institution's auditorium, were located within another building that was never completely renovated. Although both buildings were connected by an above-ground, enclosed walkway, Masten Park felt like a relatively small institution despite its population of approximately 100 juveniles.

Masten Park like other DFY facilities differs from adult prisons in several important ways. First, they are physically different. Secure facilities for juveniles are much smaller than most maximum security adult prisons. Like other juvenile facilities, there are no prison cells with iron bars in place of doors. Juvenile institutions contain a much lower staff-to-inmate ratio. Masten Park's daily average of 100 juvenile offenders contrasts sharply with another correctional facility in western New York, Attica, which houses over 2,000 adult inmates.

Thus the cost of operating secure facilities for juveniles is much higher than that of running an adult prison. They require a fully equipped school with classrooms, computers, and certified teachers to meet state mandated educational requirements. For institutions like Masten Park, the total cost averaged as high as $80,000 a year per incarcerated juvenile (Schulman & Ciotta, *Buffalo News*, October 8, 1986, p. B-2). This amount is substantially higher than the average adult facility, where the cost might reach an average of $20,000 per year.

Despite the amount of money that the state is willing to expend in the name of treatment, there is much about Masten Park that makes it look like an ordinary prison. As with all prisons, officials are most concerned with security – they want to maintain order and prevent escapes. Every resident, staff member, and visitor is regularly reminded by the over 20-foot, double-edged barbed-wire walls, locked doors, and constant security checks that Masten Park is a prison. Juveniles are there to do time as mandated by their criminal court sentences.

At this point I wish to relate how I became intimately acquainted with Masten Park, its residents, and staff. I first discovered Masten Park, and consequently New York's JO law, upon moving to Buffalo and seeing a maximum security institution located within a few miles of my home. Several months later I asked for a tour of the facility, and several years later I then volunteered as a summer-school teacher. This I did for a 6-week period; five mornings a week I taught history to twelve juvenile offenders. I am not a certified high-school teacher, but I gather that the fact that I taught at the university qualified me in the view of the director to teach in the institution.

The class I taught was considered an elective on the history of juvenile justice. My students were preselected and consisted of twelve of the better residents in the facility. Most of them were convicted of homicide and were lifers in the sense that their minimum sentence ranged from 9 years to a maximum of life in prison. I became, as I hoped, personally familiar with most of the juveniles in my class, and that provided me with the rapport I needed later to talk in detail with them and other juveniles in the facility. At the same time, I spent several weeks with juvenile offenders on the "wings" during their leisure time. During school hours, when I was not having lunch with the juvenile offenders, I listened and talked to staff informally often in the teacher's lounge.

Since my summer-school experience, I have remained in touch with several former student/residents, some of whom are still serving sentences in adult facilities. I returned to Masten Park regularly to give class tours to my university students. Also, I became part of Masten Park's citizen advisory board, which allowed me to maintain an inside view of the facility. Although this may have compromised my objectivity as a sociologist, I viewed it as critical to learning the intimate story of juvenile offenders and the institutions that were created to control and prevent their continued violent behavior.

In the pages to follow, I relate some of my interviews with juvenile offenders and officials. Interviews with officials also draw on the observations of Colleen A. Connoly, who also worked as a summer-school teacher at Masten Park. I then relate major events that transpired in Masten Park, and an all-too-familiar story of institutional crisis and reform.

Interviews with Incarcerated Juvenile Offenders

At the time of my interviews in 1983, there were 88 juveniles incarcerated in Masten Park. The mean age of these juveniles was 16.5, and their average age of arrest was 15.5. By race, the population of juveniles consisted of 53 black juveniles (60 percent), 20 white juveniles (23 percent), 14 Hispanics (16 percent), and one Native American. The percentage of white juveniles is higher at Masten Park than at other DFY secure facilities because of its distance from the New York City area, where most juvenile offenders originally resided. By offense characteristics, 12 juveniles were convicted of murder, 9 rape/sodomy, and the rest other designated felony offenses. The vast majority of juveniles were from the densely populated counties of New York City.

Masten Park's residents fit many of the offender characteristics of convicted and incarcerated juvenile offenders as reported in the DCJS data. The small proportion of white juveniles were in Masten Park for more serious violent offenses and for longer sentences, while black juveniles were incarcerated for shorter periods of time for less serious offenses.

For many, Masten Park was just another residential facility on a long list of state institutions in which they had previously served time. Some fit the definition of chronic delinquents merely by the fact that, like Bosket, they were raised by the state in one institution after another. For these repeatedly institutionalized juveniles, Masten Park was just another stop along the way to adult corrections.

A small segment of juvenile offenders seemed initially frightened by their experiences in Masten Park. Doing time was difficult. The first several weeks seemed like years. For these juveniles, doing time was still difficult – but they seemed to have adjusted to life in the institution. Among the ones who never seemed to adjust to confinement, there were repeated attempts to escape or to commit suicide.

In the next two sections, I have organized parts of my recorded interviews with eleven juvenile offenders to show their perceptions of justice and crime. Most of the juvenile offenders I interviewed in private were students in my summer-school class, and they do not randomly represent the total residential population. However, my impressions of Masten Park and its juvenile offenders are based on my contact with the larger residential population of juvenile offenders in a variety of settings.

A Sense of Criminal Injustice. Juvenile offenders talk constantly about the legal injustice related to their conviction in criminal court. Although they do not deny guilt for some offense, they generally see their conviction in criminal court as unfair. This is because of the legal technicalities related to their case and their status as juveniles. They did not invent these arguments; they heard them elsewhere – over and over again – from their lawyers and from a culture that emphasizes techniques for neutralizing the "moral bind" of the law. According to Matza (1964), neutralization occurs when the delinquent's sense of injustice is heightened by his standards. His standards of justice are rigorous, though not peculiarly so. His statements often seem unduly legalistic, and we infer that he is simply indulging in self-service (103).

The self-serving reaction of juvenile offenders is one that restates the technicalities of formal law.

As Matza suggests, the juvenile's interpretation of justice draws on what is seen as fair. Are the official decision makers consistent and competent? Consistency refers to being "treated according to the same principles as others of my status" (Matza 1964: 196). Competency reflects the offender's belief in the ability or authority of officials to pass judgment on his or her criminal responsibility.

In criminal court, juvenile offenders are caught between their legal status as adults and their status as juvenile delinquents. In passing judgment on criminal justice officials, juvenile offenders can draw on their handling as either criminal offenders or juvenile delinquents. At times they can draw on their subjective status as delinquents in arguing that their cases should have been removed to juvenile court. At other times, they can emphasize that their due process rights were compromised through the criminal justice process.

A critical element of proceedings in a traditional juvenile court is the confidentiality of the delinquents' identity and official record. Juvenile offenders, like adults in criminal court, may have their identity broadcast throughout the media. This would appear related to the seriousness of the offense, because ordinary, designated felony offenses may be of little interest to the media in large jurisdictions.

Of the eleven I interviewed in detail, only four said their cases received media attention. All four were convicted of homicide offenses. One juvenile offender from an upstate urban area complained that the judge and prosecutor used his case as a means to achieve higher political office; each pointed out that both officials won their election campaigns because of the publicity attached to his trial. Another juvenile offender spoke about how everyone in the small city where he lived knew about his crime.

> At the trial when they were interviewing for the jury, everyone said that they had heard of the crime. I don't think that I was tried fairly.

Although the above statement is not entirely accurate, because jurors are not technically required to be ignorant of the crime, it reflects a part of the juvenile's perception of justice.

That perception is also related to the severity of penalties and the administration of justice for other juvenile offenders. A few juvenile offenders felt that they were not granted their full procedural rights. Some rights are explicit in the stated legal rules, such as the right to legal representation or the right to a trial by jury. Five of the eleven juveniles said they were not informed of their right to remain silent and to have a lawyer present at the time they were questioned by the police. The vast majority of juvenile offenders plead guilty and were not provided with a trial by jury. Several juvenile offenders said they had no other choice but to plead guilty or risk more severe penalties.

But other rights are less explicit in the legal rules, such as the right to negotiate a plea. Where the severity of the offense precludes officials from negotiating the terms of the charge and penalties, juvenile offenders, even when they admit their guilt, will go through the motion of a trial by jury. Among those who went through a trial by jury, one juvenile convicted of homicide was told that he could not expect any sentence reduction in prison time from the prosecutor even if he pleaded guilty.

> The DA gave me no choice, I could either plead guilty and get 9 to life, or go to trial and get a maximum of 9 to life. I figured I might as well put the state through some expense even though I admitted having committed the crime.

In response to the question "Were you treated fairly by the criminal justice system?" five said they were. As expected, these juveniles were charged with the least serious designated felony offenses. But others cited examples of the manner in which procedural unfairness in the criminal justice system resulted in their conviction and incarceration.

> The police didn't have proper cause to pick me up. My parents should have been present, if possible, at the time of the arrest. The police also failed to read me my rights, and they also searched my house.

Another juvenile offender who was especially adept at identifying procedural violations spoke of other technicalities that should have led to the dismissal of his case from criminal court:

> The size of the room in which a juvenile can be questioned is governed by statute. The size of the room in which I was questioned was not of the prescribed dimensions. The number of persons who can question the juvenile at one time is also determined by statute. Also, the law states that a lawyer or a parent of the accused juvenile must be present at all times during questioning. I was in a room no more than five by seven, and there was three

or four officers questioning me at the same time, and there was no lawyer or parent there at the time of questioning. We were also told that we could leave at any time during the questioning but we had no way of leaving because the police picked us up at the house in a police car. We really were not free to go anywhere without the consent of the police. According to the law, anything I told them then was inadmissible in court. I had no right to waive my rights because I was a minor, and there was no adult present to advise me as to what I should do. It was an emotional time for me and I was very impressionable. They could have told me anything and I would have believed them in my condition.

The ability to articulate the specific details of their cases is specific to juvenile offenders subject to a trial by jury. Because of their lengthy sentences, a few juvenile offenders remained hopeful that appellate courts would overturn their convictions. This itself turned into an education for several juvenile offenders, because at a relatively young age they had already become jailhouse lawyers and were intimately acquainted with all the legal arguments related to their criminal court convictions.

In the opinion of juvenile offenders, the question of ultimate guilt or innocence for their violent offenses is irrelevant to the legal requirements for a conviction in criminal court. Most of the juveniles who pleaded innocent did not deny their actual guilt for some offense. Instead, they distinguished actual guilt from legal guilt by noting that they should not have been convicted in criminal court, because they were "technically" innocent of the alleged offenses. In their words, they saw themselves as "legally screwed." As one juvenile offender who committed murder at the age of 13 noted:

> I feel that I got what I deserved because I was guilty. I did what I did and I got what I deserved. But legally, I was screwed by the criminal justice system. In a legal sense, they shouldn't have convicted me because of the legal technicalities.

I later asked juvenile offenders how the experience in criminal court might have differed from their earlier arrest and disposition in juvenile court. Four of the eleven juveniles said they were previously adjudicated in juvenile court. Among these four juveniles, two said the criminal court process was more formal.

> SINGER: How did the criminal court experience differ from the family court?
>
> JO: Family court just had my parents and the judge. In the criminal court the public was involved.

SINGER: What kind of effect do you feel the criminal court experience had on your family?

JO: They were in shock and it was very hard on them. They were very disappointed in me.

SINGER: Were they surprised that you were processed in adult court?

JO: They thought that I would be in family court.

Six of the eleven juveniles responded to the question, "What length of sentence would you give to a juvenile who committed a murder?" Only one said 9 to life, and another said 3 to life. The remaining juveniles indicated maximum sentences of 5 to 9 years, with minimums ranging from probation to 3 years. As might be expected, none of the juvenile offenders serving 9 to life indicated that a maximum of life was an appropriate sentence for a juvenile. One said:

> There is a lot of time. And we're talking about 14- and 15-year-old kids who come in and see no light at the end of the tunnel. And the attitude is that as long as I'm not going to get it for 10 years, I may as well fuck up because it won't make any difference. So they just get worse instead of getting rehabilitated. From the initial phase of when the emphasis is on the rehabilitation, the kid no longer has an interest in getting rehabilitated. It's not the same as one would expect from an adult who could relate to the time. The kid feels that his life is over at that point.

Although most juvenile offenders felt that their punishment was much too severe, several stressed that conviction in criminal court was appropriate for some violent offenses. In regards to the JO law, one juvenile who was convicted for a sodomy and murder he committed at the age of 13 commented:

> I feel that the JO law is not totally a bad law. The intent was correct but the sentencing a bit stiff. Giving a 13-year-old 9 to life at such a young age is a traumatic experience which could psychologically do more harm than good. He is more likely to become a career felon than to become rehabilitated. The youth feels his life is over and many times wants to commit suicide.

On the Determinants of Violent Juvenile Crime. No juvenile offender I spoke to saw anything innate about his past criminal behavior. They repeatedly expressed the view that their criminal behavior was due to their prior institutional placements, delinquent friends, and families.

SINGER: How about the idea of punishment – do you think that it prevents kids from going out and getting into trouble?

JO: No. Look at me. They put me in lock-up. That didn't do anything for me. They keep you away from your family in with bad people. That's where you learn more things from them. It makes you worse. You could have been in for little petty things and they put you in with people who did many bad things. When you get out on the street the next time you know more.

SINGER: You don't think that it [prison] scares kids into staying out of trouble?

JO: No.

SINGER: How long were you sent away for the first time you were convicted?

JO: Five years.

SINGER: Where were you for those 5 years?

JO: All around. Different places. That's what messed me up.

SINGER: What are some of the facilities that you've been to?

JO: I was in Queens [facility] for a while and then I went to Staten Island [facility]. Then I went back to Queens [facility] and to Yonkers [facility], they had me going all around. The more serious the institution, the more serious the stuff I was doing.[1]

SINGER: These were open facilities where you could leave most of the time?

JO: Yes. On weekends. We weren't locked up or anything like that. We could walk around and things.

SINGER: How could you steal when you were in these places?

JO: When you walk around you could steal from places inside the facility.

SINGER: Do you feel that you needed a lot more control than you were getting there?

JO: If they would have let me be with my family it might have been better. That's what it does when you run away from it and go to the facility. And you meet somebody who robs, and then you start following him and stealing too, and it grows. It's like germs; it spreads. When you let people in here they catch the germ. It just grows bigger. People who never robbed trains or banks listen to people who have done it, then they go out and do it themselves.

SINGER: So you feel that you've learned a lot of crime here.

JO: Yes. And once you get used to the time, you can deal with it; it doesn't bother you any more.

SINGER: Would you say that you also learned how to commit crimes from your friends at home?

JO: I learned it here. How to hot-wire a car and things like that.

SINGER: Did you do the burglary by yourself or did you have a co-defendant?

JO: I had two co-defendants.

For some juvenile offenders, however, there seemed to be greater security in the environment of Masten Park than in their home environments. An interview with a white juvenile convicted of first degree robbery reflects some of the deeper familial difficulties that juvenile offenders may have faced. He is what is known in the institution as a *cut-up* – his body displays the scars from numerous attempted suicides. Unfortunately, the attempts are so common that they are rarely taken seriously by the institution's officials.

SINGER: How does life in a secure facility such as this differ from learning in a public school?

JO: I think this is better than the public school. I didn't like the public school very much. I attended a lot of special ed classes there. It wasn't so much for academic reasons as for hyperactive behavior. Here there is that special control. The public school couldn't handle me. This is all right, and now I feel different. I feel much better. When I get out I will probably be attending . . . County Community in . . . , and from there I will try to get into a better school such as . . . University. I know I have it mentally, and now I feel that I have the discipline which I didn't have before I came here.

This same juvenile reported that his home environment was a source of much of his anger and frustration.

JO: I was getting into marijuana in seventh grade and I got suspended. That weekend we had a foster kid at the house. His name was Brian. I was getting into bad arguments with him. I had a nervous breakdown because I couldn't handle the pressure of what was going on. I was in an institution for about 3 months and then I got released. We were working things out with a psychiatrist and a social worker. When I got home that was when I was put into special ed at school. I would see the shrink on and off then. When I was seeing him I was doing good. Then they would stop it and, I don't know, it was more like a family thing.

SINGER: And your parents were there too?

JO: I didn't like some of the things that he [the psychiatrist] was saying though.

SINGER: Is there anything in particular that stands out in your mind about what he said?

JO: Well, I would stay out late with my older brother a lot and they said that I was too young and not responsible. But when I was with him and his friends I would behave. But they soon gave into me and it was all right. Then I got into stealing. I was about 12 or 13 and I was stealing everything in sight.

SINGER: If they were tougher on you, do you think that the outcome might have been different?

JO: I think it would have been worse. Something definitely would have happened that, to this day, well the feelings I have with them now, we don't talk much even. I haven't called them since I've been here. I tried calling them when I was in Riverhead and they wouldn't talk to me any more. They say I'm not their son no more. I had feelings about killing them a lot of times. When I get mad a lot I'll think of them, and I'll get madder, and a lot of times I'll cut myself. I get mad at them so much and I want to kill them. I'm seriously thinking of killing them but I've been overcoming that these last couple of months cause I've been thinking strong about my freedom and that I should just leave them alone and say that they never were. Just like they said that I never was. So I'll just try to make it on my own and pick my own friends and do my own thing.

When juveniles cut themselves every time they think about their parents, there are deep psychological problems that defy the simple solution of a punishment-oriented criminal justice system. Unfortunately, Masten Park fails to provide the intensive counseling that so many of its residents obviously require. Masten Park and other secure facilities provide only temporary relief for society from the problems or frustrations of juvenile offenders by keeping them away from their home environments.

How juveniles see their treatment and punishment reflects their reality. For most of the juvenile offenders I talked to, the impact of criminal court is only marginally different from juvenile court. Most juvenile offenders expressed the opinion that their sentences were fair and not out of the ordinary.[2] They accepted their chronic status as delinquents or as juvenile offenders. They expressed legal ignorance as well as legal injustice. Their legal ignorance stemmed from their perception of a negotiated legal process that seemed similar to what they experienced in juvenile courts. In criminal court they pleaded guilty to their offenses in the same way they pleaded guilty in juvenile court.

Legal injustice was confined to the small segment of offenders who felt the more severe sanctions of criminal court. Their penalties were substantially more severe than what they might have received for the same offense in juvenile court. These juvenile offenders viewed their sentences not just as a product of their offenses; they questioned the motives and competencies of criminal justice officials. They compared themselves not with adult offenders but with other juveniles. They resisted for good reason the idea that they were criminally responsible for their offenses.

Finally, it is important to bear in mind that the reaction of juvenile offenders might not differ that dramatically from incarcerated adult offenders. Casper (1972) shows that adult offenders expressed their feeling of injustice when their sentences went beyond the going or expected sentence for the crime. Adult offenders can also compare what they got to other adult offenders in criminal court. Juvenile offenders, however, are in a unique position. Their source of comparison is not confined to juvenile offenders in the criminal court but to other juveniles sentenced or placed as delinquents in the juvenile court.

Meeting Mandated Treatment Objectives

The only requirements at Masten Park are to attend school, to perform assigned work chores, to act in a nonviolent manner at all times, and not to venture outside of the institution's walls. As can be gleaned from a variety of DFY policy statements, the goals of the institution are

1. to improve basic skills in reading, math, and written communication;
2. to accumulate high-school units needed toward grade achievement or high-school graduation;
3. to prepare for General Equivalency Tests and the Regents' Competency Tests in Reading, Writing, and Math when eligible;
4. to provide vocational/career counseling;
5. to provide vocational, multi-occupational shop experience;
6. to develop marketable vocational skills to be utilized upon release;
7. to modify negative behaviors;
8. to provide mechanisms for developing decision-making skills.

An explicit goal of the facility that might not be documented easily is that of maintaining the institution's custodial orientation. Security is an important concern and at times conflicts with the institution's treatment-oriented mandate. The most explicit ways in which treatment is implemented are through Masten Park's level system and techniques of education. Masten Park's treatment mandate is also implemented through the services of a full-time psychologist who meets regularly with groups of juvenile offenders. The groups are voluntary, and they are generally specialized around particular kinds of problems. Juvenile offenders are also free to meet with the psychologist on an individual basis, although it is not a requirement. In the sections that follow, I first discuss the level system and then techniques of education.[3]

The Level System. Institutional control is maintained through a "progressive level system." A resident's level is considered by the parole board when deciding if the juvenile should be released after the minimum time served. How well juvenile offenders perform socially and academically is directly measured by their level within the institution. Juvenile offenders start at D level and can move in reverse alphabetical order to A level. After success at A level, juvenile offenders can graduate to trustee status, commonly known as *T level*.

The rewards at each level come in the form of late-night privileges, additional room decorations, and additional long-distance phone calls. Juvenile offenders at D level start out with no privileges in a standard room without decorations. They are locked in their rooms by 10 P.M. They may have one 10-minute phone call a week. If they graduate to A level, they can have three posters, one rug, a stereo, and two phone calls each week. A-level residents can have eight late nights a month when they may stay up till 1:30 in the morning. If they reach the level of trustee, they may decorate their rooms any way they wish and are granted three phone calls per week.

Advances in levels are dependent on satisfactory behavior. Satisfactory behavior ratings, Ss, are assigned in each 8-hour shift provided juveniles do not violate any of the institutional rules of conduct. More serious, illegal types of violations, such as causing injury to another resident, can result in sanctions as well as a reduction in level. The institutional rules that residents are to follow are presented verbally and in written handout to each entering juvenile offender.

Juvenile offenders can also advance in level if they perform well in school. Youth Division Counselors (YDCs) and the facility administration link advances in level to significant school success, such as a GED or high-school diploma. All As during a 10-week marking period are worth 4 weeks of satisfactory behavior (Ss), and Bs 3 weeks of Ss. A high-school general educational diploma is worth 5 weeks of Ss. So, like public schools, the progression within the institutional setting is linked to grade performance. Furthermore, parole boards consider level advances as an indicator of progress in the overall program.

According to the assistant facility director, while progress in school programming was important to the parole board, other factors counted as well:

> They looked for overall progress. School is so small in light of a youth's overall improvement as a person. Was school important? Yes. But, the importance of school is all very relative to a person's perspective. So many grade levels of reading improvement was hardly as important as acting nonviolently.

Acting nonviolently was not only important to the parole board members but also to facility administrators. By acting nonviolently, juveniles could progress in the level system, which was critical to maintaining security and techniques of education.

Techniques of Education. The importance of education is reflected in the fact that the education director answers directly to the director of the facility. Juvenile offenders are taught the basics, but the teaching of basics is generally within the context of special education. Twenty-five percent of the facility's youths were classified for special education. Of these youths, two-fifths were classified on the basis of learning disabilities, another two-fifths as emotionally disturbed youth, and the last fifth as mentally retarded.

But perhaps like in a regular school, teachers expressed difficulty at not being able to provide the individual attention that some juveniles appeared to need. As one English teacher explained:

> There's no time in the day to give any extra help beyond the 45 minutes; it's too bad there isn't an after-school study hall on the units.

In their home environment, school homework might not have been possible because of distractions related to a disorganized family situation. In Masten Park, the routine procedures of a secure facility might initially be viewed as conducive toward extra-school work. However, this was usually not the case. The two Youth Division Aides (YDAs) on each wing were not in a position to supervise approximately fourteen residents and enforce a school homework policy. Some teachers tried to assign homework, but they had little expectation that it would be completed. Staff on the units are not obliged to require that students do homework.

One YDA explained that a barrier to a homework policy was the constant changes on the living units. She explained:

> Our populations could change daily due to the shifting of residents from unit-to-unit. Or, we might need to have double group sessions because of some problem in the facility or on the unit. Or, there could be a special evening TV program which we'd decided to require youths to view. Or, everyone might have early bed due to an infraction. There were too many things to prevent a policy from working when it came to homework.

Another YDA explained that

> pushing homework on top of a bad school day was worthless because it just made kids angrier. We didn't maintain any homework expectation. There was no guarantee that it would get done.

Security was also given as a reason for not giving homework:

> I didn't want my guys carrying anything in the corridors. Having a book, pens or folders gave them more places to hide contraband.

But one YDC complained that there was plenty of opportunity for supervised homework:

> If teachers wanted to come up to work with kids they could, they just never did.

There is no record of any initiative to create more opportunities for increased student–teacher contact. Many teachers indicated that by the end of classes they were tired. They needed the afterschool time for their preparation and committee work, but they would have welcomed a study hall woven into the day's schedule. Other problems related to the structure of the facility, such as not enough open classrooms in too poorly ventilated summer-school settings. In times of a heat wave, the school was closed for the afternoons because the classrooms were much too hot.

The minimum expectation at Masten Park led one teacher to note that

> I reprioritized. My students were low readers so there was no way that they could pass that text. I did have some kids who were high readers, but I figured that they could benefit from the reading lessons, too. I gave high readers other activities at the conceptual level to work on while I worked on the low kids' vocabulary skills.

At Masten Park much was left to the individual teacher.

> It wasn't like a "real school." Everyday, I did what I could do with materials and kids in front of me. Aside from RCT or GED pressure, there was no accountability in terms of the curriculum I was teaching.

As one math teacher explained:

> My class was supposed to be for Math, not group therapy. The best thing I could do was teach and if there was a problem, kids had to handle that with staff on the unit. Once I let them bring it into my class, I'd lose them for the whole class period.

On the other hand, another teacher responded:

> I let them talk about their fights and get it out of their systems: sometimes, that was more important to them than sentence structure rules.

By and large the expectations to achieve the stated educational goals appeared to vary with educational directors. As one of Masten Park's facility directors indicated:

These teachers had worked summers prior to . . . when I was appointed. They'd basically do whatever they wanted with the curriculum and then show movies on Friday. This was a poisonous habit to try to break.

The VCR became a common educational tool.

They'd bring in tapes they'd made off HBO; the tapes weren't screened at the security check because the teachers were friends of the YDAs working the desk. They'd show films in the first period which would always run into the second period. Students wouldn't want to leave in the middle of a film so they'd pressure other teachers to release them from class. This was a real problem, because if students weren't permitted to watch films, they'd be disruptive in class. The YDAs were inconsistent. Often, they were watching the films, too, so they didn't like moving to another classroom.

There were suggestions for change to make the school setting work better. These were expressed in the following statement:

A secure center is just not a public school setting. If you wanted to make progress with those kids who were really indifferent about school, you should've changed the schedule. No one learned much after lunch. Run academics in the morning, recreation and phys ed in the afternoon and shops at night.

But such a schedule change would have been a huge facility disruption. No one wanted to give up the current hours that they worked. It was inconvenient for the school officials and the teachers to try to duplicate their former public school educational setting.

We could not as an organization withstand a schedule change that would alter the lives of staff. There was a constant morale problem so we kept our focus on keeping the program in the education unit going. I supported education strongly when I came in here; other people didn't. So, there was no way that I could get everyone convinced that a schedule change would work.

And indeed morale problems did surface, especially with a series of newspaper reports about repeated acts of violence and abuse within the Masten Park Secure Facility.

Institutional Crisis

A picture of the troubles at Masten Park appeared on Oct. 5, 1986 in a front-page *Buffalo News* headline stating that "Even the Guards Have Records." The staff members' previous arrests and convictions for a wide range of offenses, including the use and sale of drugs, were listed (Schulman & Ciotta 1986). The *Buffalo News* revealed that of the 92 guards (YDAs), 21 had been arrested while working at the facility or shortly before getting their jobs there. Of those 21, 8 were charged and 3 were convicted of violent felonies.

The *Buffalo News* series[4] also listed the political affiliation of many of the staff members and showed their political connection to Assemblyman Arthur Eve. Most of the jobs at Masten Park were filled by a process that was outside the civil service system. For example, Arthur Eve's son and several people who worked on the Assemblyman's campaign, including the institution's first director, were on Masten Park's payroll. Although Eve denied that he controlled the hiring of staff, he insisted that he recommended to the facility's director only persons that he thought were qualified.

An audit by the state comptroller confirmed the problems of Masten Park. The audit by Comptroller Edward V. Regan covered a period from January 1983 to May 1985, and reported that security problems at Masten Park produced an inordinate number of violent or criminal incidents. The audit further cited inadequate training of staff members and a poorly administered security program. During the 29-month period ending May 1985, auditors counted 86 critical incidents, including 31 fights between staff and youths, 23 fights among youths, 4 cases of weapons possession, 6 attempted escapes, and 22 incidents related to suicide attempts, destruction of property, drug use, and harassment of employees.

In subsequent years, more news reports on serious incidents of violence by residents and guards produced demands for administrative reform. The first director of the institution was required to resign when it was further alleged that his staff appointments were directly linked to political patronage. According to one teacher, the effect of institutional turmoil impacted on the school's ability to teach.

> By midsummer, I was just ready to finish off the program and get out of there; you never knew what was going to happen next and some of the fights indicated that the kids were being used or were trying to get control.

After 1986, Masten Park became a limited-secure facility. Reorganizing Masten Park for a population of juvenile delinquents required officials to divide the institution into secure and limited-secure buildings. The division continued not only by type of adjudication but also by type of offense. Some juvenile offenders were isolated into a sex offender unit. The unit was created in part as a consequence of the proactive treatment efforts of one of the two psychologists at the time who had an active interest in the treatment of sex offenders. The assistant facility director explained:

We have one of the few sex offender treatment units in the state. No matter what a youth's special education status is, he's assigned to the sex offenders unit. Our staff on that unit has special training to deal with those issues in group sessions and they can be more easily scheduled to see the psychologist as a unit. This is definitely more important than their school schedules.

Thus, as the long and familiar history of juvenile justice shows, education became more ceremonial than real. It was secondary to the objectives of the institution to maintain control and to avoid crisis.

Conclusion

The labeling and tracking of juveniles as offenders deserving of incarceration in maximum security institutions does not end with their imprisonment. Rather, it continues in the form of the institution's systems of education and control. As I mentioned, the level system worked to control juveniles by tracking them into a behavioral modification program in which they began at D level and then progressed possibly to T level. Ironically, juvenile offenders were more likely to be rewarded with being a trustee if they committed a very serious offense and received long-term incarceration. The trustee level could only be obtained over time, and the institutional adjustment of residents naturally appeared far better among those juveniles who spent considerable amounts of time at Masten Park.

Masten Park followed the same techniques of treatment that generally existed in the world outside of the institution. Techniques of classification in which troubled juveniles are divided as they were in their public school setting and in the juvenile justice and criminal justice systems are duplicated over and over again. They reflect modern-day institutions that like to classify juveniles into A, B, C, & D levels, not-so-bad, bad, and very bad students, status offenders, delinquents, youthful offenders, juvenile offenders, and sex offenders.

But it would be too easy to dismiss the treatment-oriented mission of Masten Park. There is an ancient conflict between society's legal need to punish the offender as reflected in the JO law and to treat the offender as reflected in the stated objectives of DFY. The task of Masten Park's officials was a difficult one given their legal mandate to treat juveniles with the violent juvenile offender label. But Masten Park might be viewed as successful in breaking the cycle of locating institutions for treatment far from the urban areas where juvenile offenders reside. It was founded with the best of intents, and the staff that worked in the institution was largely motivated to provide for the best interests of its resident population.

Still the task of administrators and staff simultaneously to treat and to punish juvenile offenders is an extremely difficult one, especially in the artificial community or family atmosphere that officials attempted to create. Like all prisons, including adult facilities operated by Departments of "Corrections," there is a bottom-line concern with maintaining discipline, order, and security. Juvenile offenders by definition are proven rebels, and their resistance to authority does not end once they enter the barbed-wire walls of a maximum security institution. Moreover, the additional sense of injustice that some juvenile offenders expressed as a consequence of their sentencing in criminal court may have further fueled their resistance to institutional treatment. Contrary to the intent of officials, the values and norms conducive to committing acts of violent crime may have been strengthened by the juvenile offender's prison experience.

Another part of the problems that emerged in Masten Park is related to management issues. Officials were ill prepared to deal with apathy, frustration, and even the violence that arose among the staff. There was no sense of the complex reasons why Masten Park was created, and why its residents were labeled as juvenile offenders. In-service training was exclusively devoted to crisis management as defined by short-term problems, such as an attempted escape or what to do when a juvenile hits another juvenile.

Of course, Masten Park was not alone in its inability to maintain a crisis-free atmosphere in which to treat and to punish juveniles. It is part of the familiar history of juvenile justice reforms. Other DFY institutions were subject to investigation for incidence of abuse. In explaining the high level of violence at the Austin MacCormick Residential Center, the New York Office of State Inspector General (1993: 21) stated in a forty-one-page report that

> strict control of the residents has been a strong theme at MacCormick. Origins of this can be traced, in part, to the 1977 fire that destroyed most of the facility and in staff's experience with former resident Willie Bosket, a notoriously dangerous and manipulative youth.

Willie Bosket again? We return full circle to where we started with crisis and then reform. The direction of those reforms is not easily predicted by the good intentions of reformers. They involve specific organizational needs and interests. Those interests stem from pockets of power deposited in the hands of white and black legislators concerned not only about crime but also about other important matters, such as employment for constituents.

Policymakers and the public must address the balancing of legal requirements for both punishing and treating in loosely coupled subsystems of justice.[5] Doing justice and doing good requires us to look more deeply at our legal bureaucracies in action. If our institutions for treatment are to work, they will have to continue to require some consistent accounting of their purposes. Subsystems will continue to send conflicting messages to staff and to delinquents or offenders if they continue to ignore each others' stated purposes. For example, every juvenile offender sentenced to a DFY facility knows that it is not really a division *for youth* facility but actually a juvenile prison operated by a division *for the state.* The euphemistic terms of juvenile justice send a conflicting message of treatment and punishment for juvenile offenders.

If there is a risk to be taken toward treatment, it must be explicit to the public, officials, and juvenile offenders themselves. That requires an acknowledgment of the risks of treatment. As every good business person and smart criminal knows, without taking chances there is little opportunity for success. Increasing security to create more well-managed prisons for juveniles is the wrong path to pursue if officials want DFY institutions to meet their treatment-oriented mandate. In such institutions, I believe the warehousing of juvenile offenders to just doing their time will most likely haunt the public in the form of more violent adult offenders.

On January 8, 1994, the *Buffalo News* reported that Masten Park would be shutting down by the end of March. During the previous year, the *Buffalo News* reported that the U.S. Justice Department was investigating allegations that the civil rights of residents were repeatedly violated because of beatings and the failure to supervise. Under investigation is a "wake-up club," which regularly delivered beatings to youngsters who misbehaved or failed to show respect for the guards. One incident involved four guards who were reported to have punched and kicked a juvenile offender until he vomited, spit blood, and fell to the floor (Ciotta 1993; Ciotta & Sorenson, 1994; Gryta, 1994).

Perhaps the real reason for the rise and fall of Masten Park is stated in the following letter to the editor by a former employee (Piccillo, *Buffalo News,* January 22, 1994).

> As a former officer of the original Masten Park Rehabilitation Center (1968 to 1977), I am sorry yet pleased to finally see it all come to an end. Those of us who were "original staff" did, for the most part, serve the "clients" very well and did accomplish what the facility was intended for.
> Common Council President George Arthur was one of the officers on board at that time, and both officers and inmates, more so than not, re-

spected each others' positions. But the atmosphere began to take on a different status when politics and politicians got involved.

Arthur Eve, who is a supporter of the facility, allegedly was influential in the hiring of some of the later staff.

There is no doubt Mr. Eve means well in wanting to keep the facility open, but perhaps he is also looking for those precious votes and the power that comes with the territory.

Supposed drug dealing, physical abuse and the lack of professionalism has been alleged to have been the root of Masten Park's demise. If those in control of the center did not respect either the position of staff members or the inmates they were there to supervise, then it's time to pull the plug.

Mr. Eve, in trying to play the part of "savior" of this project, no doubt means well, but not when he is instrumental in obtaining jobs there for people who did not perform well.

Mr. Eve should funnel his energy in the field of politics and leave the privilege of accepting patronage jobs to those who sincerely appreciate having the job given them and will respect it.

Peter R. Piccillo, Buffalo

So once more we see that our institutions for punishing and treating juveniles often are susceptible to the same political interests that led to their creation. It is the familiar history of decriminalization and criminalization. It is an expensive history not only for the wasted dollars in reconstructing institutions that are later to be closed but also for the lost opportunities to provide juvenile offenders with the secure environments that for their sake, as well as ours, are so desperately needed.

Concluding "Real" Reasons
for Recriminalizing Delinquency

BOTH THE REAL AND LEGAL REASONS for recriminalizing delinquency go beyond the case of Willie Bosket and sudden concerns about violent juvenile crime. While legal rules for waiver reforms draw on the logic of deterrence and past precedents for mandating criminal responsibility, I have argued that the real reasons for their creation and implementation are political and organizational. Real reasons for recriminalization emerge as a consequence of political and organizational concerns and interests in maintaining the legitimacy of loosely coupled systems of juvenile and criminal justice. In response to modern-day crisis, they produce the unique legal avenues for classifying and tracking juveniles as offenders.

In suggesting that there are real reasons for recriminalization that go beyond the legally stated ones, I do not pretend to know all the political and organizational concerns and interests that have led to the creation and implementation of waiver legislation. I have repeatedly argued, however, that the reforms are not purely symbolic, generated merely to satisfy immediate political interests in doing something about violent juvenile crime. In the pages that follow, I list first the reasons for recriminalization as generated from my case study of the creation and implementation of New York's JO law. Then I discuss policy implications and future research directions.

Real Reasons for Recriminalization

The reasons for the particular shape of recriminalization in New York stem first from its unique history of juvenile justice reforms. These reforms began to redefine delinquents and delinquency in the early part of the nineteenth century as a way of providing a more acceptable legal alternative to criminal justice for offending juveniles. They were responses to earlier crises in the administration of justice, leading New Yorkers to favor houses of refuge as an alternative to other institutional settings such as state prisons or orphan asylums. Houses of refuge became less acceptable alternatives to treating serious delinquent behavior because they were increasingly perceived as ineffective in their ability to do good and to do justice.

When the house of refuge was seen as a less desirable institutional setting, a crisis developed in the system's ability to treat delinquents. Alternative legal avenues were sought namely in the form of probation and juvenile court. The road toward decriminalization was marked not only by reformatories and juvenile courts but also by a diverse set of other institutions that were created to deal with the deviant behaviors of juveniles in settings that were increasingly separated from that of adults. Juvenile justice became dependent on the decision making of not only juvenile court judges and probation officers but also officials in public schools and mental health clinics.

With the diverse set of agencies that came under the increasingly large umbrella of juvenile justice, a complex system of doing good emerged in diverse and less visible negotiated orders of justice. Legal and other institutional attempts to do good and justice expanded the parameters of juvenile justice, producing new and related forms of crisis. Again the solution in the shape of legal reform became part of the reason for subsequent forms of crisis. For example, the problem that New York's prosecutors addressed in having to charge 15-year-old juveniles in criminal court for murder was solved in 1958 through the complete decriminalization of capital offenses. But that solution, which seemed reasonable to the legislators at the time, became a part of the problem when 15-year-old juveniles, such as Willie Bosket, could not be brought into New York's criminal courts for brutal acts of murder.

Real reasons for recriminalization are located within not only the temporal context of a history of reforms but also the boundaries of urbanization. Houses of refuge, juvenile courts, legal aid, media stories, commission hearings, Willie Bosket, and legislative debates all point to the problem of violent juvenile crime and juvenile justice in New York City. From the beginning of the nineteenth century to the end of the twentieth century, officials all expressed concerns about juvenile crime and justice in densely populated urban areas. Systems of juvenile justice first emerged in cities where they reproduced a multitude of agencies to deal with urban crime and disorder. As a consequence, the real story of juvenile justice is an uneven one that belies the uniform quality of state laws mandating a system of juvenile justice.

The negotiated order of juvenile justice is another reason for recriminalization. The loosely coupled quality of past juvenile justice systems produced new opportunities for waiver and the criminal court as another subsystem in an already complex juvenile justice process. Thus jurisdictional concerns and interests are related not only to an uneven story of juvenile justice reforms but also to variation in the implementation of the legal rules related to waiver legislation.

The implementation data led me to suggest that some counties assigned criminal responsibility to juveniles in a more tightly coupled manner than other counties. For example, I noted that in Albany County decision making appeared more tightly coupled in that a higher proportion of juveniles were arrested, convicted, and incarcerated for a wider range of designated felony offenses than in other counties. Tight coupling, in the form of higher rates of conviction for less serious designated felony offenses, supports Zimring's (1991: 275) contention that in systems of legislative waiver "discretion can be removed only at the price of a rigidity that increases the punitive bite of legal policy toward youth crime."

The loose and tight fit between the various subsystems of juvenile and criminal justice can also produce higher arrest, conviction, and incarceration rates for less serious designated felonies committed by black juveniles. The greater likelihood of black juveniles receiving the juvenile offender label suggests that criminal justice decision making, like juvenile justice decision making, is rooted in the principle of individualized justice especially for juveniles charged with less serious designated felony offenses. The effect of race on the assignment of criminal responsibility to juveniles in New York supports the view that the legal decision making of criminal justice officials in waiver decisions can be just as arbitrary as that of juvenile justice officials (Thomas & Bilchik 1985: 479). A possible explanation for the effect of race is the greater likelihood that black juveniles reside in single-parent households. Perceptions of moral character, parental support, and residential availability are the factors that I suggested qualify legal decision making for juveniles not only in juvenile court but also in criminal court.

The diverse set of political and organizational concerns and interests leading to recriminalization, I argued, produced multiple indicators of success. In routine decision making, success may be defined in the police officer's ability to make an arrest, while success may be defined by prosecutors in terms of their ability to convict. Police officials know the advantages and disadvantages in booking a juvenile as offender in their particular county of jurisdiction. Similarly, prosecutors are well aware of the probability that their county's criminal court judges will look favorably at their presentation of a juvenile's case. And so too are criminal court judges aware of the advantages and disadvantages of incarcerating juveniles as offenders. In other words, the negotiated order of juvenile and criminal justice requires that success be continually redefined to include a diversity of organizational concerns and interests.

The real or organizational reasons for treating juveniles as offenders in criminal court cannot be separated from the related legal rules of recriminalization. Sentencing in criminal court was modified the year following passage of the JO law by allowing officials to offer eligible juveniles youthful offender status. In a less direct way, the JO law was also modified by an unpublicized 1982 amendment changing the county's proportional cost for incarcerating juveniles. Rates of conviction and incarceration were related to the gradual implementation of an increase in the county's cost sharing. The less known administrative rules related to recriminalization reflect the less visible practical concerns of officials in their filtering and rubber-stamping of each other's decisions. Those decisions are based on their intimate knowledge of the jurisdictional consequences of prosecuting and sentencing juveniles in criminal court.

Diverse sets of interests and concerns produced a cycle of reforms that are more complex than those which might be envisioned as a clearly visible form of legal control. There are deep-seated and hidden pockets of power and control that simply cannot be measured with state agency data. In a more blurred vision of legal control, juvenile justice and its treatment-oriented dispositions are not eliminated through waiver legislation. Recriminalization does not reduce the workload of juvenile court judges nor does it dismantle or eliminate treatment programs. Instead, it produces alternative legal avenues within and between systems of juvenile and criminal justice. For example, probation is still the preferred disposition for juveniles charged with less serious designated felony offenses whether in juvenile court or criminal court.

But the intended effects of recriminalization are not purely ceremonial. One openly stated purpose of the JO law was to reduce rates of violent juvenile crime. Based on a controlled time-series analysis of monthly juvenile arrests for New York City and non–New York City counties, I concluded that the JO law failed to influence crime rates. Violent juveniles were not responsive to the increased certainty and severity of punishment promised by the JO law. New Yorkers were still at risk of serious violence by juveniles, and sensational acts of juvenile violence were still regularly reported in the media. But this time when the story of Willie Bosket was replaced by the story of a gang of juveniles that repeatedly assaulted and raped an affluent woman jogging in Central Park (Gibbs 1989), criminal court was there to charge and convict the juveniles as offenders instead of as delinquents. New York already had its JO law, and there was little motivation to get even tougher on violent juveniles. In a sense, there was success in the wake of failure because recriminalization temporarily calmed public criticism of juvenile justice.

Success in the wake of evidence of failure is contained in the maximum security institutions designed to treat and punish juvenile offenders. Recriminalization was related to several sources of perceived injustice among convicted juvenile offenders. The sources of comparison are no longer confined to what other delinquents received in juvenile court but include what offenders could have received if they were placed in juvenile court as delinquents instead of criminal court as juvenile offenders. A segment of incarcerated juvenile offenders is well aware of the possible political and organizational concerns and interests that led to their conviction independent of the objective characteristics of their offenses.

Organizational interests in maintaining the custodial objectives of a secure facility repeatedly conflicted with its treatment mission. The institution classified juveniles in ways that mirrored their experiences inside and outside formal systems of juvenile justice. The level system, special education, and sex offender units reflected the kinds of classifications and tracks that the institution appeared to need more for maintaining control than for the sake of rehabilitation. The institution's educational objectives were modified to fit the convenience of staff and the institution's need for maintaining security. Psychological treatment was based on a system of behavioral modification that could work only within the institution's walls.

And the list goes on. The political and organizational interests that led to the creation of Masten Park produced a familiar story of abuse. Cynicism, political patronage, and ultimately the kind of violence that led to the arrest and indictment of several staff members, all superseded the institution's high hopes of rehabilitating juvenile offenders. The problem is not just one of mismanagement. There are deeper issues that are related to recriminalization and the determinants of delinquency and crime. They have to do with the legal labels that isolate juvenile offenders, producing an even more resistant and rebellious population of juveniles whom society has defined by their past conduct as extremely dangerous.

Despite the closing of Masten Park, other maximum security institutions remain to meet the legal demands of recriminalization. Juvenile offenders are legally defined as dangerous juveniles requiring the more exclusionary institutions generated by the state division for youth. But juvenile justice and criminal justice systems did not create their population of chronic violent juvenile offenders. The chronic violent delinquent appeared and reappeared in academic research, conservative ideologies, media stories, committee hearings, and legislative debates. As a consequence, recriminalization and its waiver policies went beyond acts of murder by juveniles such as Willie Bosket to be inclusive of a broader array of potential juvenile murderers who were characterized as violent juveniles based on a wide range of designated felony offenses. This broad range of violent felony offenses justified the type of tracking that would allow criminal justice officials to identify chronic violent delinquents at younger ages in the adult criminal justice system. In the end, organizational convenience worked in tandem with ideology to produce the diverse legal avenues that recriminalization has created.

Policy Implications

If my son or daughter were in the unfortunate circumstance of having committed a violent crime, I would want them treated for whatever psychological or sociological quirk led to their aberrant behavior. I would passionately describe their past good behavior and stress that the criminal act was out-of-keeping with their normal behavior. If the problem were to continue, despite my best efforts to convince them to change their friends or to obtain professional counseling, I would accept and seek comprehensive help, such as a good residential treatment facility might provide. My image of residential treatment, however, is not a Masten Park, no matter how serious their offense. Rather, I would want what the rich are able to afford for their troubled children in the form of elite boarding schools. If discipline were the issue, I would want for them the same kind of treatment that General Norman Schwarzkopf received at a preparatory military academy. Of course, I would want to treat my son or daughter in a different manner than state divisions for youth treat juveniles because I am more knowledgeable about my children and can better identify with them than someone else can.

At this point, I am drawn back to Judge Julian Mack and his optimistic image of a juvenile court in which the juvenile court was supposed to act as a wise parent in treating or coordinating the services needed to help juveniles. But beliefs on how to deal with one's own children do not translate well into public policy. The poor do not have the means to provide their youth with private psychological counseling or with expensive boarding schools. For the poor the juvenile justice system is too often the first as well as the last resort. The poor do not have houses to mortgage or access to insurance or credit to provide for their troubled children. Besides, officials cannot make decisions about juveniles as if they were their own children, because legal decision making is embedded in a complex bureaucracy where routine decisions must be made quickly without the time and resources to discover all there is to know about juveniles as individuals. And even if they wanted to, officials would complain that the resources are not there to provide delinquent juveniles with the services they need.

The image of a wise parental role for juvenile court judges is further tarnished by the complex bureaucracy that juvenile court judges find themselves in, particularly in large urban counties. Treatment services require a degree of coordination that is not easily overcome by the organizational interests of a diverse set of agencies and officials. Judge Mack's bureaucratic juvenile court never became the tightly coupled middle-class household where decisions could be made for troubled children in the best interests of the child. But in rereading the words of Judge Mack, it is apparent that he envisioned a more narrow juvenile court and juvenile justice system than the one that emerged in New York and in other states. Juvenile justice was only for those delinquents "treading the path that leads to criminality" (Mack 1909: 107). Willie Bosket had already arrived in the adult world of criminality the moment he murdered his first subway passenger. And, as noted earlier, the fact that he was placed in juvenile court in 1978 instead of criminal court reflected the unique organizational rules, concerns, and interests that at the time produced New York's expanding systems of juvenile justice.

A more narrow set of legal rules can be envisioned for states that wish to respond to violent juvenile crime by both doing good and doing justice. A more tightly coupled system of juvenile justice is needed in which recriminalization is more narrowly focused and confined to the most serious of violent offenses. A combination of legislative and judicial waiver procedures might provide the mix of administrative rules that would maintain the principle of offense and at the same time provide criminal justice officials the ability to track serious violent delinquents. Legislative waiver has the advantage of being offense-based and of preventing juveniles from entering criminal court for nonviolent offenses. For example, in New York no juvenile under the age of 16 has been convicted in criminal court of a nonviolent property offense, as is the case in other states. By restricting legislative waiver to murder, Willie Bosket would have been taken care of in criminal court and juvenile justice and criminal justice systems spared the burden of dealing with less serious designated felony offenses.

But what about juveniles who rape and rob? For these designated felony offenses, it seems more appropriate to begin tracking their violent behavior in juvenile courts so that when they appear in criminal court at the age of 16 it is not as first-time offenders. In this sense, a combination of legislative and judicial waiver would set limits as to the kinds of offenses for which juveniles would enter criminal courts. At the same time, a tightly coupled system of juvenile and criminal justice would require that criminal court officials be aware of an adult's earlier juvenile court convictions for violent designated felonies.

The problem of juvenile crime and justice falls into that category of intractable social problems that defy any simple solutions (Levine & Perkins 1987: 52). They require a constant evaluation of the reasons for doing good as well as for doing justice. The feeling among many New Yorkers – that it simply was not right for Willie Bosket to receive a 5-year indeterminate placement for the murder of two subway passengers – cannot be ignored in modern-day attempts to do both good and justice. It reflects the belief among some New Yorkers that juveniles who kill strangers on the city's subways should be convicted in criminal court as adult offenders. Juvenile justice policies like crime control policy in general should be in reference to the collective interest of society in maintaining its highest set of values (Cohen 1985: 271).

But in suggesting a more tightly coupled system of juvenile and criminal justice that balances the need to do good with the need to do justice, I do not wish to confine accountability to the behavior of delinquents. I also want to hold officials equally accountable for their dispositions and related treatment services. I want to hold officials accountable for what goes on in offices of probation and parole as well as in residential facilities. This is the more difficult task to implement in that it involves opening the too often closed and less visible doors of juvenile justice.

Research Directions

There is much to be learned by opening the doors of juvenile justice. We need to know more about the institutions that the rich have created to deal with their troubled children (Miller 1979 and 1991). What is it about the system of treatment from military academies to psychological counseling that is significantly different from the services of state juvenile justice agencies? The answer may cause us to dwell on the obvious fact that these institutions are more tightly coupled around a singular goal of helping children. But comparative research might also produce some surprises, such as the possibility that treatment for more affluent juveniles is not necessarily more expensive than the cost of state divisions for youth. It might also show that we know very little about how to treat deviance, and that there is little that can be done to prevent repeated violence through exclusionary types of control.

There are other relevant ways in which comparative research can better inform public policy on juvenile justice systems. A more complete analysis would have led me to follow the case processing decisions of juvenile offenders removed to New York's juvenile court. Such data would have provided a comparison of the capacity of juvenile and criminal justice systems to convict and incarcerate violent juveniles. Research is also needed to see if violent juveniles in criminal court are actually sentenced less severely than comparable juveniles in juvenile court. Not much has changed since Farrington et al. (1986) noted that we "only have fragmentary evidence as to the effect – in sentence length and later criminality – of transferring juveniles to adult court" (11).[1]

We also know little about the long-term effects on juveniles when they are processed in the adult criminal justice system. Waiver allows criminal justice officials to create a juvenile's official record at an earlier age. How well the criminal justice system is able to use that information later when juveniles graduate to adult offending requires more comparative data than I have been able to generate.

The other side of implementation is the impact of recriminalization in different states with their varying forms of waiver legislation. How do these states differ in the short- and long-term consequences of bringing juveniles into criminal court with different types of waivers? Waiver reform subjects juveniles to lengthy periods of incarceration. What happens to these long-termers as a consequence? Do they turn out to become chronic violent adult offenders, or have they matured into nonviolent adults? Specifically, what happened to the juveniles as young as 13 sentenced to a maximum sentence of life in prison? Are they still incarcerated, or have they been paroled after serving their minimum sentence? If they are still incarcerated, is it because of their poor adjustment to maximum security prisons at a relatively young age? And is the adjustment of incarcerated juveniles related to their unique institutional setting? Although high schools and colleges can be quite good at keeping track of their alumni and their successes, we know little about the successes, or failures, of those who graduate from other kinds of institutional settings.

It is also important to bear in mind that the cycle of juvenile justice reforms continues to repeat itself. Recently, Queens and Manhattan have recreated youth courts within criminal courts to provide judges with the specialized opportunity to handle juvenile offenders (Corriero 1990). The judges that I observed in these specialized adult–juvenile courts appear to have much of the same treatment-oriented philosophy that once characterized the judges of traditional juvenile courts. Youth courts may be the middle ground that would lead to a compromise between treatment and punishment advocates. But we need research to evaluate case processing decisions for juveniles placed in specialized and general courts of criminal, as well as juvenile, jurisdiction. The ultimate question concerns the degree to which courts are effective in meeting their stated treatment- or punishment-oriented objectives.

In making my call for comparative research, I recognize the need for remaining sensitive to the rights, privacy, and confidentiality of juveniles. But confidentiality seems to have worked against systems of juvenile justice in that the public has become ignorant as to the reasons for its treatment- and punishment-oriented mandates. We need just as much public discussion devoted to issues of juvenile justice as is devoted to the knee injury of a star football player. By opening the doors of juvenile justice, we can learn more about its real purpose in preventing and controlling serious delinquent behaviors.

Juvenile and criminal courts are only one element in a complex set of interacting subsystems of juvenile justice. To examine the less visible, negotiated parts of juvenile and criminal justice, we need sets of data that greatly improve upon the available information presented in this book. Otherwise, it will continue to be difficult to evaluate what works and does not work in juvenile justice. By expanding our understanding of juvenile justice, we may be able to better respond to juvenile violence with reforms that are not only humane and fair but which do not continue to ignore the real reasons for recriminalizing delinquency.

Definitions of Designated Felony Offenses

Murder (125.25 A-1 Felony)

A person is guilty of murder when:

1. With intent to cause death of another person, he causes the death of such person or of a third person; except that in any prosecution under this subdivision, it is an affirmative defense that:

(a) The defendant acted under the influence of extreme emotional disturbance for which there was a reasonable explanation or excuse, the reasonableness of which is to be determined from the viewpoint of a person in the defendant's situation under the circumstances as the defendant believed them to be. Nothing contained in this paragraph shall constitute a defense to a prosecution for, or preclude a conviction of, manslaughter in the first degree or any other crime;

(b) The defendant's conduct consisted of causing or aiding, without the use of duress or deception, another person to commit suicide. Nothing contained in this paragraph shall constitute a defense to a prosecution for, or preclude a conviction of, manslaughter in the second degree or any other crime; or

2. Under circumstances evincing a depraved indifference to human life, he recklessly engages in conduct which creates a grave risk of death to another person; or

3. Acting either alone or with one or more other persons, he commits or attempts to commit robbery, burglary, kidnapping, arson, rape in the first degree, sodomy in the first degree, sexual abuse in the first degree, aggravated sexual abuse, escape in the first degree, or escape in the second degree, and, in the course of and in furtherance of such crime or of

immediate flight therefrom, he, or another participant, if there be any, causes the death of a person other than one of the participants; except that in any prosecution under this subdivision, in which the defendant was not the only participant in the underlying crime, it is an affirmative defense that the defendant:

(a) Did not commit the homicidal act or in any way solicit, request, command, importune, cause or aid the commission thereof;

(b) Was not armed with a deadly weapon, or any instrument, article or substance readily capable of causing death or serious physical injury and of a sort not ordinarily carried in public places by law-abiding persons;

(c) Had no reasonable ground to believe that any other participant was armed with such a weapon, instrument, article or substance; and

(d) Had no reasonable ground to believe that any other participant intended to engage in conduct likely to result in death or serious physical injury.

Aggravated Sexual Abuse (130.70 Class B Felony)

1. A person is guilty of aggravated sexual abuse in the first degree when he inserts a foreign object in the vagina, urethra, penis or rectum of another person causing physical injury to such person:

(a) By forcible compulsion;

(b) When the other person is incapable of consent by reason of being physically helpless;

(c) When the other person is less than eleven years old.

2. Conduct performed for a valid medical purpose does not violate the provisions of this section.

Arson-1 (150.20 A-1 Felony)

1. A person is guilty of arson in the first degree when he intentionally damages a building or motor vehicle by causing an explosion or a fire and when (a) such explosion or fire is caused by an incendiary device propelled, thrown or placed inside or near such building or motor vehicle; or when such explosion or fire is caused by an explosive; or when such explosion or fire either (i) causes serious physical injury to another person other than a participant, or (ii) the explosion or fire was caused with the expectation or receipt of financial advantage or pecuniary profit by the actor; and when (b) another person who is not a participant in the crime is present in such building or motor vehicle at the time; and (c) the defendant knows that fact or the circumstances are such as to render the presence of such person therein a reasonable possibility.

2. As used in this section, "incendiary device" means a breakable container designed to explode or produce uncontained combustion upon impact, containing flammable liquid and having a wick or similar device capable of being ignited.

Arson-2 (150.15 Class B Felony)

A person is guilty of arson in the second degree when he intentionally damages a building or a motor vehicle by starting a fire, and when (a) another person who is not a participant in the crime is present in such building or motor vehicle at the time, and (b) the defendant knows that fact or the circumstances are such as to render the presence of such a person therein a reasonable possibility.

Assault-1 (120.10-1,2 Class C Felony)

A person is guilty of assault in the first degree when:
1. With intent to cause serious physical injury to another person, he causes such injury to such person or to a third person by means of a deadly weapon or a dangerous instrument; or
2. With intent to disfigure another person seriously and permanently, or to destroy, amputate or disable permanently a member or organ of his body, he causes such injury to such person or to a third person.

Attempt Murder-2 (125.25 Class B Felony)

There is no such crime as attempted murder when the charge is attempting to commit murder in the 2d degree by recklessly engaging in conduct that endangers another person. An attempt occurs when a person displays behavior that insinuates the commission of a crime.

Attempt Murder-2 (120.35 Class B Felony)

A person who engages in behavior that constitutes a murder attempt *may not* be convicted of attempt to commit murder unless s/he causes the murder to occur.

Burglary-1 (140.30 Class B Felony)

A person is guilty of burglary in the first degree when he knowingly enters or remains unlawfully in a dwelling with intent to commit a crime therein, and when, in effecting entry or while in the dwelling or in immediate flight therefrom, he or another participant in the crime:

1. Is armed with explosives or a deadly weapon; or

2. Causes physical injury to any person who is not a participant in the crime; or

3. Uses or threatens the immediate use of a dangerous instrument; or

4. Displays what appears to be a pistol, revolver, rifle, shotgun, machine gun or other firearm; except that in any prosecution under this subdivision, it is an affirmative defense that such a pistol, revolver, rifle, shotgun, machine gun or other firearm was not a loaded weapon from which a shot, readily capable of producing death or other serious physical injury, could be discharged. Nothing contained in this subdivision shall constitute a defense to a prosecution for, or preclude a conviction of, burglary in the second degree, burglary in the third degree or any other crime.

Burglary-2 (140.25 Class C Felony)

A person is guilty of burglary in the second degree when he knowingly enters or remains unlawfully in a building with intent to commit a crime therein, and when:

1. In effecting entry or while in the building or in immediate flight therefrom, he or another participant in the crime:

(a) Is armed with explosives or a deadly weapon; or

(b) Causes physical injury to any person who is not a participant in the crime; or

(c) Uses or threatens the immediate use of a dangerous instrument; or

(d) Displays what appears to be a pistol, revolver, rifle, shotgun, machine gun or other firearm.

Kidnapping-1 (135.25 A-1 Felony)

A person is guilty of kidnapping in the first degree when he abducts another person and when:

1. His intent is to compel a third person to pay or deliver money or property as ransom, or to engage in other particular conduct, or to refrain from engaging in particular conduct; or

2. He restrains the person abducted for a period of more than twelve hours with intent to:

(a) Inflict physical injury upon him or violate or abuse him sexually; or

(b) Accomplish or advance the commission of a felony; or

(c) Terrorize him or third person; or

(d) Interfere with the performance of a governmental or political function; or

3. The person abducted dies during the abduction or he is able to return or to be returned to safety. Such death shall be presumed, in a case where such person was less than sixteen years old or an incompetent person at the time of the abduction, from evidence that his parents, guardians or other lawful custodians did not see or hear from him following the termination of the abduction and prior to trial and received no reliable information during such period persuasively indicating that he was alive. In all other cases, such death shall be presumed from evidence that a person whom the person abducted would have been extremely likely to visit or communicate with during the specified period were he alive and free to do so, did not see or hear from him during such period and received no reliable information during such period persuasively indicating that he was alive.

Manslaughter-1 (125.25 A-1 Felony)

A person is guilty of manslaughter in the first degree when:

1. With intent to cause serious physical injury to another person, he causes the death of such person or a third person; or

2. With intent to cause the death of another person, he causes the death of such person or of a third person under circumstances which do not constitute murder because he acts under the influence of extreme emotional disturbance, as defined in paragraph (a) of subdivision one of section 125.25. The fact that homicide was committed under the influence of extreme emotional disturbance constitutes a mitigating circumstance reducing murder to manslaughter in the first degree and need not be proved in any prosecution initiated under this subdivision; or

3. He commits upon a female pregnant for more than twenty-four weeks an abortional act which causes her death, unless such abortional act is justifiable pursuant to subdivision three of section 125.05.

Rape-1 (130.35-1,2)

A male is guilty of rape in the first degree when he engages in sexual intercourse with a female:

1. By force; or

2. Nonconsensual by reason of helplessness.

Robbery-1 (160.15 Class B Felony)

A person is guilty of robbery in the first degree when he forcibly steals property and when, in the course of the commission of the crime or of immediate flight therefrom, he or another participant in the crime:

1. Causes serious physical injury to any person who is not a participant in the crime; or

2. Is armed with a deadly weapon; or

3. Uses or threatens the immediate use of a dangerous instrument; or

4. Displays what appears to be a pistol, revolver rifle, shotgun, machine gun or other firearm; except that in any prosecution under this subdivision, it is an affirmative defense that such pistol, revolver, rifle, shotgun, machine gun or other firearm was not a loaded weapon from which a shot, readily capable of producing death or other serious physical injury, could be discharged. Nothing contained in this subdivision shall constitute a defense to a prosecution, or preclude a conviction of robbery in the second degree, robbery in the third degree or any other crime.

Robbery-2 (160.10-1,2 Class C Felony)

A person is guilty of robbery in the second degree when he forcibly steals property and when:

1. He is aided by another person actually present; or

2. In the course of the commission of the crime or of immediate flight therefrom, he or another participant in the crime:

(a) Causes physical injury to any person who is not a participant in the crime; or

(b) Displays what appears to be a pistol, revolver, rifle, shotgun, machine gun or other firearm.

Sodomy-1 (130.50-1,2 Class B Felony)

A person is guilty of sodomy in the first degree when he engages in deviant sexual intercourse with another person:

1. By forcible compulsion; or

2. Who is incapable of consent by reason of being physically helpless.

Survey to Measure
Prosecutorial Attitudes

Please circle your responses to the following incidents:

THE FIRST SCENARIO

A juvenile is accused of stabbing another youth with a knife. As a result, the victim dies. The juvenile claims that the victim was mistakenly assumed to be someone who had earlier threatened the juvenile's life.

1) If it is the adolescent's first arrest for a violent offense, how likely would you be to prosecute in criminal court?

1	2	3	4	5	6	7	8	9	10	11
Very unlikely   Very likely

2) If it is the adolescent's third arrest for a violent offense, how likely would you be to prosecute in criminal court?

1	2	3	4	5	6	7	8	9	10	11
Very unlikely   Very likely

3) If it is the adolescent's sixth arrest for a violent offense, how likely would you be to prosecute in criminal court?

1	2	3	4	5	6	7	8	9	10	11
Very unlikely   Very likely

THE SECOND SCENARIO

A juvenile steals an elderly woman's purse, with the threat of a knife. In the process, she is knocked to the ground. Upon arrest the juvenile claims that the victim's injuries were not intended.

1) If the victim received a minor injury such as a scratch or bruise, how likely are you to prosecute in criminal court?

1	2	3	4	5	6	7	8	9	10	11
Very unlikely									Very likely	

2) If the victim received overnight hospitalization, resulting from a broken arm, how likely are you to prosecute in criminal court?

1	2	3	4	5	6	7	8	9	10	11
Very unlikely									Very likely	

3) If the victim received extensive injuries, a complex fracture resulting in hospitalization for at least six months, how likely are you to prosecute in criminal court?

1	2	3	4	5	6	7	8	9	10	11
Very unlikely									Very likely	

The following information about yourself would also be helpful:

Date of Birth   Sex   Years Working as D.A. or Ass't

_____   _____   _____

Offense Severity Weights

Offense Severity Weights

Offense	Severity Score
A Felonies	
Murder	36
Arson	22
Kidnapping	22
Attempted Murder	19
Attempted Kidnapping	12
B Felonies	
Rape	26
Forcible Sodomy	26
Manslaughter	28
Sexual Assault	26
Robbery First	17
Burglary First	16
Arson Second	13
C Felonies	
Assault	12
Robbery Second	10
Burglary Second	10

Notes

INTRODUCTION

1. The legal and policy issues related to juveniles in the criminal court are discussed in the extensive writings of Barry Feld (1980; 1981; 1983; 1984; 1987; 1988; 1990; 1993). This book has been stimulated by the scholarly questions that Feld has raised, particularly in his 1987 article reviewing legislative changes in the rules of waiver. Champion and Mays (1991) also provide a general survey of the diverse ways in which juveniles can be brought to criminal court.
2. The increasing percentage of juvenile arrests ending in juvenile court or criminal court may be an artifact of earlier selection processes. Still, the number of juveniles brought to criminal court has increased dramatically from 11,534 in 1971 to 62,180 in 1992 according to UCR arrest data.
3. The act proposed to treat 13-year-olds as adults if they committed a serious crime with a gun. It was sponsored by Senator Carol Moseley-Braun, Democrat from Illinois. It listed the following offenses for which juveniles could be treated as adult offenders: murder, attempted murder, armed robbery with a gun, aggravated assault with a gun, and aggravated sexual assault with a gun. The act was approved by the majority of the Senate, although juvenile and criminal justice are largely a responsibility of state legislators (Povich 1993).

1. RECRIMINALIZING VIOLENT JUVENILE CRIME

1. My description of Willie Bosket and the events that led to his shooting of two subway passengers is based largely on news reports that appeared in the *New York Times* (e.g., Gallanter 1989; Hays 1988; Kaiser 1978a & 1978b). I

also draw on Peter Noel's (1989) five-part series of articles, "The Monster In Willie Bosket," which appeared in the newspaper *The City Sun.*

2. In Family Court, delinquency cases are just one part of the custody, divorce, and other civil family matters that family court judges can see. To be more consistent with the research literature that deals with delinquency and juvenile justice, I will refer to New York's Family Courts as Juvenile Courts.

3. Bosket claimed to have committed over a thousand offenses during the few years that I estimate he spent outside of state institutions. Some news reports place the quoted figure at 2,000. I think the numbers have taken on a life of their own; they are presented to fit the media's image of Bosket as an extremely dangerous, chronically violent juvenile.

4. Detailed legal descriptions and analyses of New York's Juvenile Offender Law are contained in numerous law journal articles (e.g., Levy 1979; Peyser 1978; Salkin 1981; Sobie 1981; Woods 1980).

5. For an analysis of case processing decisions and YO status in New York, see Peterson (1988).

6. Bortner (1986: 69) makes the important point that "political and organizational factors, rather than concern for public safety, account for the increasing rate of remand."

7. My purpose here is not to review the longitudinal research on delinquency but to illustrate how that research helped to direct public policy toward waiver legislation. It is also important to note that there are numerous problems with public policy based on the Wolfgang et al. cohort study. These problems are reviewed by Blumstein and Moitra (1980), who note that the chronic offenders are not such a small proportion of the total cohort population. Actually, 18 percent of offenders accounted for 52 percent of arrests.

8. The breadth of Mark Moore's work on juvenile justice is not reflected in the cited report. A much more sensitive analysis to the complex problem of juvenile justice is presented in Moore's (1987) book.

9. Some would argue that Durkheim was wrong about primitive societies, which appeared at times to stress restitution instead of retribution. For example, Spitzer (1975: 631) concluded that the "severity of punishment does not decrease as societies grow more concentrated and complex" and that "greater punitiveness is associated with higher levels of structural differentiation."

10. For a detailed explication of Mead's (1961) essay and modern-day systems of juvenile justice, see Miller (1974).

11. In several generations of published research, John Hagan (1975; 1980; 1988; 1989) has detailed the manner in which loosely coupled criminal justice systems produce legal decision making that fit neither instrumental, functional, nor Marxian perspectives. Hagan et al.'s (1979) study is an

especially insightful application of the loosely coupled concept to criminal justice decision making.

12. The organizationally specific nature of first- and last-resort sanctions is examined in much greater theoretical detail than I can provide in my use of these very important terms. For a detailed discussion of the sociological significance of first- and last-resort sanctions, see Emerson's (1981) seminal article "On Last Resorts."

13. Based on his inside perspective on juvenile justice, Ira Schwartz supports two important points that I have repeatedly raised. First, Schwartz (1989) in his book *In Justice for Juveniles: Rethinking the Best Interests of the Child* shows repeatedly how juvenile justice reforms are driven by political concerns that take precedence over the so-called "best interests" of juveniles. Also Schwartz et al. (1984) show how the process is complex, involving a "hidden" system of juvenile justice.

2. TAKING STOCK OF JUVENILE JUSTICE REFORMS

1. There is an important point here that is too easily overlooked: systems of juvenile justice are not determined exclusively by the interests of the so-called ruling elite. Other interests that stem from "the power of the powerless" (Sutton 1994: 238) helped to shape our institutional responses to deviance.

2. Platt (1977: 175) states that the "participation of lawyers in juvenile court is likely to make the system more efficient and orderly, but not substantially more fair or benevolent." I agree with Platt that the introduction of lawyers to juvenile court did not necessarily make the process more fair, but I disagree that legal representation for juveniles has made the juvenile court more efficient.

3. RECRIMINALIZATION ON THE MOVE AND ITS LEGAL RULES

1. The report does not mention which detectives were responsible for which part of the quotes, so I cannot associate names with the specific testimony.

2. According to victimization surveys, age appears inversely related to the risk of assaultive violence (Hindelang 1976: 150). The category of indoor robbery victimization is an artifact of data tabulating procedures to produce higher rates of victimization among the elderly. This is because younger adults are more often outside of the home and, as a consequence, less likely to encounter an offender during a burglary attempt.

3. The number of uniformed officers in the New York City Police Department

by year is based on a letter from Michael J. Farrell, Deputy Commissioner, New York City Police Department, dated January 26, 1995.

4. Since passage of the JO law, several modifications appeared in the juvenile court's stated rules of confidentiality. Still, names are usually withheld by the media to preserve the anonymity and confidentiality of juveniles.

5. In effect, the "downward waiver" scheme implicit in the JO law creates a heavy presumption that a "juvenile offender" should be tried as an adult. As the New York Court of Appeals observed in *Vega* v. *Bell* (1979), explaining why "juvenile offenders" are not automatically entitled to a transfer hearing:

> This is a matter best left to the sound discretion of the court in which the removal decision is made. We note that the Legislature has already decided that in most cases juveniles charged with certain serious crimes are to be prosecuted with the criminal justice system. It is not for the courts to question the wisdom of this legislative decision, nor to seek to undermine its operation by removal to Family Court in the "typical" case. [U]nder the present scheme it will only be in the unusual or exception[al] case that removal will be proper, and thus a hearing will be necessary only if it appears for some special reason that removal would be appropriate in the particular case (460–1).

6. I quote from the debates as obtained from the record (New York State Assembly Debates 1978, July 19; New York State Senate Debates 1978, June 27).

7. In contrast to the 1978 JO law, the 1979 amendment was considered in a regular session of the Assembly and Senate. The amendment proposed several organizational changes in the case processing of juvenile offenders. The first set of provisions emphasized the amendment's due process orientation:

> . . . require that the parent or other person legally responsible for the care of an alleged juvenile offender be notified of his arrest and the location of the facility in which he is being detained;

> . . . provide that the testimony of an alleged juvenile offender at a removal inquiry may not be used against him except for impeachment purposes at a later proceeding;

> . . . provide for a removal inquiry in the superior court, rather than the local criminal court, either before or after indictment, at the defendant's option;

> . . . expressly provide that once a court has ordered removal of a juvenile offender case, no further proceedings may be had in any criminal court;

> . . . set forth specific factors to be considered by the superior court in determining whether removal of a case to the Family Court is in the interests of justice;

> . . . limit criminal responsibility of a juvenile offender for the crime of felony murder to cases in which the juvenile offender is criminally responsible for the underlying felony. . . .

The second set of provisions solidified the power of criminal justice officials in deciding the fate of juvenile offenders. The prosecutor's discretion to determine the removal process for juvenile offenders charged with murder is expanded. DFY is authorized to act in the same manner as adult correctional services to determine whether to incarcerate juvenile offenders in local jails. And finally, the state's criminal justice system is required to collect information on the arrest process for juvenile offenders:

> . . . provide that the district attorney may recommend the acceptance of a plea by a 13-year-old juvenile offender charged with murder in the second degree to a designated felony listed in Section 712 (h) of the Family Court Act and removal of the case to the Family Court;

> . . . authorize the Division for Youth to approve, on a case by case basis, the detention of an alleged juvenile offender in a local jail, provided that the Division states its reasons for such approval;

> . . . require that a probable cause hearing be held in a case removed to the Family Court if such a hearing was not held in the criminal court; and

> . . . require the court to provide the Division of Criminal Justice Services with more complete information concerning the cases in which removal to the Family Court is granted.

8. The law was amended in 1982 to read as follows:

> Expenditures made by the division of youth for care . . . [of] . . . juvenile offenders committed pursuant to section 70.05 of the penal law . . . shall be subject to reimbursement . . . by the social services district in which the juvenile offender resided at the time of commitment, in accordance . . . with the following schedule: twelve and one-half percent of the amount expended for care, maintenance and supervision of juvenile offenders from July first, nineteen hundred eighty-three through June thirtieth, nineteen hundred eighty-four; twenty-five percent of the amount expended for care, maintenance and supervision of juvenile offenders from July first, nineteen hundred eighty-four through June thirtieth, nineteen hundred eighty-five; thirty-seven and one-half percent of the amount expended for care, maintenance and supervision of juvenile offenders from July first, nineteen hundred eighty-five through June thirtieth, nineteen hundred eighty-six; fifty percent of the amount expended for care, maintenance and supervision of juvenile offenders after June thirtieth, nineteen hundred eighty-six (NY Executive Law S. 529, McKinney 1982, Amended L.1983 c.15, Subd.2 S. 139; Subd.6 S. 145).

4. CONTEXTUAL AND LEGAL REASONS FOR IDENTIFYING JUVENILES AS CRIMINAL OFFENDERS

1. Kitsuse and Cicourel (1963) provide the theoretical justification for considering official data as excellent measures of crime and other forms of deviant conduct.

2. Of course, judges are technically the only legal officials who can assign criminal responsibility. I use the legal concept of criminal responsibility to discuss various stages of decisions that can ultimately lead to conviction in criminal court. The police and prosecutors in charging juveniles are critical to the assignment of criminal responsibility to juveniles but are not legally in a position to adjudicate guilt or innocence.

3. Ordinary least-squares procedures are inappropriate given that the dependent variable is dichotomous – that is, indicating whether or not juveniles were certified for a grand jury indictment. Logistic regression allows for estimates of the effects of a set of independent variables on a nominal dependent variable without violating any major statistical assumptions. Moreover, a logistic regression provides a direct analogy with ordinary least-squares regression.

   The exponentiation (exp) of the coefficient (Beta) can be interpreted as an odds ratio. It is actually the ratio of two odds and is an estimate of the risk in two groups: one group at risk and another group not at risk. A ratio greater than 1 indicates that the risk factor is associated with higher rates, and a ratio less than 1 indicates that the group with the risk factor is at lower risk. That is, a positive logistic coefficient indicates greater odds, while negative coefficients indicate reduced odds (Dawson-Saunders & Trapp 1994: 169–71).

   Ordinary and logistic regression estimates were calculated with the LIMDEP program (Green 1991).

5. THE CASE PROCESSING OF JUVENILE OFFENDERS: FROM ARREST TO DISPOSITION

1. For an early analysis of the DCJS data based on the first several years of the JO law's implementation, see Royscher and Edelman (1981).

2. Sharon Lansing of DCJS, in a letter dated May 12, 1994, noted several problems with the DCJS data on juvenile offenders. She found that JO removals were sometimes incorrectly reported as dismissals, while "not arraigned" dispositions were occasionally reported as JO removals or dismissals. I believe this occurs because of confusion about the pre- versus post-arraignment dispositional status of JO arrests when processing is terminated in adult court.

3. As is the case with offender and jurisdictional characteristics, the linear increase in the mean seriousness of arrests by year follows an ordinal measure of seriousness based on felony arrest categories (A, B, and C felonies coded as 3, 2, and 1). Based on type of designated felony offense, the seriousness of arrest charges rose from 1.89 in 1978 to 2.08 in 1982. Whether measured on an ordinal or interval scale of severity, the seriousness of arrests gradually increased from the time of the JO law's initial implementation.

4. Although legally it is not possible to receive YO status for an A felony, such as homicide, recall that I am analyzing the most serious arrest charge along with the most severe adjudication. It is possible that in homicide–robbery incidents, the homicide charges were dismissed or reduced to B felonies, allowing for YO and JO status.

5. Based on the informed judgment of the director and assistant director of a DFY facility for juvenile offenders, I reduced the maximum sentence length by one-third. This one-third reduction in sentence length is routinely based on good time, conditional release, and parole. My two-thirds of maximum sentence rule is modified for homicides in which juveniles received a maximum of 9 years to life. In those cases, I added one-third of the minimum for a sentence of 12 years (144 months). Again, this is based on the informed view of institutional officials who report that juveniles convicted of homicide (9 to life) are usually rejected by the parole board after their minimum sentence.

6. As is the case in the previous multivariate analyses, the separate analysis of Hispanic juveniles produced no substantive difference in the estimated coefficients.

7. Selection bias correction procedures appear to make a significant difference in only a proportion of generated estimates (Stolzenberg & Relles 1990).

8. The operating cost of one maximum security prison is estimated at $80,000 a year per incarcerated juvenile offender (Schulman & Ciotta, *Buffalo News*, October 8, 1986, p. B-2). This figure might appear extremely high, but Chapter 7 will provide some details for why this is the case. For ease of computation, let us assume that 100 fewer juveniles incarcerated translates into a saving of $8 million. Based on a 50 percent cost-sharing formula, then New York City would have saved approximately $3,400,000 a year since it produces about 85 percent of the juvenile offender population.

6. RECRIMINALIZATION AND ORGANIZING FOR DETERRENCE

1. Zimring (1984) studied the effects of the JO law on homicide arrests in New York City using annual data. Monthly arrest series are much longer than the series available to him and so permit a more accurate estimate of the law's possible effects. However, Zimring's findings are in accord with those presented here.

2. The analysis reported here does not allow for the effects of the JJRA of 1976. In a preliminary analysis, models were estimated that included effects for both the JJRA and JO law, and models that included effects for the JJRA alone. None of these models suggested conclusions different from those presented.

3. The upstate data is based on continuously reporting jurisdictions which is

one in which there were UCR reports for at least 11 months of data each year. Among the larger upstate cities, Buffalo was the only one to be excluded because of a large apparent discrepancy in its reports for 1975.
4. This is the pattern that would be expected if initial publicity caused a change in the series that wore off over the course of time.

7. CONVICTED JUVENILE OFFENDERS IN A MAXIMUM SECURITY INSTITUTION

1. The juvenile is explaining that he resided in an open facility where he was free to commit repeated offenses outside the institution.
2. The surveyed view of delinquents that the juvenile justice process is essentially fair can be found in Smith's (1985) study of delinquents' understanding and sense of legal fairness in a juvenile court.
3. I am indebted to the research assistance of Colleen A. Connolly for her help in securing the official interview data. Dr. Connolly also worked as a summer-school teacher at Masten Park, and her analysis of the institution's educational program is presented in her dissertation (1991) "A Case Study of Educational Policy Implementation in a New York State Division for Youth Maximum and Limited Secure Center."
4. The *Buffalo News* series of articles on Masten Park that I base this section on are by Ciotta (1993), Ciotta & Schulman (1986a,b & 1990a,b), Ciotta & Sorensen (1994), Schulman (1986), and Schulman & Ciotta (1986).
5. See Levine and Levine (1992: 110–13) for a description of an "ideal" residential program. Zimring (1984) deals with the complex issue of considering a gradual definition of legal responsibility.

8. CONCLUDING "REAL" REASONS FOR RECRIMINALIZING DELINQUENCY

1. My call for comparative research on juvenile justice can be traced to Aaron Cicourel (1968) and his now classic book *The Social Organization of Juvenile Justice*. Lemert (1986) presents an excellent cross-cultural model for juvenile justice research. More recently, John Sutton (1994: 239–40) stresses the need for comparative research on juvenile justice and delinquency by "comparing societies" and their varying "institutional sectors."

References

Allen, Francis A. 1981. *The Decline of the Rehabilitative Ideal: Penal Policy and Social Purpose.* New Haven: Yale University Press.

Almy, Frederick. 1902. "Juvenile Courts in Buffalo." *American Academy of Political and Social Science Annals* 20:279–85.

Andriot, Donna. 1993. *Population Abstract of the United States.* McLean, Virginia: Documents Index Incorporated.

Austin, James, & Barry Krisberg. 1981. "Wider, Stronger, and Different Nets: the Dialects of Criminal Justice Reform." *Journal of Research in Crime and Delinquency* 18:165–96.

Beaumont, Gustave de, & Alexis de Tocqueville. 1964. *On the Penitentiary System in the United States and Its Application in France.* Carbondale: Southern Illinois University Press.

Ben-Yehuda, Nachman. 1990. *The Politics and Morality of Deviance: Moral Panics, Drug Abuse, Deviant Science, and Reversed Stigmatization.* New York: State University of New York Press.

Berk, Richard. 1983. "An Introduction to Sample Selection Bias in Sociological Data." *American Sociological Review* 48:386–97.

Bernard, Thomas J. 1992. *The Cycle of Juvenile Justice.* NY: Oxford University Press.

Bishop, Donna M., & Charles E. Frazier. 1991. "Transfer of Juveniles to Criminal Court: A Case Study and Analysis of Prosecutorial Waiver." *Notre Dame Journal of Law, Ethics and Public Policy* 5:281–302.

Blumstein, Alfred, & S. Moitra. 1980. "The Identification of 'Career Criminals' from 'Chronic Offenders' in a Cohort." *Law and Policy Quarterly* 2:321–34.

Bortner, M. A. 1986. "Traditional Rhetoric, Organizational Realities: Remand of Juveniles to Adult Court." *Crime & Delinquency* 32:54–74.

Box, G. E. P., & G. M. Jenkins. 1976. *Time Series Analysis: Forecasting and Control (Rev. Ed.)* San Francisco: Holden Day.

Butts, Jeffrey A., & Eileen Poe. 1993. "Offenders in Juvenile Court, 1990." U.S. Department of Justice, Office of Juvenile Justice and Delinquency Prevention.

Casper, Jonathan D. 1972. *American Criminal Justice: The Defendant's Perspective.* Englewood Cliffs, NJ: Prentice-Hall.

Casper, Jonathan, & David Brereton, 1984. "Evaluating Criminal Justice Reforms." *Law and Society Review* 18:121–44.

Chambliss, William. 1974. "The State, the Law and the Definition of Behavior as Criminal or Delinquent." In Daniel Glaser (Ed.), *Handbook of Criminology* (pp. 7–42). Indianapolis: Bobbs-Merrill.

Chambliss, William J., & Robert B. Seidman. 1971. *Law, Order, and Power.* Reading, MA: Addison-Wesley Publishing.

Champion, Dean J., & Larry G. Mays. 1991. *Tranferring Juveniles to Criminal Court: Trends and Implications for Criminal Justice.* New York: Praeger.

Chesney-Lind, M., & R. Shelden. 1992. *Girls: Delinquency and Juvenile Justice.* California: Wadsworth Publishing Co.

Cicourel, Aaron. 1968. *The Social Organization of Juvenile Justice.* New York: John Wiley.

Cohen, Stanley. 1980. *Folk Devils and Moral Panics: The Creation of the Mods and Rockers.* New York: Basil Blackwell.

Cohen, Stanley. 1985. *Visions of Social Control.* Oxford: Blackwell.

Cohen, Stanley, & J. Young. 1981. *The Manufacture of News: Social Problems, Deviance and the Mass Media.* Beverly Hills: Sage.

Cook, T. D., & Donald T. Campbell. 1979. *Quasi-Experimentation: Design and Analysis Issues for Field Settings.* Chicago: Rand McNally.

Corriero, Michael A. 1990. "Outside Counsel-Youth Parts: Constructive Response to the Challenge of Youth Crime." *New York Law Journal* 1–7.

Cressey, Donald, & Robert A. McDermott. 1973. *Diversion from the Juvenile Justice System.* Ann Arbor, MI: National Assessment of Juvenile Corrections, University of Michigan.

Dannefer, Dale, & Russell K. Schutt. 1982. "Race and Juvenile Justice Processing in Court and Police Agencies." *American Journal of Sociology* 87:1113–32.

Dawson-Saunders, Beth, & Robert G. Trapp. 1994. *Basic & Clinical Biostatistics.* Norwalk, CT: Appleton & Lange.

Durkheim, Emile. 1933. *The Division of Labor in Society.* New York: Macmillan. Originally published in 1893.

Eigen, Joel. 1981. "Punishing Youth Homicide Offenders in Philadelphia." *The Journal of Criminal Law and Criminology* 72:1072–93.

Eisenstein, James, Roy Flemming, & Peter Nardulli. 1988. *The Contours of Justice: Communities and Their Courts.* Boston: Little Brown and Company.

Emerson, Robert M. 1969. *Judging Delinquents*. Chicago: Aldine Publishing Company.

Emerson, Robert M. 1974. Role Determinants in Juvenile Court. In Daniel Glaser (Ed.), *Handbook of Criminology* (pp. 621–50). Chicago: Rand McNally College Publishing Co.

Emerson, Robert. 1981. "On Last Resorts." *American Journal of Sociology* 87:1–22.

Emerson, Robert. 1983. "Holistic Effects in Social Control Decision Making." *Law and Society Review* 17: 425–55.

Emerson, Robert M. 1991. "Case Processing and Interorganizational Knowledge: Detecting the 'Real Reasons' for Referrals." *Social Problems* 38:198–211.

Ericson, Richard V., Raptricia M. Baranek, & Janet B. L. Chan. 1987. *Visualizing Deviance: A Study of News Organizations*. Toronto: University of Toronto Press.

Erikson, Kai T. 1966. *Wayward Puritans: A Study in the Sociology of Deviance*. New York: John Wiley and Sons, Inc.

Fabricant, Michael. 1983. *Juveniles in the Family Courts*. Lexington, MA: Lexington Books.

Fagan, Jeffrey, & Elizabeth Piper Deschenes. 1990. "Determinants of Judicial Waiver Decisions for Violent Juvenile Offenders." *Journal of Criminal Law and Criminology* 81:314–47.

Farrington, David P., Lloyd E. Ohlin, & James Q. Wilson. 1986. *Understanding and Controlling Crime: Toward a New Research Strategy*. New York: Springer-Verlag.

Feeley, Malcolm M., & Mark H. Lazerson. 1983. Police-Prosecutor Relationships: An Interorganizational Perspective. In Keith O. Boyum & Lynn Mather (Eds.), *Empirical Theories About Courts* (pp. 216–41). New York: Longman.

Feld, Barry C. 1980. "Juvenile Court Legislative Reform and the Serious Young Offender: Dismantling the 'Rehabilitative Ideal.'" *Minnesota Law Review* 65:167–242.

Feld, Barry C. 1981. "Legislative Policies Toward the Serious Juvenile Offender: On the Virtues of Automatic Adulthood." *Crime and Delinquency* 27:497–521.

Feld, Barry C. 1983. "Delinquent Careers and the Criminal Policy: Just Deserts and the Waiver Decision." *Criminology* 21:195–212.

Feld, Barry C. 1984. "Criminalizing Juvenile Justice: Rules of Procedure for the Juvenile Court." *Minnesota Law Review* 69:141–276.

Feld, Barry C. 1987. "Criminal Law: The Juvenile Court Meets the Principle of the Offense: Legislative Changes in Juvenile Waiver Statutes." *Journal of Criminal Law and Criminology* 78:471–533.

Feld, Barry C. 1988. "The Juvenile Court Meets the Principle of Offense: Punishment, Treatment and the Difference It Makes." *Boston University Law Review* 68:821–915.

Feld, Barry C. 1990. "Bad Law Makes Hard Cases: Reflections on Teen-Aged Axe-Murderers, Judicial Activism, and Legislative Default." *Law and Inequality: A Journal of Theory and Practice* 8:1–101.

Feld, Barry C. 1993. "Juvenile (In) Justice and the Criminal Court Alternative." *Crime and Delinquency* 39:403–24.

Ferdinand, Theodore N. 1989. "Juvenile Delinquency or Juvenile Justice: Which Came First?" *Criminology* 27:79–106.

Fishman, Mark. 1978. "Crime Waves as Ideology." *Social Problems* 25:531–43.

Foucault, Michel. 1977. *Discipline and Punish: The Birth of the Prison.* New York: Pantheon Books.

Garland, David. 1985. *Punishment and Welfare: A History of Penal Strategies.* Vermont: Gower.

Gilbert, James. 1986. *The Cycle of Outrage: America's Reaction to the Juvenile Delinquent in the 1950s.* New York: Oxford University Press.

Glassman, Robert B. 1973. "Persistence and Loose Coupling in Living Systems." *Behavioral Science* 18:83–98.

Glassner, Barry, Margret Ksander, Bruce Berg, & Bruce D. Johnson. 1983. "A Note on the Deterrent Effect of Juvenile vs. Adult Jurisdiction." *Social Problems* 31:219–21.

Green, William H. 1991. *Limdep: User's Manual and Reference Guide.* New York: Econometric Software, Inc.

Guggenheim, Martin. 1976. "Juvenile Justice and the 'Violent' Juvenile Offender." *New York State Bar Journal* 48:550–5.

Hagan, John. 1975. "The Social and Legal Construction of Criminal Justice: A Study of the Pre-Sentencing Process." *Social Problems* 22:620–37.

Hagan, John. 1980. "The Legislatiion of Crime and Delinquency: A Review of Theory, Method, and Research." *Law and Society Review* 14:603–28.

Hagan, John. 1988. *Structural Criminology.* NJ: Rutgers University Press.

Hagan, John. 1989. "Why Is There So Little Criminal Justice Theory? Neglected Macro- and Micro-Level Links between Organization and Power." *Journal of Research in Crime and Delinquency* 26:116–35.

Hagan, John, John D. Hewitt, & Duane F. Alwin. 1979. "Ceremonial Justice: Crime and Punishment in a Loosely Coupled System." *Social Forces* 58:367–97.

Hagan, John, & Jeffrey Leon. 1977. "Rediscovering Delinquency: Social History, Political Ideology and the Sociology of Law." *American Sociological Review* 42:587–98.

Hall, John C., Donna Martin Hamparian, John M. Pettibone, & Joseph L. White. 1981. *Major Issues in Juvenile Justice Information Training: Readings in Public Policy.* Washington, DC: U.S. Department of Justice.

Hamparian, Donna, Linda K. Estep, Susan M. Muntean, Ramon R. Priestino,

Robert G. Swisher, Paul L. Wallace, & Joseph L. White. 1982. *Major Issues in Juvenile Justice Information and Training, Youth in Adult Courts: Between Two Worlds.* Washington, DC: U.S. Department of Justice.

Hart, Hastings H. 1910. *Juvenile Court Laws in the United States.* Philadelphia: William F. Fell Co.

Hassenfeld, Yeheskel, & P. Cheung. 1985. "The Juvenile Court as a People-processing Organization: A Political Economy Perspective." *American Journal of Sociology* 90:801–25.

Hay, Douglas. 1975. Property, Authority and the Criminal Law. In Douglas Hay, Peter Linebaugh, John G. Rule, E. P. Thompson, & Cal Winslow (Eds.), *Albion's Fatal Tree: Crime and Society in Eighteenth-Century England* (pp. 17–63). New York: Pantheon Books.

Hindelang, Michael J. 1976. *Criminal Victimization in Eight American Cities: A Descriptive Analysis of Common Theft and Assault.* Cambridge, MA: Ballinger.

Horowitz, Donald L. 1977. *The Courts and Social Policy.* Washington, DC: The Brookings Institution.

Horwitz, Allan, & Michael Wasserman. 1980. "Formal Rationality, Substantive Justice, and Discrimination: A Study of a Juvenile Court." *Law and Human Behavior* 4:103–15.

Jackson, Bruce. 1984. *Law and Disorder: Criminal Justice in America.* Urbana, IL: University of Illinois Press.

Jacobs, Mark D. 1990. *Screwing the System and Making It Work.* Chicago: University of Chicago Press.

Kitsuse, John, & Aaron V. Cicourel. 1963. "A Note on the Use of Official Statistics." *Social Problems* 12:131–9.

Knell, B. E. F. 1965. "Capital Punishment: Its Administration in Relation to Juvenile Offenders in the Nineteenth Century and Its Possible Administration in the Eighteenth." *British Journal of Criminology* 5:198–207.

LaFree, Gary. 1989. *Rape and Criminal Justice: The Social Construction of Sexual Assault.* CA: Wadsworth.

Landau, Simha F., & Gad Nathan. 1983. "Selecting Delinquents for Cautioning in the London Metropolitan Area." *British Journal of Criminology* 23:128–49.

Lemert, Edwin M. 1986. "Juvenile Justice Italian Style." *Law and Society Review* 20:509–44.

Lempert, Richard. 1982. "Organizing for Deterrence: Lessons from a Study of Child Support." *Law and Society Review* 16:513–68.

Levine, Murray, & Adeline Levine. 1992. *Helping Children: A Social History.* New York: Oxford University Press.

Levine, Murray, & David V. Perkins. 1987. *Principles of Community Psychology: Perspectives and Applications.* New York: Oxford University Press.

Levy, Harlan A. 1979. "Violent Juveniles: The New York Courts and the Constitution." *Columbian Human Rights Review* 11:51–62.

Lindsey, Ben B. 1925. Colorado's Contribution to the Juvenile Court. In Jane

Addams (Ed.), *The Child, the Clinic, the Court* (pp. 274–90). New York: Johnson Reprint Corp., 1970.

Liska, Allen E., and Mark Tausig. 1979. "Theoretical Interpretations of Social Class and Racial Differentials in Legal Decision-Making for Juveniles." *Sociological Quarterly* 20:197–207.

Mack, Julian. 1909. "The Juvenile Court." *The Harvard Law Review* 23:105–26.

Martinson, Robert. 1974. "What Works? – Questions and Answers About Prison Reform." *The Public Interest* 35:22–54.

Matza, David. 1964. *Delinquency and Drift.* New York: John Wiley.

McCarthy, Belinda R., & Brent L. Smith. 1986. "The Conceptualization of Discrimination in the Juvenile Justice Process: The Impact of Administrative Factors and Screening Decisions on Juvenile Court Dispositions." *Criminology* 24:41–64.

McDowall, David, Richard McCleary, Errol Meidinger, & R. A. Hay, Jr. 1980. *Interrupted Time Series Analysis.* Beverly Hills: Sage.

McGarrell, Edmund F. 1988. *Juvenile Correctional Reform: Two Decades of Policy and Procedural Change.* Albany, NY: State University of New York Press.

McGarrell, Edmund F. 1989. "The Ideological Bases and Functions of Contemporary Juvenile Law Reform: The New York State Experience." *Contemporary Crises* 13:163–87.

Mead, George Herbert. 1961. The Psychology of Punitive Justice. In T. Parsons (Ed.), *Theories of Society* (pp. 876–86). Glencoe, IL: Free Press.

Mennel, Robert M. 1973. *Thorns and Thistles: Juvenile Delinquents in the United States, 1825–1940.* Hanover: The University of New Hampshire Press.

Meyer, John W., & Brian Rowan. 1977. "Institutionalized Organizations: Formal Structure as Myth and Ceremony." *American Journal of Sociology* 83:340–63.

Miller, Jerome G. 1974. The Dilemma of the Post-Gault Juvenile Court. In Robert H. Bremner (Ed.), *Children and Youth: Social Problems and Social Policy* (pp. 229–39). NY: Arno Press.

Miller, Jerome G. 1979. The Revolution in Juvenile Justice: From Rhetoric to Rhetoric. In LaMar T. Empey (Ed.), *Future of Childhood and Juvenile Justice* (pp. 66–111). Charlottesville: University Press of Virginia.

Miller, Jerome. 1991. *Last One Over the Wall.* Columbus: Ohio State University Press.

Mohr, Lawrence B. 1976. "Organizations, Decisions, and Courts." *Law and Society Review* 10:621–42.

Moore, Mark H. 1987. *From Children to Citizens: Volume 1. The Mandate for Juvenile Justice.* New York: Springer-Verlag.

Osbun, Lee Ann, & Peter A. Rode. 1984. "Prosecuting Juveniles as Adults: The Quest for 'Objective' Decisions." *Criminology* 22:187–202.

Peterson, Ruth. 1988. "Youthful Offender Designations and Sentencing in the New York Criminal Courts." *Social Problems* 35:111–30.

Peyser, A. 1978. "The New Juvenile Offender Law in New York: A Comparison with Other Jurisdictions." *New York Law Journal* 27:1–18.

Pickett, Robert S. 1969. *House of Refuge: Origins of Juvenile Reform in New York State, 1815–1857.* Syracuse, NY: Syracuse University Press.

Platt, Anthony M. 1977. *The Child Savers: The Invention of Delinquency,* Second Ed. Chicago: University of Chicago Press.

Prescott, Peter S. 1981. *The Child Savers: Juvenile Justice Observed.* New York: Alfred A. Knopf, Inc.

Rothman, David J. 1971. *The Discovery of the Asylum: Social Order and Disorder in the New Republic.* Boston: Little, Brown.

Rothman, David J. 1980. *Conscience and Convenience: The Asylum and Its Alternatives in Progressive America.* Boston: Little, Brown.

Royscher, Martin, & Peter Edelman. 1981. Treating Juveniles As Adults in New York: What Does It Mean and How Is It Working? In John C. Hall, Donna Martin Hamparian, John M. Pettibone, & Joseph L. White (Eds.), *Major Issues in Juvenile Justice Information and Training: Readings in Public Policy* (pp. 265–93). Columbus, OH: Academy for Contemporary Problems.

Ryerson, Ellen. 1978. *The Best-Laid Plans: America's Juvenile Court Experiment.* New York: Hill and Wang.

Salkin, Barbara. 1981. "Down The Up Staircase: Due Process and Removal from Criminal Court." *New York Law School Law Review* 26:643–75.

Sampson, Robert J. 1986. "Effects of Socioeconomic Context on Official Reaction to Juvenile Delinquency." *American Sociological Review* 51:876–85.

Sampson, Robert J., & John H. Laub. 1993. "Structural Variations in Juvenile Court Processing: Inequality, the Underclass, and Social Control." *Law and Society Review* 27:285–311.

Schinitsky, Charles. 1962. "The Role of the Lawyer in Children's Court." *The Record of the Association of the Bar of the City of New York.* 17:10–26.

Schlossman, Steven L. 1977. *Love and the American Delinquent: The Theory and Practice of "Progressive" Juvenile Justice, 1920–1925.* Chicago: University of Chicago Press.

Schwartz, Ira. 1989. *In Justice for Juveniles: Rethinking the Best Interests of the Child.* Lexington, MA: Lexington Books.

Schwartz, Ira M., M. Jackson-Beeck, & R. Anderson. 1984. "The 'Hidden' System of Juvenile Control." *Crime and Delinquency* 30:371–85.

Scull, Andrew T. 1977. *Decerceration, Community Treatment and the Deviant: A Radical View.* Englewood Cliffs, NJ: Prentice-Hall, Inc.

Sellin, T., & Wolfgang, M. E. 1964. *The Measurement of Delinquency.* New York: John Wiley and Sons.

Singer, Simon I. 1993. "The Automatic Waiver of Juveniles and Substantive Justice." *Crime and Delinquency* 39:253–61.

Singer, Simon I., & Charles P. Ewing. 1986. "Juvenile Justice Reform in New York State: The Juvenile Offender Law." *Law and Policy* 8:457–83.

Singer, Simon I., & David McDowall. 1988. "Criminalizing Delinquency: The Deterrent Effects of the Juvenile Offender Law." *Law and Society Review* 22:521–35.

Smith, Charles P., P. S. Alexander, G. L. Kemp, and E. N. Lemert. 1980. *A National Assessment of Serious Juvenile Crime and the Juvenile Justice System: The Need for a Rational Response.* Washington, DC: National Institute for Juvenile Justice and Delinquency Prevention.

Smith, Trudie F. 1985. "Law Talk: Juvenile's Understanding of Legal Language." *Journal of Criminal Justice* 13:339–53.

Sobie, Merril. 1981. "The Juvenile Offender Act: Effectiveness and Impact on the New York Juvenile Justice System." *New York Law School Law Review* 26:677–721.

Sobie, Merril. 1987. *The Creation of Juvenile Justice: A History of New York's Children's Laws.* Albany, NY: The New York Bar Foundation.

Spitzer, Steven. 1975. "Punishment and Social Organization: A Study of Durkheim's Theory of Penal Evolution." *Law and Society Review* 9:613–37.

Stanko, Elizabeth A. 1981. "The Arrest versus the Case." *Urban Life* 9:395–406.

Stapleton, Vaughan, David P. Aday Jr., and Jeanne A. Ito. 1982. "An Empirical Typology of American Metropolitan Juvenile Courts." *American Journal of Sociology* 88:549–64.

Stolzenberg, Ross M., & Daniel A. Relles. 1990. "Theory Testing in a World of Constrained Research Design: The Significance of Heckman's Censored Sampling Bias Correct for Nonexperimental Research." *Sociological Methods and Research* 18:395–415.

Sutton, John R. 1988. *Stubborn Children: Controlling Delinquency in the United States, 1640–1981.* Berkeley: University of California Press.

Sutton, John R. 1994. Children in the Therapeutic State: Lessons for the Sociology of Deviance and Social Control. In George S. Bridges & Marth A. Myers (Eds.), *Inequality, Crime, and Social Control* (pp. 227–48). Boulder, CO: Westview Press.

Tappan, Paul W. 1949. *Juvenile Delinquency.* New York: McGraw Hill.

Thomas, Charles, & Shay Bilchik. 1985. "Prosecuting Juveniles in Criminal Courts: A Legal and Empirical Analysis." *The Journal of Criminal Law & Criminology* 76:439–79.

Thornberry, Terrance P. 1973. "Criminology: Race, Socioeconomic Status and Sentencing in the Juvenile Justice System." *Journal of Criminal Law and Criminology* 64:90–8.

Thorpe, Mara T. 1979. "Juvenile Justice Reform." *Trial* 15:26–30.

Tittle, Charles R., & Debra A. Curran. 1988. "Contingencies for Dispositional Disparities in Juvenile Justice." *Social Forces* 76:23–58.

van den Haag, Ernest. 1975. *Punishing Criminals: Concerning a Very Old and Painful Question.* NY: Basic Books.

Weber, Max. 1946. *From Max Weber: Essays in Sociology.* New York: Oxford University Press.

Weber, Max. 1954. *Max Weber on Law in Economy and Society.* Cambridge: Harvard University Press. Originally published in 1925.

Weick, Karl E. 1976. "Educational Organizations as Loosely Coupled Systems." *Administrative Science Quarterly* 21:1–19.

Wheeler, Stanton, & Leonard S. Cottrell. 1966. *Juvenile Delinquency: Its Prevention and Control.* New York: Russell Sage Foundation.

Wolfgang, Marvin E., Robert Figlio, & Thorsten Sellin. 1972. *Delinquency in a Birth Cohort.* Chicago: University of Chicago Press.

Wolfgang, Marvin E., Robert Figlio, Paul Tracey, & Simon I. Singer. 1985. *The National Survey of Crime Severity.* Bureau of Justice Statistics. Washington, DC: Government Printing Office.

Woods, J. P. 1980. "New York's Juvenile Offender Law: An Overview and Analysis." *Fordham Urban Law Journal* Winter:1–50.

Zimring, Franklin E. 1982. *The Changing Legal World of Adolescence.* New York: The Free Press.

Zimring, Franklin E. 1984. "Youth Homicide in New York: A Preliminary Analysis." *Journal of Legal Studies* 13:81–99.

Zimring, Franklin E. 1991. "The Treatment of Hard Cases in American Juvenile Justice: In Defense of Discretionary Waiver." *Notre Dame Journal of Law, Ethics and Public Policy* 5:267–80.

NEWSPAPER REPORTS

Butterfield, Fox. 1989. "A Boy Who Killed Coldly Is Now a Prison 'Monster.' " *New York Times*, March 22.

Ciotta, Rose. 1993. "State Claims Abuse at County Youth Home." *Buffalo News*, October 10.

Ciotta, Rose, & Susan Schulman. 1986a. "Violence Is a Way of Life for Youthful Inmates." *Buffalo News*, October 6.

Ciotta, Rose, & Susan Schulman. 1986b. "Changes at Secure Facility Offer Signs of Hope." *Buffalo News*, October 7.

Ciotta, Rose, & Susan Schulman. 1986c. "Don't Judge System by Masten, Official Says." *Buffalo News*, October 10.

Ciotta, Rose, & Susan Schulman. 1990a. "Runaways from Youth Homes Prey on the Public." *Buffalo News*, October 1.

Ciotta, Rose, & Susan Schulman. 1990b. "Agency's Lax Supervision Kept Runaway on Course to Slaying of Buffalo Priests." *Buffalo News*, October 2.

Ciotta, Rose, & Jon R. Sorensen. 1994. "Center for Troubled Youths to Shut Down." *Buffalo News*, January 8: B-2.

Gallanter, Martin. 1989. "Bosket's Law: Trouble Sets You Free." *New York Times*, April 21.

Gibbs, Nancy. 1989. Wilding into the Night. *Time Magazine.* May 8:20–1.

Gryta, Matt. 1994. "Ex-Guards at Youth Facility Indicted." *Buffalo News*, March 12.

Hays, Constance L. 1988. "Man Who Killed 2, Leading to New Law, Is Held in Prison Attack." *New York Times,* April 18.

Kaiser, Charles. 1978a. "Youth Held in 2 Murders Asked for Placement in a Foster Home." *New York Times,* July 20.

Kaiser, Charles. 1978b. "Subway Slayer's Accomplice, 17, Is Sentenced to 8 Years in Prison." *New York Times,* August 21.

Morgan, Ted. 1975. "They Think I Can Kill Because I'm Fourteen." *New York Times Magazine,* January 19.

New York Times. 1978. "Juvenile Justice in State of Disarray." March 2.

Noel, Peter. 1989. "The Monster in Willie Bosket." Five part series, in *The City Sun,* March 1–April 4.

Piccillo, Peter R. 1994. "Masten Rehabilitation Center Dies a Just Death." *Buffalo News,* January 12.

Povich, Elaine S. 1993. "Senate OKs Teen-Crime Amendment." *Chicago Tribune,* November 6.

Prichard, Peter S. 1993. "Get Tough on Teen Crime? Look Close; There's a Catch." *USA Today,* October 29.

Schulman, Susan. 1986. "Official Seeking Stiffer Rules on Masten Guards." *Buffalo News,* October 17.

Schulman, Susan, & Rose Ciotta. 1986a. "Even the Guards Have Records." *Buffalo News,* October 5.

Schulman, Susan, & Rose Ciotta. 1986b. "Youth Division to Study Center Workers' Records." *Buffalo News,* October 8: B-2.

Silver, Roy R. "Alleged Rape by Freed Inmate, 17, Intensifies Criticism of State Aide." *New York Times,* July 22, 1978.

Tomasson, R. E. 1976. "Proposed Bill Would Be Tougher on Juveniles Who Attack Elderly." *New York Times,* December 14.

Treaster, J. B. 1976. "Justice for the Young: Unjust." *New York Times,* March 21.

RELEVANT LEGAL STATUTES

Juvenile Justice Reform Act of 1976. 1976 N.Y. Laws S. 878.

Kent v. *United States.* 1966–1967. 383 U.S. 541, 555.

Murray v. *Owens.* 341 Federal Supplement. 722 (1972) reversed on appeal at 465 F.2d 289. Albany: William Press, Inc.

NY Executive Law S. 529. McKinney 1982. Amended L.1983 c.15, Subd.2 S. 139; Subd.6 S. 145.

New York State Assembly Debates. 1978. July 19.

New York State Crime Package Bill of 1978. 1978 N.Y. Laws Chapter 481.

New York State Senate Debates. 1978. June 27.

Vega v. *Bell.* 1979. 419 N.Y.S. 2d 454.

UNPUBLISHED WORKS

Bucci, E. M. 1985. "Knowledge, Understanding and Perceptions of the Juvenile Offender Law: Youth Perspectives." Independent Study Paper. School of Social Work: Syracuse University.

Connolly, Colleen A. 1991. "A Case Study of Educational Policy Implementation in a New York State Division for Youth Maximum and Limited Secure Center." A dissertation submitted to the Faculty of the Graduate School of State University of New York at Buffalo.

GOVERNMENT REPORTS

Carey, Hugh L. 1976. *Special Message on Children and Youth.* State of New York: Executive Chamber, April 29.

Department of Justice. *Uniform Crime Reports for the United States.* 1971; 1992. Washington, DC: Government Printing Office.

Marino, Senator Ralph J. 1977a. *The Juvenile Justice System and the New Delinquent.* Report of the New York State Senate Committee on Crime and Correction and New York State Select Committee on Crime.

Marino, Senator Ralph J. 1977b. *Part One: Violent Juveniles and Their Older Victims in New York State.* Report of the New York State Senate Committee on Crime and Correction and New York State Select Committee on Crime.

Marino, Senator Ralph J. 1977c. *Part Two: Criminal Victimization of Minority Groups and the Elderly.* Report of the New York State Senate Committee on Crime and Correction and New York State Select Committee on Crime.

Marino, Senator Ralph J. 1977d. *Crime Against the Elderly.* Report of the New York State Senate Committee on Crime and Correction and New York State Select Committee on Crime.

Moore, Mark, James Q. Wilson, & Ralph Gants. 1978. "Violent Attacks and Chronic Offenders: A Proposal for Concentrating the Resources of New York's Criminal Justice System on the 'Hard Core' of the Crime Problem." New York State Commission on Management and Productivity in the Public Sector. Albany, NY.

New York State Division for Youth. 1980–1990. *Annual Statistical Report.* Albany, New York: State of New York.

New York Office of State Inspector General. 1993. "Inspector General Report of Investigation Concerning: Austin MacCormick Residential Center." Albany, NY: State of New York.

Office of Court Administration, Annual Reports, New York, 1975 and 1978.

Proceedings of the Seventh Annual Conference of the New York State Association of Judges of Children's Courts. 1929. Albany: New York State Department of Correction Division of Probation.

United States. 1967. President's Commission on Law Enforcement and Administration of Justice. *The Challenge of Crime in a Free Society.* Washington, DC: Government Printing Office.

Young People in the Courts of New York State. 1942. New York State. Legislative Document. (No. 55).

Index